The Portuguese

The Portuguese

A Modern History

Barry Hatton

Interlink Books

An imprint of Interlink Publishing Group, Inc.
Northampton, Massachusetts

This book is for my family, British and Portuguese
—B.H.

First American edition published in 2011 by

INTERLINK BOOKS
An imprint of Interlink Publishing Group, Inc.
46 Crosby Street, Northampton, Massachusetts 01060
www.interlinkbooks.com

Library of Congress Cataloging-in-Publication Data
Hatton, Barry, 1963-
  The Portuguese : a modern history / by Barry Hatton. — 1st American ed.
    p. cm.
  Includes bibliographical references and index.
  ISBN 978-1-56656-844-9 (pbk.)
  1. Portugal—History. 2. National characteristics, Portuguese. I. Title.
  DP538.H37 2011
  946.9—dc22   2011012311

Cover Design: Baseline Arts
Cover Images: vanbeets/istockphoto; TMAX/fotolia
Illustrations: Wikipedia Commons: i, x, 2, 12, 18, 24, 26, 31, 39, 46, 49, 54, 58, 69, 74, 88, 96, 101, 105, 111, 114, 124, 163, 168, 178, 200, 209, 214, 223, 228, 235, 247, 252; purl.pt: 197; Shakeoutblog.com: 184

Printed and bound in the United States of America

Contents

Contents

Preface

As a Lisbon-based foreign correspondent for more than two decades I have written thousands of articles about Portugal but I am forced to acknowledge—it feels like a rebuke—that this country remains little-known abroad, even in the rest of Europe, even in Spain. That was one of the reasons for writing this book: to fill a gap, I hope, and to wake foreigners up to Portugal's enduring appeal. Wider recognition is owed to its fascinating history, which includes the first steps towards globalization and a spell as the world's richest nation; its climate, which is as agreeable as the gentle and hospitable Portuguese people; a captivating variety of countryside within a relatively small space; and food that is so good that overeating is always a temptation.

Another motive for this book was that I had built up a "critical mass" of intimate knowledge about the Portuguese way of life which needed to find expression. Selfishly perhaps, I had to put it somewhere, tidy it away. Almost daily reporting on Portugal has filled countless notebooks, and much of what I have recorded over the years had to be left out of newspaper and magazine articles for reasons of space. Some of the evidence set out here is anecdotal, the fruit of years of travel around Portugal and to its former colonies, and drawn from enlightening conversations with Portuguese friends and family. In that way, I hope to provide a view from the inside and the outside.

A third cue for this account was to offer solutions to an abiding puzzle. I have often been asked by my editors abroad how Portugal came to fall so far from the glorious days of the fifteenth and sixteenth centuries. Even Portuguese friends prod me for theories: "What happened to us?" they ask, eager for a concise explanation of why Portugal is today Western Europe's poorest country—in cash terms, anyway. It is a big question, though, and it could never begin to be addressed in a single newspaper article, nor in a passing conversation. Possible answers can be teased out only in a whole book.

The riddle of Portugal's economic misfortune is all the harder to figure out because while the Portuguese are marvellously cordial and affable people it is notoriously difficult for outsiders to get closer to them, to step into their intimate and tightly-wrapped social circles where many of the answers lie. Some twelve million tourists come to Portugal each year, but many of them head straight to the many delightful beaches. Most could probably name a Portuguese soccer player, or identify port wine as a Portuguese product. But beyond that foreigners know little of the real Portugal, and find it very hard to fathom. In this effort they are handicapped, first of all, by unfamiliarity. How often do you read about Portugal in your daily paper? How much does the general public abroad know about, say, the Age of Discovery and Portugal's four-continent empire, António Salazar's prolonged twentieth-century dictatorship, or the Carnation Revolution that brought democracy in the 1970s and laid the foundations for Portugal to blossom as part of modern Europe?

This country can be all the more baffling if it is approached on the premise that it must be like Spain, which it is not. The seemingly impenetrable language, the sound of which was once likened to windsurfing from consonant to consonant, is another barrier. My intention, then, is to shine a light on this enigmatic corner of Europe, describe the idiosyncrasies that make this lovable and sometimes exasperating country unique, and seek explanations by surveying the historical path that brought the Portuguese to where they are today.

Dangers lurk, of course, in any attempt to synthesize an entire country in a few hundred pages. Broad brush strokes cannot capture the whole story, and some may be stung by generalizations they feel do not apply to them. Nevertheless, I have sought to convey the differences in Portugal between the urban elite and the largely overlooked countryside, and the generation gap between young people who have grown up as members of the European Union and their parents.

All that is between these covers was compiled in good faith by an author who owes some of the best years of his life to Portugal. My Portuguese colleagues have expressed astonishment at my refusal of job offers in New York, London, Brussels, and Madrid. They think I am mad. But I wanted to stay because Portugal, in some vital respects, beats those places hands-down. Many will agree. Others will discover Portugal and come to the same conclusion.

I must acknowledge the contribution to this work of my wife Carmo, who at times had to set me straight and whose cheerful optimism kept me going; my parents Roy and Rita Hatton for their encouragement and curiosity; my mother-in-law Luísa Beltrão, who invited me to co-author the first biography of Portugal's only ever woman prime minister, which came out in 2007; my valued friends Sandy Sloop, and Axel and Aida Bugge, for their unstinting support, wisdom and enthusiasm; and my children João, Maria, and Madalena, who just generally make the world a better place.

Introduction
Wrestling with Bulls

At the third bugle call bullfights in Portugal climb to their climax.

In the shirt-sleeve nights of the summer bullfighting season the circular arena blazes with bright light like a boxing ring. A lone bugler standing on a platform in the steeply-terraced stands announces the start of the event, and the crowd's excited chatter thins to an expectant murmur. A second burst from the bugle brings out a bullfighter on horseback. Heavy wooden gates are drawn apart and a bull bursts into the enclosure. A lively beast elicits a hum of approval from the crowd. With theatrical skill, the flamboyant horseman keeps his horse just beyond the reach of the horns as, in repeated charges, he sticks half-a-dozen barbed darts between the bull's shoulders. He salutes the cheering crowd and sidles triumphantly from the ring, leaving the panting bull alone.

Then the bugle sounds for a third time. On cue, eight young men vault over the arena's painted boards, their legs together, tidily, like gymnasts, and stride towards the bull. They are *forcados*, a group sometimes described by wide-eyed foreigners as the "Suicide Squad." They are impeccably attired in spotless white, knee-length stockings, skin-tight trousers, clipped waistcoat and jacket (traditionally blessed at a special Mass), a crimson length of cloth wrapped around their midriffs, a prim white shirt and tie. These amateur entertainers have been watching the bull's movements intently from the ringside while the horseman performed his tricks. They solemnly approach the fearsome beast in single file so it can only see the man at the front, lest it be scared it off by weight of numbers. The one at the front, who wears a floppy wool cap pulled down to his eyebrows, proceeds with dramatically paused paces towards the bull on the far side of the ring. He puffs out his chest, places his hands on his hips and bellows *Toiro! Toiro!* ("Bull, bull!") to taunt the half-ton of muscle and bone into charging at him. The crowd tenses up and mutters in anticipation. Some spectators cover their eyes. The bull snorts and, before long, it arches its back and dips its head, horns parallel to the ground, and kicking up bursts of sand with its stubby legs pounds towards the man who coolly steps into the gap between the horns, falls forward and grabs the bull around its tree-trunk of a neck. He hangs on for dear life as it flips him around like a rag doll. The crowd gasps. Sheer momentum means that the bull and his passenger plough full-tilt into the others behind who ricochet off the beast like skittles. Quickly they regroup and smother the bull's head and eventually it slows to a standstill. They do not always pull it off at the first attempt. Sometimes they have to dust themselves off, wipe away blood, and line up again. Occasionally, bones are broken and flesh is torn. It is a display of nerve that merits a standing ovation.

Wrestling a huge bull into submission with your bare hands is a uniquely Portuguese endeavor and a centuries-old tradition that invites parallels with how the Portuguese perceive themselves and their place in the greater scheme of things. They long ago took the role of indomitable underdogs arrayed against more potent forces that would submerge them but which, with varying degrees of success, they resist. The adversary, in historical terms, may be the perilous ocean or bigger, rival countries. It might be their own national leaders. The foe could also be identified as something vaguer, such as cruel fortune. Or they may recognize their antagonist as residing in their own temperament, because their way of life sometimes collides with their best interests— they do not, for instance, lack the valor and pluck for great accomplishments, but pooling their strength like the *forcados* does not always come naturally.

A common sentiment among the Portuguese is that the odds are stacked against them, that they are playing a losing game with fate. Since the glorious Age of Discovery—also called the Age of Exploration or Expansion—in the fifteenth and sixteenth centuries, when Portuguese seafarers valiantly met peril and menace head-on and took a lead in shaping the modern world, Portugal has mostly been riding at anchor. Fernando Pessoa, regarded as one of the country's greatest poets, in 1928 described the nation as "slumbering" since those maritime feats. There is a residual sense of loss.

Crushing historical setbacks, such as the catastrophic 1755 Lisbon earthquake and a stunting four-decade dictatorship in the middle of the twentieth century, kept a brighter future beyond Portugal's reach, or snatched it away. In the early years of the twenty-first century a recurring mood of despondency took hold once more as a cascade of miserable news and bad omens engulfed the Portuguese.

At a big NATO gathering in Prague in 2002, where the organization's new members from behind the former Iron Curtain were being anointed, each head of government sitting at the polished round table was granted a two-minute slot to expound on the weightiness of the historical moment. After each of the three dozen leaders had had their say they all started shuffling their papers and getting down to business. Then it dawned on someone: they had forgotten Portugal, one of the alliance's founding members. The Portuguese prime minister at the time, José Manuel Barroso, laughed off the gaffe and read out his prepared speech. But the bungle drew Portuguese minds back to a warning Barroso himself had delivered at home when he took office a few months earlier: "Portugal is in danger of becoming irrelevant," he said. Barroso, a former foreign minister who two years later would take the European Union's top job in Brussels, was keenly aware of his country's shrinking stature and how much ground it had lost in its effort to keep up with its continental peers.

He was not the only one who was worried. José Gil, the country's leading philosopher, picked up the same theme in his 2004 book *Portugal Today: The Fear of Existing*. "Portugal is at risk of disappearing," he concluded. This observation was not necessarily meant to be taken literally, though the perennial Portuguese debate about possibly joining Spain as a single Iberian nation had been amplified by the bleak times. Rather, it was a reference to the growing sentiment that Portugal was doomed to be a B-list country.

As a small nation, Portugal's fate is scripted in large part by its bigger partners and by events that happen elsewhere—a circumstance that exacerbates feelings of vulnerability.

Like a Stopped Wheel

Portugal, once an envied world power and, in the sixteenth century, arguably the world's wealthiest nation, has become an unheralded land. And there is something tragic in how this could happen to such a charming people who so conspicuously delight in the good things in life and who undeniably possess some enviable traits. As many who know the country will insist, although there is something deeply amiss in modern Portugal there is also something wonderfully right about its people. And Portugal's is a fascinating story. Dorothy Wordsworth Quillinan, the poet's daughter Dora, remarked in her 1847 book on the Iberian Peninsula that Portugal has "the most romantic of histories."

It appeared that Portugal had put its protracted difficulties behind it when it joined the European Union, then called the European Economic Community, in 1986. Economic boom years gave the impression that the country had finally found its path to prosperity and parity with the rest of the continent. It blossomed and came to be viewed as a model European state. Portugal silenced its detractors by racking up triumphs—making the grade, for example, to be allowed into the club of countries adopting the common euro currency after northern European officials had mockingly dismissed its chances.

Foreign tourists came to look for themselves and were delighted to discover the pleasant and easygoing Portuguese, their agreeable lifestyle and their peaceful and enchanting land. As the former newspaper editor Sérgio Figueiredo notes: "We look, at first sight, as if we don't have a worry in the world. Foreign visitors are impressed."

But the sense of well-being was short-lived. Portugal was ambushed by the EU's late twentieth-century eastward expansion, which saw the bloc's balance of power see-saw back away from the continent's southwestern corner, and by globalization, which drew back the curtain on apparently immutable Portuguese weaknesses.

As Western Europe's poorest country, accounting for only around 1 percent of the EU's GDP, Portugal has had a very hard time navigating the obstacles of the twenty-first century, at one point prompting *The Economist* magazine to brand it "the sick man of Europe." In the late twentieth century Portugal's per capita wealth crested at over 78 percent of the EU average. After that, it stalled and stumbled until by 2008 it was back at 76 percent. It was like a stopped wheel.

The new century brought with it Portugal's most prolonged economic woes in almost a hundred years, and a deep sense of malaise darkened the national mood. From 1985 to 2000, Portugal's economy grew above the average EU rate; between 2001 and 2008 it grew half as fast as the rest of the bloc.

The evidence of sclerosis in its economy—and, by extension, in its society and culture—was all around. Little wealth was generated. By 2009 the Portuguese average monthly salary stood at just under a measly €900 and the minimum monthly wage, taken home by several hundred thousand Portuguese, was—embarrassingly—under €500 (in Luxembourg it was about €1,500). The Organization for Economic Cooperation and Development (OECD), exposing continental inequalities, states that the Portuguese earn on average about 40 percent less than workers in other Western European countries. The European Union reported in 2008 that about 18 percent of the Portuguese population—roughly two million people—were living below the point where it drew the bloc's poverty line. Only Poland and Latvia were worse off.

The economic feebleness subtracted from Portugal's diplomatic clout. Portugal's shadow, once cast across four continents, was ever shorter. Some media in other European countries snorted at the 2004 appointment of a former Portuguese prime minister as European Commission president, tacking to Barroso the uncharitable nickname "Mr. Nobody"—because no one from Portugal, the thinking went, could possibly have much leverage.

After periods of recession in 2003 and 2004, the global crisis delivered a further heavy blow to the anemic Portuguese economy. It stagnated in 2008 and then shrank by 2.7 percent in 2009. Greece's economic woes preyed on Portuguese minds as the country's debt load climbed close to similarly unsustainable levels. But the mild-mannered Portuguese, accustomed to hard times in recent centuries, stoically took emergency austerity measures in their stride. There was none of the street violence witnessed in Athens.

At the start of the twenty-first century, Portugal is in limbo. The future has gone out of focus and the past seems to add little to the present. As they have tried to figure out why they are still bringing up the rear, the Portuguese have come up with caustic diagnoses and have sardonically pinned the responsibility on themselves. "The problem is inside us. Us as a people. Us as a country's raw material," Eduardo Prado

Coelho, a leading intellectual, wrote introspectively of the troubled times. "Yes, I have decided to find out who's to blame and I'm sure I will find who it is when I look in the mirror."

The glum times may have eclipsed, for the moment, the hopeful mood that appeared in the 1990s, but the truth is the Portuguese possess—in abundance—qualities such as resilience, adaptability, and forbearance that portend better times. In some fields of endeavor, such as shifting to renewable energy sources and online services, Portugal is showing Europe the way forward. Around the globe, there are Portuguese expatriates whose outstanding talents have won them top jobs in multinational companies. Inside Portugal, too, despite being stifled by some outdated ways, a new generation is breaking through and could soon take the helm. They are young people who have grown up with different experiences and consequently different presumptions from those of their parents. This generation is unlikely to settle for anything less than EU standards and it is they who are starting to refashion Portugal and restore its fortunes.

The Portuguese are also an amiable, easygoing people with a lifestyle and culture, as well as delightful landscapes, which draw praise from millions of tourists every year. As Foreign Minister Luís Amado noted in early 2010, betraying some exasperation about his country-men's habit of accentuating the negative: "I only hear people saying bad things about Portugal in Portugal."

And one thing is for sure: any country which wrestles bulls for fun can never be written off.

Chapter One
561 by 218
Small Space, Big Contrasts

A few years ago I was driving with a Portuguese colleague in north-west Germany when we came to a junction. The signposts offered us a series of destinations: either Paris, Brussels, or Frankfurt, all of them a manageable car-ride away. A self-evident but arresting fact struck us both at the same time: we were at the heart of European political and economic power, and Portugal was miles away. To get to Lisbon, we would have to drive down through France, over the Pyrenees and, getting further and further away, across Spain and then across Portugal. On the face of it, this was no eureka-magnitude revelation. But the cold geographical fact astonished and briefly silenced us. A mundane signpost had brought home the fundamental remoteness that conspires to make Portugal a low-profile country and breeds a sense of apartness.

Portugal lives in Europe's suburbs, far from where the action is, clamped into a corner by Spain and confronted by the earth's second-largest ocean, whose vastness makes anyone feel small. Portugal seldom shows up on the radar screen of world news. The Portuguese are infuriated by the way international television channels regularly omit their little southwestern rectangle in continental weather forecasts and take it as a snub. They also bristle when foreign media depict Portugal as a place where old men with flat caps and old women in black shawls ride clapped-out donkeys across narrow fields. A British television channel did just that when illustrating where soccer manager José Mourinho came from, despite the fact that he is from Setúbal, an industrial port city rich in drab factories and unattractive apartment blocks. The Portuguese are determined to be seen that way no longer, and as part of a sustained effort to dispel such outdated impressions the government wheeled out one of the capital's slick new trolleys, instead of the quaint old ones, to ferry European leaders at the glitzy signing ceremony of the Lisbon Treaty in 2007.

When I told my eldest, Portuguese-born daughter, then fifteen, that I was writing this book her immediate response was: "Oh dad, don't

The south portal of the sixteenth-century Jerónimos Monastery in Lisbon

make us out to be a bunch of yokels. That's what everyone thinks of us."
She had a point. Even the Portuguese sometimes concur. It is not
uncommon to hear a Lisbon taxi driver ranting about his compatriots'
poor driving skills, along the lines of "We're a bunch of country folk
living in a city." And when a planeload of Portuguese breaks into spontaneous applause at the successful landing of their aircraft, the embarrassment of some of their countrymen is palpable.

Correcting mistaken foreign perceptions is a battle against the
national legacy, however, and it will not be won quickly. Portugal has no
big companies a European might effortlessly list, and few Portuguese
personalities are household names outside of soccer. A foreigner's
appraisal of Portuguese literature would maybe yield mention of authors
such as the epic sixteenth-century poet Luís de Camões, the twentieth-
century poet Fernando Pessoa, who also wrote in English, and the 1998
Nobel literature laureate José Saramago, but few, if any, beyond that. And
while people could rattle off the name of at least one famous monument in most European capitals without difficulty (Big Ben, the Eiffel
Tower, etc.), what Lisbon landmark would trip off anyone's tongue?

Pessoa, the poet, wanted to rescue Portugal from obscurity and with
that aim in mind wrote a guidebook in English in 1925 called *Lisbon:
What the Tourist Should See*. He noted: "For the average Britisher, and,
indeed, for the average anything (except Spaniard) outside Portugal,
Portugal is a vague small country somewhere in Europe, sometimes
supposed to be part of Spain..."

It is taken for granted that Portugal is an unconsidered country in
global affairs. It is why the American satirical magazine *The Onion*,
during the 2008 US presidential election, could make a joke out of it
in a spoof questionnaire for candidates: "How would Hillary Clinton
deal with a nuclear-capable Portugal?" Then there was Homer's threat
in an episode of *The Simpsons* when he went to watch a soccer game
between Portugal and Mexico: "I'll kill myself if Portugal doesn't win!"
The joke, apparently, lies in the question: how could anyone take so
seriously a place that many would find hard to locate on a world map?
Truth is stranger than fiction: a friend who works for a global US media
organization was discussing a story idea on the phone with an American
editor in New York who after ten minutes interrupted with the ques-

tion, "Where did you say Portugal was again?"

The sense of feeling unheeded is perhaps why the Portuguese make so much fuss when their country occasionally does merit some media coverage abroad. Respected Portuguese newspapers publish articles about articles about Portugal published in foreign newspapers and magazines. It has a certain novelty value. Conversely, the Portuguese, while quick to criticize their own country, are easily stung by disapproving foreigners. That has long been the case as they felt disparaged and disregarded by bigger countries, and it is no less true now amid the mood of dejection and low self-esteem that set in after the country's early twenty-first-century difficulties.

The singular language is another handicap to a more intimate acquaintance with Portugal. Travel through Europe and people cannot identify what language you are speaking, much less what you are saying. Brows furrow when people hear Portuguese, as if they are trying to place a rare smell or flavor. Once, a Dutch woman asked me and my family what we were speaking. When we told her, she said, "Oh! I thought it was Hebrew or something."

On the one hand, this ignorance rankles. Some 220 million people around the world speak Portuguese as their native tongue. If more people speak Portuguese as their first language than speak French, German, Italian or Japanese, how can it be deemed "minor"? The great bulk of Portuguese-speakers are in the remnants of the bygone empire: Brazil and the five former Portuguese colonies in Africa as well as East Timor in Asia. On the other hand, the Portuguese find such linguistic incomprehension flattering. It makes them feel special. They hold dear a famous phrase by Pessoa: "My homeland is the Portuguese language." They love the way foreigners find it so hard to speak well. They fondly describe their language as "treacherous." Like other peoples with lesser-known languages, the Portuguese have developed a creditable knack for speaking other tongues. A foreign visitor can usually get by with English, French, or Spanish.

Geographic detachment has kept Portugal at a remove from continental influences, perhaps most crucially the Industrial Revolution but also European trends in philosophy and science. When I moved to Portugal more than two decades ago, I had little more than a romantic notion of the country, some vague ideas rooted in the exotic unknown, like a distant destination listed on an airport departure board. My imagination had been captured by a passing reference in Bob Dylan's song "Sara": "Sleepin' in the woods by a fire in the night/Drinkin' white rum in a Portugal bar." But stepping off the train in Lisbon in the mid-1980s was like stepping back in time. I had come from London, a postmodern city of punks, to a country where a 1950s retro style appeared to be all the rage. I was mistaken. The latest fashions simply had not spread this far. I had the distinct sensation I had washed up in a European backwater.

Spontaneous Generosity

There was, nevertheless, a spell in the late 1980s when Portugal was in vogue. This newcomer to the European Economic Community, as the European Union was then called, excited a lot of curiosity among foreign media. For centuries it had been standing on the continent's sidelines. Now, by joining the bloc on 1 January 1986, it had been called into the first team. Still, Portugal—along with Spain, Italy, and Greece—was viewed by some northern European diplomats as an incorrigible slacker, and they condescendingly lumped the southern European countries together under the moniker "Club Med." It hinted at a certain disdain, or superciliousness, which would surface again in the 2009 financial crisis when the term PIGS—denoting Portugal, Italy, Greece, and Spain—was employed to describe the countries seen as fiscally lax, even though the four were not alone in overstepping the line.

The spate of interest faded, however, and just about vanished when Eastern European countries began to draw the limelight after the fall of the Berlin Wall. Portugal—unfortunately for foreign correspondents in Lisbon—stirs little interest nowadays. It does not possess the economic, and consequently diplomatic, weight that would make it a player on the world stage.

Anyone who spends any length of time getting to know Portugal, though, might conclude that Western Europe's poorest country is in some ways its wealthiest. Large swathes of undeveloped countryside make for a rare natural idyll, likened by the medieval epic poet Camões—in a poetic flourish guaranteed to appeal to national sentiment—to "a garden growing by the sea." In truth Portugal possesses some of the most stunningly beautiful places you have never heard of.

For a start, its geography offers a fascinating mosaic of contrasting features. Continental Portugal, up to just 561 kilometers (350 miles) long and 218 kilometers (135 miles) wide, packs a lot of unexpected variety into a small space. Francisco Manuel de Mello Breyner wrote in the nineteenth century: "Few countries of a similar size have such a varied landscape as Portugal nor show such sensitive differences in their spontaneous local flora and farming practices." Ramalho Ortigão, a writer from the same period, remarked that a person suddenly transported from the Minho province in the far north to the Alentejo province in the south would think they were many more leagues distant, such is the dissimilarity. Orlando Ribeiro, a twentieth-century geographer and historian who described the Portuguese landscape at length, judged it to be "Mediterranean by nature and Atlantic by location"—a feature that adds to the country's fascination.

Given the rich diversity, Francisco da Cunha Leal in his 1960 book *The Portuguese Enigma* thought it "intriguing" that national bonds had survived intact. He had a point. Regions of Portugal look much more suitably matched with their neighboring Spanish provinces than with other Portuguese ones. The Algarve, for example, is much more like Andalucia than the Minho, which in turn is more like Galicia.

The historian José Mattoso explains that Portugal is not determined by a single ethnic source but is a political/administrative circumstance that dates from its birth. It slowly expanded into a nation that was an aggregate of distinct territories with very different ways of life. So the unity of Portugal as a land and language contrasts with its territorial diversity. Portugal was the first European nation to adopt its local tongue as its official language. Latin was used by the royal courts and the courts of law during the Middle Ages but Portugal's sixth king, Dinis (1261-1325), decreed Portuguese the official language of government.

Still, the local differences lingered and contribute to that tribal Portuguese tendency called *bairrismo*—a reference to *bairros* or neighborhoods—but a word that also stands as a metaphor for small defensive groupings in business, politics, or society. Mattoso recounts that one day nineteenth-century King Luís called out from his yacht to some fishermen in a boat, asking if they were Portuguese. "Us? No, my Lord," they replied. "We're from Póvoa de Varzim," a town near Porto. That local outlook manifests itself still. A classic, indignant rebuff to a stranger's presumption is the expression, *Não o conheço de nenhum lado* ("I don't know you from anywhere"). It is a clannish sentiment, which speaks of a people who have been oppressed to a point that that they are reflexively wary of outsiders and stick together for safety. Detached houses in Portugal, too, are inevitably cloistered behind high walls, as if on guard against the world.

The suspicion of outsiders also stems from the remoteness of large parts of the interior. Though just a couple of hours' drive from Lisbon, they seem a world away. In a small southeastern town called Amareleja, hard on the border with Spain, a colleague and I walked down a long street lined with low houses where several groups of people were sitting outdoors. As we neared them they got up smartly, took their chairs indoors and shut the front door. At the end of the street I glanced over my shoulder and saw they had all come back out. I had a flashback to those old cowboy films where the saloon piano player stops playing and everyone falls silent when strangers walk in.

Rural cultures, of course, tend to be very local in their outlook, and Portugal was a largely rural country until the second half of the twentieth century, when migration and better roads changed its complexion. Even so, migrating workers took their rural mentality to the cities with them. At the same time, these people can be tremendously accommodating, and small acts of generosity are not uncommon. The traveller, after all, could be a fellow sufferer. A Spanish friend of mine once had a flat tire on a Sunday in a place like Amareleja and needed a mechanic's help. He asked at the local café and the owner stepped out from behind the counter and walked with him to the house of the village mechanic who, it turned out, was having his afternoon nap. Without a grumble he got up and went to help the person in need. That unmatched British travel writer of the past century, V. S. Pritchett, in his 1964 book *Foreign Faces*, described himself, in proverbial fashion, as being "as obliging as a Portuguese." A popular song called *Uma Casa*

Portuguesa ("A Portuguese Home") celebrates this spontaneous, heart-warming generosity, eulogizing the manner in which people are invited into a humble abode for a drink and something to eat: "The happiness of poverty/Lies in the great wealth/Of giving, and the pleasure it brings."

This small country with tightly-knit communities and a strong web of kinship may no longer produce the large Catholic families of yore with a dozen or more children. However, when people usually have three or four surnames after their Christian name, and can tack on as many as eight, it is easier to tease out the threads of shared history. The author and university professor João Medina, describing Portugal as "a little island clamped onto a peninsula," commented, with his tongue only partly in his cheek: "We're all each other's cousins. We're a country where if two people get on a train in (Lisbon), by the time they reach Coimbra, they find out that they have numerous friends in common or live 100 meters apart on the same street. And if they keep going as far as Porto, they'll disembark convinced they're very close cousins."

Portuguese families, especially those outside the cities anyway, tend to stick together. It is not only a matter of emotional comfort but is in part a question of economic feasibility. Children live at home longer than, say, in Britain. Low incomes make it hard to buy a house, and low education levels limit job opportunities. And the Portuguese tend to dote on their children. The essayist Eduardo Lourenço noted the "permanent and spectacular adoration of the child-king (especially the male)," thereby perhaps exposing the roots of a male-dominated culture. The spontaneous kindliness also has to do with the need for self-help in response to the inadequate care furnished by the welfare state. "The Portuguese are so good because their State is so bad," a longtime Swedish resident once commented. ✓

Cunha Leal observed that Portugal, despite the cracks, has sustained its national cohesiveness by dint of what he called "a demonstration of sheer will-power." The Portuguese like it this way. The Portuguese court was itinerant, of no fixed abode, up to the late sixteenth century and the regal progression around the country, historians say, helped weave the social fabric tighter. When in the late fourteenth and early fifteenth centuries King João I and his queen Filipa journeyed through the kingdom they encountered no private fiefdoms, no breakaway movements, everyone speaking the same language without dialects, united under the Crown. That said, the country's relatively small size also facilitated a modern system of political centralism. Lisbon remains the political citadel. And the centralization of power has not always been helpful.

Capital and Countryside

Porto, Portugal's second-largest city, has long chafed at Lisbon's dominance. The two Atlantic port cities share about half the country's population and engage in teasing one-upmanship that mirrors the rivalry between Madrid and Barcelona. Porto portrays itself as a city of hard work and enterprise and Lisbon as a city that likes to sit around giving orders and spending the country's money. Porto begrudges the capital its cosmopolitan glamour and scoffs at its apparent blithe high-living. "Porto works while Lisbon plays," the saying goes. The region around Porto is home to the country's major textile and footwear industries.

In Lisbon, Porto people are sniggeringly caricatured as coarse and parochial, as people who curse a lot (they do, and they are very funny with it) and who in their pronunciation swap the letter "v" for "b" (Porto's inner-city ring-road is the VCI, which comes out as BCI; and you hear "baca" for cow instead of "vaca.") Porto, however, comes across as better-balanced than Lisbon, not as dressy and not as international in its flavor but firmer in its sense of self—an authenticity that seems at one with the city's solid granite buildings. Porto's sophistication feels more muted, more sensible than Lisbon's.

Porto, like the north of Portugal generally, is markedly more conservative and traditional than Lisbon and the south—a feature that generated so much friction after the 1974 Carnation Revolution that a civil war looked to be in the cards. On maps showing voting trends the north is colored blue. The south is mostly red. And in the north, even the smallest villages seem to have several churches. They call Lisbon people Moors, after the Arab occupiers from North Africa who held Lisbon much longer than Porto. In other words, they view them as heathens.

Lisbon has long basked in its national primacy and privilege. Eça de Queirós, the great nineteenth-century Portuguese novelist, made famous a phrase that is still apt and a commonplace observation: "Portugal is Lisbon. The rest is countryside." It is an opinion that maintains its resonance. A Portuguese friend remarked to me not long ago: "Lisbon bleeds the country dry." (He was from Porto.)

The general feeling, not just in Porto, is that Lisbon, as the seat of government, rakes in taxes, splashes out on itself and hands out the crumbs to rural areas. The notion is backed up by statistics. Lisbon is the only Portuguese region whose per capita income is above the EU's average. Northern areas of Portugal, by contrast, barely reach 60 percent of that average. Cross the border, where regional authorities have more power, and the contrast is plain: rural Spanish towns are much better equipped.

Portugal's development has been strikingly lopsided. The cities, most of them on the coast, profited from the sporadic boom times in recent decades but rural areas largely missed out. Reflecting on this, the sociologist António Barreto says, "Most of the EU is made up of wealthy countries with pockets of poverty. Portugal is a poor country with pockets of wealth."

A former prime minister, Pedro Santana Lopes, acknowledged in 2008 that there had been unfairness in the distribution of generous EU development aid. "We had the EU funds and we have the country that stands before us," he said. "A large part of the country is worse off now than it was twenty years ago. It's poorer, more remote, has an elderly population and is vulnerable." Take the largely rural southern Alentejo province, for instance. Official statistics showed that in 2004 almost half its population lived on an old-age pension that averaged €266 a month. On top of that, the illiteracy rate was 15 percent.

The lack of economic development can be misleading, however. It is a temptation to assume that country folk are out-of-touch bumpkins. One Sunday afternoon I stopped at a café in a one-horse village about an hour north of Lisbon, well off the beaten track, and as I walked in I noticed everyone inside was intently watching a TV screen above the door. I turned around and looked up and saw it was showing the final of some major international tennis tournament. I settled at the bar and started watching the match. At one point, the ruddy-faced, pot-bellied farmer next to me shook his head, turned to his friend and sighed, "Agassi's got to work on that backhand."

The great Portuguese poet Miguel Torga described in 1950 how Lisbon stands aloof from the rest of the country. It is an attitude that has brought mutual hostility, he said. The capital disdains the countryside, embarrassed by the backwardness of rural areas that through its own neglect it helped to create. Meanwhile, people outside the capital seethe at Lisbon's rapture with things foreign.

Torga, a northerner, conceded that for all its faults Lisbon is "pretty." Few would disagree. Lord Byron, in his nineteenth-century narrative poem *Childe Harold's Pilgrimage*, exclaimed, "What beauties doth Lisboa first unfold!" Approached from the south bank at dusk in the summer, after a long, lazy day on the beach at Caparica across the River Tagus, Lisbon shimmers with a delightful pink glow. It is a rare beauty. A bright, white city, it shows depth in its shades of ochre and the tilting shadows of its narrow streets. Fernando Pessoa, in his Lisbon guidebook in English, wrote:

> For the traveller who comes in from the sea, Lisbon, even from afar, rises like a fair vision in a dream, clear-cut against a bright blue sky which the sun gladdens with its gold. And the domes, the monuments, the old castles jut up above the mass of houses, like far-off heralds of this delightful seat, of this blessed region.

Pessoa, who wrote under three main pseudonyms as well as his own name and has been described as "Portugal's best four poets of the twentieth century," is identified with Lisbon in the same way James Joyce is associated with Dublin. There is a sense of drawing on the essence of the place. Pessoa, who on his walks through the city cut a diminutive figure in a black hat and suit and wore a moustache and wire glasses, termed the capital his *aldeia* ("village"), cherishing its small, familiar scale. He said the downtown district furnished "village streets in a city" and was particularly fond of empty squares because, he said, they were "a village thing in the city."

Pessoa was born and died in Lisbon and, like many Portuguese,

travelled a lot of miles in-between. He spent ten years of his youth in South Africa, where he learned English, after his mother married a Portuguese consul there. He returned to Lisbon alone aged seventeen and moved in with his grandmother. From 1905 to his death in 1935 Pessoa lived at sixteen different addresses in Lisbon. He never married. He started a printing business but gravitated towards writing and criticism, co-founding a literary magazine called *Orpheu*, which produced just two editions and was widely mocked for its avant-garde poetry but remains a milestone in Portuguese culture. There is a bronze statue of Pessoa sitting alone at a table, one leg crossed over the other, outside the capital's downtown Chiado district's Brasileira café where he was a regular. His fondness for a strong drink, especially a spirit called *aguardente* (literally: firewater), gradually took a toll on his liver and by his mid-forties he was gravely ill. The last phrase he penned was in English: "I know not what tomorrow will bring." One of Portugal's most prestigious contemporary awards for outstanding work in the fields of science and the arts is the Pessoa Prize.

The view from Lisbon's giant suspension bridge, which bears a striking resemblance to San Francisco's Golden Gate Bridge, is deeply enchanting. It offers a panorama of the graceful city's hills, rolling from St. George's castle down to the Tagus, the peninsula's longest river at more than 1,100 kilometers (680 miles), and the quays from where the maritime explorers sailed. Nearby is the elegant sixteenth-century Jerónimos Monastery. As the writer José Cardoso Pires said, in Lisbon the river always seems to be at the bottom of the street. He likened the city to a ship docked beside the Tagus. Watching from one of the hilltops, the ferries that trail white foam across the blue river capture the city's sedate rhythm. And there are plenty of hilltops: Lisbon is a hilly city that makes your thigh muscles sting. It used to be said that Lisbon stood on only seven hills but that was a myth created in a book from 1620 by a monk keen on drawing a parallel with Rome.

An unexpected feature of the capital is the noticeable number of decrepit or abandoned buildings in the best downtown neighborhoods. There are two reasons for this urban decay: rent controls and inheritance laws. Some of the older indexed rents are a mere pittance, just a handful of euros. That is welcome for the elderly people on low pensions who have lived in the tenements all their lives, but for landlords it means there is no point investing in building upkeep because they get no return. Commercial property development has been choked for the same reason. One popular four-story, 54-room hotel in the heart of Lisbon's downtown district pays only around €600 a month in rent (about the equivalent of a few nights' stay in a single room) to the building's owners. Not surprisingly, the owners are less than happy. A new rent law introduced in 2005 was intended to change the situation, but typically lengthy bureaucratic procedures dampened early hopes. The inheritance law, meanwhile, stipulates that at least two-thirds of a bequest must go to the spouse and children of the deceased. In a country that not too long ago had big families this means that property can be split between dozens of heirs down the generations. I know of one case where ownership of a prime city center property is shared between forty members of the same family. It is crumbling because for decades they have been quarrelling over what to do with it. Only climbing real estate values are shifting such blockages.

Perhaps the Portuguese capital's greatest asset is its human scale— the hallmark that captured Pessoa's imagination. Lisbon would be a fair-sized town in a bigger European country. Skyscrapers do not grow here. As in Porto and other Portuguese cities, the vernacular architecture is small, as if deliberately abbreviated. The buildings stay close to pedestrians, helping the city cast its spell. Lisbon is low, touchable, and intimate. Closely built, it permits privacy and encourages fraternity. The narrow streets of the historic quarters and the shabby charm of their buildings bestow on the city an antique flavor.

The old quarters are like villages. Alfama, which girdles St. George's castle, is a one-time Arabic neighborhood with a warren of alleyways where the narrow buildings look poised to tumble down the hill. In Mouraria, at the foot of the castle hill and just a couple of hundred meters from Lisbon's main square, people still say, "I'm going into the city." These *bairros* possess an enigmatic complicity, an intimacy that is not easily broken into. Once you are invited in, though, the neighborliness inspires a seductive conviviality. While in Alfama and Mouraria many apartments are cramped and pokey, the façades can be deceptive: a nondescript front door with a couple of windows each side may lead into airy, high-ceilinged rooms and a terrace, garden, or patio out back.

These slices of old Lisbon are a prize for the *flâneur*. They are honeycombed with hidden patios, narrow side streets, and restaurants that make only a token effort to draw attention. The streets ambush the stroller with clouds of smoke from grilling fish and the delicate scents of jacaranda and jasmine. Equally unexpected are prim ranks of apartment blocks painted in tasteful pinks, oranges, and pale blues. In the background there is the punctuating chatter from cafés and the whirr-bang-hum of coffee machines that suggest a soundtrack from Chaplin's *Modern Times*. Lisbon at its best has a folksy feel. A walk through the old quarters can include waving aside washing hung out to dry and side-stepping legless little barbecues smoking in alleys.

The pavements are a sight themselves. They are known as *calçada portuguesa*—a unique style that uses fist-sized chunks of white and black stone that are hand-cut and used to embroider pathways. The patterns are like waves tattooed into the pavement or like ribbons twisting in an onshore wind, as if the sea had stolen inland. A foreign friend of mine—one of those who did not take to Portugal at all—once scoffed at kneeling workmen artfully putting together one of these pavements. "We can send men to the moon but here they're still building pavements by hand," he groaned, rather missing the point. This urban art form can also be found in Brazil and in the former Portuguese colonies in Africa.

Walking along these patterned pavements you abruptly come across a bright splash of pink or yellow or orange bougainvillea or spy a crumbling panel of antique hand-painted tiles called *azulejos*, which embellish old palaces and churches as well as new buildings, including Lisbon underground stations. These tiles are practical, beautiful, and versatile. They make buildings cool in summer and protect against damp in winter. Like the pavements, *azulejos* are unique to Portugal. This art came from the North African Moors (in Arabic, *al-zulaij*—the root of the Portuguese term—means small polished stone). Once the Arabs had gone the Portuguese developed their own decorative style, portraying human figures that are forbidden in Muslim art, whereas Spain stuck with the Muslim convention. The painting is in cobalt blue on a milky white background. In Mouraria, there is a tumble-down police station at the top of a flight of uneven wooden stairs that are clad with exquisite panels of *azulejos* showing scenes from a royal hunt and a stately court.

Lisbon is also a relatively peaceful city when compared to other European capitals, as is Portugal as a whole. Television news footage of violent street demonstrations elsewhere in Europe or wars in the Middle East seem far removed. Lisbon is too easygoing to permit hostile radicalism or violent tension, and Portugal is poor soil for such sentiments. Except, that is, when some aggression is called for, as happened during the Age of Discovery. Jorge Dias, the writer, observed: "The Portuguese are, above all, deeply human, sensitive, loving and caring, without being weak. They don't like causing suffering and avoid conflict, but if they take offence, they can be violent and cruel."

Lisbon has something of a summer resort town's somnolence. At 9:30 a.m. there is still ample room to park in the city center, though an hour later it is congested. There is little sense of a rat race going on. It feels—and this is intended as a compliment—more like a gentle canter towards lunch. The Portuguese work to live, they do not live to work. There is not much evidence of the cultural and economic vitality encountered in, say, London, Paris, or Berlin, but Lisbon has a magnetism which those cities cannot match. Foreigners arrive and feel like they have washed up on a pretty, peaceful shore.

Head south and the pace of life slows even further. Going into the Alentejo province from Lisbon is like wading into mud, and getting served at a café or restaurant seems to take forever. People move slowly there and put it down to the aching summer heat, when temperatures can exceed 104°F (40°C). The center of the peninsula is scorched by the sun, sending people fleeing to the coast from the Alentejo, just like in neighboring Extremadura in Spain. The heat induces a drowsy indolence. City folk find the Alentejo people amusing because of that torpor and because they seem so out of step with the rest of the world. The Portuguese tell jokes about Alentejo people in the same way the British do about the Irish or the Americans about the Polish.

The Alentejo's signature landscape consists of cork forests and olive groves riding the swells and troughs of gently undulating meadows which are coated with thin, ankle-high grass. The trees stand motionless in the hissing heat. The oldest olive trees—some are said to be as old as Christianity—are short and twisted and tightly-wound, as if wringing themselves dry. They appear to have had their innards gouged out in some kind of trunk-cracking spasm of violence but still they survive and bear fruit.

The cork trees are "unmasked" every nine to twelve years. The spongy cork comes off in featherweight slabs, with a crackling, tearing sound like an orange being peeled, to reveal the living bark beneath. Then they stand bare, showing a color perhaps best described as "startled orange," as if they had been embarrassingly disrobed. The skilled harvesters paint the final digit of the year on each stripped tree so that in nine years' time they will know which trees to return to. Cork oaks are Portugal's most common tree, covering an estimated 2,840 square miles. A cork tree said to be the world's largest is in the Alentejo. It yields enough for some 100,000 bottle corks every nine years. Portugal is the world's largest cork producer and cork is an economic mainstay of the Alentejo region, though livelihoods are in peril due to the encroachment of plastic bottle-stoppers. In small towns such as Azaruja, where about 2,000 people live, wealth from cork has enabled locals to escape the fate of other fading rural communities. The town has a school, a bank, a pharmacy, and a post office—rare blessings in such a thinly-populated area.

The Alentejo's low, whitewashed farmhouses with thick walls and small windows against the heat stand in solitude, often abandoned now because small-scale farming rarely pays. In spring these silent plains are thick with the fragrance of wild herbs and colored with vast patches of purple, yellow, and red flowers around the cork trees.

There are big plans for the Alentejo, which accounts for roughly one-third of continental Portugal. Billions of euros are destined for private tourism developments. Most projects are along the unspoiled coastal beaches, which stretch virtually unbroken from Lisbon to the Algarve, and the future shoreline around the Alqueva reservoir, which became Europe's largest man-made lake (roughly the size of Malta) when it finally filled up in early 2010, eight years after being built.

It remains to be seen whether the Alentejo tourism authorities will learn from the mistakes that were made in the Algarve, the next province down, though given that the Algarve's mistakes were made after Spain's Costa del Sol became disfigured it is easy to be pessimistic. The development of tourism in the Algarve from the late 1960s was for too long a get-rich-quick scheme that sacrificed much of the southernmost region's character. Ugly apartment blocks pushed out the picturesque. The way the private and public spheres connived in copying what had been done in the worst Spanish resorts was almost like a ritual slaughter of the goose that laid the golden eggs. Tourists may still run into that short-sightedness, which of course is not exclusive to Portugal and is often a trait of poorer countries. A Portuguese friend told me how a restaurant owner he knew duped a British couple into paying way over the price for a dish of sardines. The story was a boast. But when one of Britain's biggest tour operators pulled out because the region had become overpriced, restaurant owners went running to the government to bail them out.

The name Algarve comes from *Al Gharb* (The West), in Arabic, which is what the North African Muslims called this part of the peninsula they occupied. In Portuguese, most words starting with "al" are of Arab origin—*aldeia* for village, *alface* for lettuce, for example. There are about 1,000 of them. Also, a genetic study found that about 14 percent of the Portuguese population has North African ancestry. Anyone familiar with North African towns is taken aback by the similarity with the Algarve. Only the minarets are missing. The town of Silves was a center of Arab culture between the ninth and twelfth centuries and is said to have been known at the time as "the Baghdad of the West." The Algarve still has fantastic beaches and an appealing climate but it lacks depth, being designed with a fortnight's holiday on the beach in mind.

Tourists wanting to avoid the evidence of the despoliation of the Algarve have to make a beeline either to one of the region's upscale resorts or to the lateral extremities such as picturesque Tavira near the Spanish border or, in the west, Sagres, where the sea's mood witnessed from the windswept cliffs provides a stirring drama. Otherwise, you might duck into the hilly Algarve hinterland.

Different Textures

Not far from Lisbon is the beguiling hilltop town of Sintra. It has an embarrassment of natural riches—dewy glades, dappled clearings in shady woods with limpid pools and bubbling brooks. It is the perfect cliché of rural beauty. Lord Byron, who grew tired of Lisbon's nineteenth-century squalor ("The dingy denizens are rear'd in dirt"), described Sintra as a "glorious Eden." It also has a deliciously flamboyant, wedding-cake palace called Pena, built by Portugal's German-born King Fernando II in the nineteenth century. Visible to the west is Cabo da Roca, the westernmost point of mainland Europe and a promontory that British seafarers heading south once knew as "the rock of Lisbon."

The Mafra palace: Portugal's most important baroque monument

Close by is the old farming town of Mafra. A nondescript place, it somewhat preposterously possesses a massive convent that is Portugal's most important baroque monument. The British traveller William Beckford wrote in 1787, "The distant convent of Mafra, glowing with ruddy light, looked like the enchanted palace of a giant, and the surrounding country bleak and barren, as if the monster had eaten it desolate." This is the building that almost broke the back of the country's eighteenth-century economy. It is said that 45,000 people, overseen by 7,000 soldiers, worked on it for years. Everything that went into it was imported except for marble from nearby quarries. The tale of the forced labor and the effort to transport huge chunks of marble by ox cart (going downhill was worse than going up) are memorably captured by José Saramago, the Nobel literature laureate, in his 1982 historical fantasy *Memorial do Convento*, published in English as *Baltasar and Blimunda*. The convent's Harry Potter-style library is unmissable.

The monasteries at Batalha and Alcobaça, on the way to Porto, are equally captivating, providing plenty of material for glossy coffee-table books. Batalha, built on the orders of King João I to celebrate victory over Castile at the Battle of Aljubarrota in 1385, looks today as if it has landed by chance next to a busy road. Inside its curlicue cloisters is a monument to the Unknown Soldier commemorating military feats at Aljubarrota, during the *reconquista* when Portugal pushed out the North African Arabs, and in the First World War. Alcobaça, meanwhile, is Portugal's gothic centerpiece. It cannot boast the ornateness of Batalha but King Pedro I and Inês de Castro—known as a real-life Romeo and Juliet for their doomed fourteenth-century love affair—lie in intriguing carved tombs inside the monument of blank grandeur.

In Fátima, home to a world-famous Catholic shrine, the boundaries of good taste have been overrun by a tawdry world of trinkets—plaster saints with haloes of flashing lights or plastic saints that change color with shifts in the weather—just like Lourdes or Medjagore. The shrine marks the spot, roughly, where in 1917 the Virgin Mary is said to have appeared. Three shepherd children aged between seven and ten claimed to witness the apparitions in a field on the edge of their unremarkable farming town. The visions are said to have occurred on the 13th of the month from May to October. By the sixth apparition, thousands gathered to watch. On that day, according to accounts, cloudy skies cleared and the sun "danced" around the sky. In 1930 the Church declared the event to be The Miracle of the Sun. (Some contend it was, in fact, a visiting UFO, while others, more prosaically, have protested that the children were exploited by the Church.)

In addition to the apparitions, the children reported that Our Lady of Fátima confided three prophecies to them. The first two secrets, made public by Church authorities in 1941, together foretold the end of the First World War, the outbreak of the Second World War and the rise and fall of Soviet communism. Details of the third prophecy, however, were held back, ensuring an aura of mystery about the so-called Third Secret that fired the public imagination. What could the prediction contain that was so horrible as to be unfit for publication? On May 13, 2000, when Pope John Paul II was making his third visit to the Fátima shrine, the Vatican stunned worshippers by unexpectedly disclosing what the Third Secret revealed. It turned out to be a foretelling of the 1981 shooting of the pope. Worldwide interest in this revelation brought a spike in internet traffic that jammed the Vatican's website all day. Almost inevitably, after all the doomsday speculation, there was a general sentiment of disappointment. Nor did the Vatican's disclosure end the plethora of conspiracy theories, instead keeping interest alive. Fátima's fame, too, has shown no signs of flagging. It draws some six million visitors a year, and in 2007 the shrine was endowed with a new church that can hold close to 9,000 worshippers—the old one held just 800—and claims to be the world's fourth-largest Catholic place of worship.

Cutting across the country from east to west, starting in Spain and reaching the Atlantic at Porto, the River Douro has some of the most stunningly beautiful scenery to be found anywhere in Europe. The river snakes through steep-sided valleys, beneath ragged ridges where eagles glide, and rows of vines in regimented lines curl like ribs around the steep slopes of scree and powdery soil. In late summer, heavy bunches of grapes as sweet as jam dangle in vineyards that stretch dozens of kilometers down the valley. Centuries-old wine estates known as *quintas* stand behind thick, whitewashed walls.

The northernmost provinces of Minho and Gerês have a wholly

different texture from the southern part of the country. Here, high hills and thick forests of pine and eucalyptus and the rocky terrain demand a different type of farming. While the fields of cereal crops that stretched across the Alentejo plains earned it fame as the country's "bread basket," the far north was necessarily dissected into small, sometimes tiny, patches of farmland wherever the topography permitted.

During the invasions of Portugal by Napoleon's armies in the early nineteenth-century Peninsular War, the French General Jean-Andoche Junot, exhibiting what some might see as typical Parisian arrogance, expressed the opinion that the beauty of northern Portugal was wasted on the "barbarians" who lived there. Byron was no less impolite: "Poor, paltry slaves! Yet born 'midst noblest scenes/Why, Nature, waste thy wonders on such men?" Large parts of the northern region, including many of its towns, look like The Land that Time Forgot. Portugal may be small but a sense of remoteness still clings to rural villages. Some more isolated communities in the hills of Trás-os-Montes (literally, Behind-the-Mountains), a province in the northeast, seem preserved in amber because from the 1950s they were so poor that anyone who could left to find work. These migrants either settled around Portuguese cities or travelled to other European countries, usually France. The phenomenon, scientifically termed "desertification," has bequeathed picturesque old towns where almost nobody lives. They remain ghost towns until August, anyway, when the emigrants return home in their expensive cars to show how well they are doing (they also harbor a fondness for the alpine-style *maisons* they saw abroad and which they insist on reproducing in Portugal).

August is the month of traditional street parties known as *festas populares*, punctuated with homemade fireworks and big meals, when left-behind grandparents touchingly reunite with their visiting children and grandchildren—though the grandchildren are sometimes surly French teenagers in leather jackets resentful about being stuck in mountain villages. And often they cannot speak Portuguese, making their grandparents' efforts to reach out to them particularly poignant. Miguel Torga, the poet, wrote: "I shall die knowing two things for sure: that there is no more beautiful country than Portugal, nor one that is so sad."

Island Idylls

The Atlantic archipelagos of Madeira and the Azores are dreamscapes for anyone looking to flee a crowd. These Atlantic islands were uninhabited before being settled by the Portuguese in the early fifteenth century. They are possessions that date from the infancy of Portugal's maritime exploration, its first steps on the way to becoming an intercontinental empire—an adventure driven by the pursuit of wealth and the Roman Catholic church's proselytizing urge. The first children of Portuguese settlers born on the virgin *terra firma* of Madeira were boy and girl twins who were baptized Adam and Eve.

These islands' common denominators are remoteness, a sedate pace of life, and jaw-dropping natural beauty. It should also be said there is not a great deal to do besides appreciate that picturesque quality. In EU jargon these are "ultra-peripheral" regions—that is, a long way away from the bloc's center—and as such they merit special aid, a kind of economic life support that is doled out locally by their regional governments. Stuck on a rock in the ocean there is limited scope for betterment, and mass emigration has been a trait of these islands' history.

The Azores, Europe's westernmost outpost, have been a haven of dry land in Atlantic crossings and a useful staging post and refuelling depot since the Age of Discovery. The first transatlantic flights in the 1930s stopped over in the Azores, and the US Air Force has kept an important strategic base at Lajes on Terceira island since the Second World War. Seen from the air, after a two-hour flight from Lisbon 1,600 kilometers (995 miles) away, the nine islands punctuate the broad blue ocean like little green bubbles and look to be in imminent peril from the crowding sea.

The volcanic soil, the generous rainfall and the influence of the warm Gulf Stream make most of the Azores islands fabulously fertile. Locals say (with a touch of pride) that you can experience weather from all four seasons of the year—driving wind and rain, baking heat, blazing sunshine, and thick, chilly mist—in the space of 24 hours. The islands are exposed, scarily so, to the elements, but bear a bucolic peacefulness. The lush, expansive pastures, marked off with ancient dry-stone walls of black lava and flecked with whitewashed houses and dairy cows, are a dazzling emerald green reminiscent of Ireland. Volcanic craters are padded with bright flowers and ferns and conceal blue lagoons. Banks of hydrangeas line narrow lanes, and vehicles are scarce. There is a sense of the primitive, of otherness, in the islands that American writer John Updike picked up on in his 1964 poem "Azores": "Great green ships/themselves, they ride/at anchor forever;/beneath the tide/huge roots of lava/hold them fast/in mid-Atlantic/to the past."

Just as there is something antique about the geography, the Azoreans, too, are thought of on the mainland as old-fashioned in their ways. They are a notably religious and conservative people and have what, for a Portuguese-speaking foreigner at least, is an almost indecipherable accent. Mark Twain passed through the Azores and in his 1869 book *The Innocents Abroad* was sniffy, not to say rude, about the people he came across: "The community is eminently Portuguese—that is to say, it is slow, poor, shiftless, sleepy, and lazy." He did speak very highly of the local paved roads, however. Twain continued (and hit on, in his concluding words, an insight he could have made more of): "The donkeys and the men, women, and children of a family all eat and sleep in the same room, and are unclean, are ravaged by vermin, and are truly happy."

Whaling became a major money-earner in the impoverished Azores from the mid-eighteenth century when American ships from New England dropped anchor to recruit the hardy local sailors for their crews. By the following century Azoreans were running their own whaling businesses. They braved the Atlantic on open boats and preyed on whales close to shore using hand-held harpoons until an international ban in the 1980s. The Azores are today home to some 230,000 people, many of them living from farming and raising livestock.

Madeira's more predictable and amenable weather—freak floods notwithstanding—has helped tourism become one of the main providers of jobs. Daytime temperatures are stable at about 72°F (22°C) in summer and 60°F (16°C) in winter. A British friend recounted in amazement how he sat in shirtsleeves on his hotel veranda in Madeira's capital Funchal, watching the famous New Year's Eve fireworks display over the harbor, while a candle flame on the table barely flickered. Nor is traffic heavy here; Funchal got its first traffic lights in 1982.

Porto Santo's
celebrated beach

These islands—Madeira island proper; Porto Santo island with its seductive five-mile (8 km) beach; and others that are uninhabited because of scarce drinking water—are closer to Africa (500 kilometers or 300 miles away) than to Europe (twice that) and, like the Azores, are the peaks of underwater mountains and astonishingly fertile. Towns mostly hug the fringe of Madeira, which soars up giddy gradients to a central peak. Crossing this island through the middle is like going on a trip through the Andes, forcing vehicles to keep their windscreen wipers on as an exotic dampness hangs in the air and drips from the extravagant vegetation. There are vertiginous views from hillside *levadas* (narrow irrigation canals), which have paths for walkers, as well as dozens of unexpected and spectacular waterfalls and the second-highest cliff in the world at Cape Girão.

The away-from-it-all appeal of Madeira has drawn some improbable visitors. George Bernard Shaw practiced the tango here in 1924, and Winston Churchill kept coming back, saying it was "warm, paintable, bathable, comfortable, flowery." A less willing visitor was Cuba's President Fulgencio Batista who, after being ousted by Fidel Castro, was exiled to Madeira in 1959 when it was reachable only by sea—placing him well out of harm's way.

The main colors of the Portuguese flag are red, representing the people's combative spirit and military conquests through history; green, standing for hope; and white, to render the values of peace and harmony. Personally, I find Portugal in other colors: at the beach, in the bright blue sea and sky, in the yellow sun and sand, and in the deep green pine forests at your back.

Chapter Two
Leading Medieval Europe out of the Mediterranean
The Age of Discovery

Children hop, skip, and jump across continents at one of Lisbon's busiest tourist stops. A giant world map of inlaid marble, fifty meters across, lies flat on the ground in the riverside suburb of Belém. The map exhibits, in black, white, and ocher, the continents stamped with dates showing the year Portuguese explorers arrived there, always one step ahead of other Europeans. Small and cursed by a lack of natural resources, including good soil, Portugal needed new lands to survive and flourish and its explorers radiated across the world until the sixteenth-century empire encompassed slices of Africa, Asia, and South America. The children playfully leap between the map's numbered outposts—a metaphor for how within reach the once-distant places seem for modern generations.

Idling tour buses disgorge travellers who marvel at these accomplishments from the Age of Discovery. Some one million people a year walk over the Belém map, moving in crowds as locals did 500 years ago when they gathered here to behold the arrival of great ships heavy with the scent of spices, their cargoes worth millions of euros in today's money. You can watch the tourists milling around, looking down at their feet, trying to square now with then. They point at the dates when history was made and goggle at the breadth of the Portuguese empire. They look impressed, but it is hard to digest. The Portuguese can find it hard, too—the Age of Discovery may trip off local tongues as evidence of national stature, but after all it was a long time ago, and Portugal today is a very different kettle of fish, even if traces of those times still occasionally appear.

Visitors pan around Belém with video cameras, across the broad lawns and cypress trees and in instants capture bookends of Portuguese history: the magnificent Jerónimos Monastery and church, built as a celebration of the fabulous wealth and distinction afforded by the maritime discoveries, its ornate exoticism a salute to romantic escapism; and the Belém Cultural Center, an underwhelming building completed in

Vasco da Gama by António Manuel da Fonseca (1796–1890)

1992 to mark Portugal's first presidency of the European Economic Community in what was a modern coming-of-age. This remarkably bland building is a monument to sober endeavor and one of the great missed opportunities of modern Portuguese architecture—a flight of the imagination, like the Louvre pyramid, might have worked better.

The sky feels bigger in wide-avenued Belém, at a remove from the city center's muddle. Along this stretch of the River Tagus fleets of wooden ships gathered for momentous voyages during the rhapsodic years of empire. The glare of the sun off the river and the nearby Atlantic Ocean lends the light a distracting quality. Spanish writer Miguel de Cervantes, on a sixteenth-century visit, arrived here by ship and wrote: "Land, land! Or, better put, Sky, Sky! Because without doubt we have come to the port of call of famous Lisbon."

Perched on the riverbank, the Monument to the Discoveries is a majestic commemoration of that golden age. In pale stone, it juts out over the river, imitating the prow of a caravel—a pioneering type of sailing ship that Iberian explorers used for their unprecedented and perilous expeditions across the Atlantic and beyond. Lined up on ledges along each side of the monument are about thirty bulky stone figures representing the heroes of the time. It is a kind of open-air pantheon. The figures, with pudding-basin haircuts and chins raised to the horizon, are not life-size but appropriately outsized. At the front stands Henry the Navigator, a prince who made the big push towards new frontiers at the end of the fifteenth century, especially along the African coast where the Portuguese scooped up gold and slaves. Behind him are Bartolomeu Dias, who rounded Africa's southern tip; Vasco da Gama, who pushed on to India; and Pedro Álvares Cabral, who claimed Brazil for the Portuguese Crown. Ferdinand Magellan, a Portuguese whose fleet was the first to circumnavigate the earth, is there too, though inconveniently, he made that trip in Spain's name. Magellan had fought for the Portuguese Crown in the East and in African campaigns in the sixteenth century and was wounded in Morocco by a lance that struck him on a knee, leaving him with a limp for the rest of his life. A difficult man but an inspiring leader who always wore black, Magellan's personal fortunes waned after King Manuel I came to the throne. The monarch refused to increase Magellan's military pension, they fell out and Magellan packed his bags for Madrid.

Never mind that the historic celebrities jostling on the Monument to the Discoveries are staring at the other bank just a few hundred meters away. The point is, they are facing south. When the Portuguese sailed out of the Tagus into the Atlantic, they made a left turn that changed the world. It would prove to be a watershed between the medieval and modern eras.

The tale of those accomplishments is contained in *Os Lusíadas* (*The Lusiads*), a rhyming epic poem almost 9,000 lines long by Luís de Camões. Published in 1572, it is one of the touchstones of Portuguese literature and a classic of the European Renaissance. Camões, perfunctorily classified as "Portugal's Shakespeare," also stands in line on the monument. His classic poem has for many generations been a compulsory subject in Portuguese schools. It chronicles the valor and derring-do of the era when the Portuguese breached the horizon. The work's archaic vocabulary and barnacled grammar make it a pretty joyless slog for schoolchildren, though they warm to the sea monsters and the "Pirates of the Caribbean"-type glamour.

Camões had an adventurous life, which provided him with the first-hand experiences that helped him compile his narrative of Portugal's maritime accomplishments. He lost his right eye in a skirmish with Muslim forces in Ceuta, in North Africa, in 1549 and is often portrayed wearing an eye-patch. From a poor background (his father set off for Goa, a Portuguese territory on India's west coast, to make his fortune but died there), Camões was repeatedly in trouble with the law for brawling and debts and lived most of his life in penury. His early education by Dominicans and Jesuits introduced him to the classics and primed his literary gift. Arrested during a scrap in downtown Lisbon, he was freed from jail on condition that he sailed to the East in the service of the Crown. He went on the same route as his father and served with the militia in Goa. There—"always with one hand on my quill and the other on my sword," he said—Camões ran a sideline producing poems-on-demand for his amorous countrymen and writing letters home for illiterate Portuguese soldiers. Moving on to Macau, a Portuguese enclave on the southern China coast, he began *The Lusiads*. He was shipwrecked in the mouth of the Mekong river where his Chinese lover drowned but, legend has it, swam ashore holding above the waves the only manuscript copy of *Os Lusíadas*. After a stay in Mozambique he returned to Lisbon with a Javanese slave he had purchased and the pair moved in with his mother, in the Mouraria quarter of Lisbon. He was so poor his slave had to go out begging for him in the street. Camões' great work was finally published in 1572 but he died of bubonic plague on June 10, 1580 before he could reap the rewards of its slowly rising reputation. June 10 is a national holiday—the Day of Camões, of Portugal and the Portuguese Communities Abroad. His tomb is in the Jerónimos Monastery.

The Monument to the Discoveries was originally built in wood, in 1940, as part of a fabled exhibition. Portugal was clinging to its neutrality during the Second World War but the conflict threatened to engulf it and times were wretched. Basic commodities were hard to come by. Prices climbed beyond the reach of many. Portugal's twentieth-century dictator, António Salazar, needed something to help his restless people keep their nerve and shore up their self-esteem. What better than a remembrance of the intrepid deeds of the fifteenth and sixteenth centuries when against the odds Portugal, barely three centuries old, and one of Europe's smallest nations, ripened into one of the continent's most prosperous countries? Salazar's Exhibition of the Portuguese World, a seven-month event, celebrated the feats of the great maritime explorers three centuries earlier. For good measure, the presentation also glorified the establishment of the Portuguese nation in 1143 and the treasured 1640 restoration of independence after Spain's chafing sixty-year ascendancy. It was a propaganda stunt that Salazar devised to reinforce his insistence on Portugal's stand-alone fortitude— a virtue flowing from the legendary boldness of its early kings and seafarers.

The message was easy to grasp for a people steeped in nostalgia. The flattering story of Portugal's formative years and the distant days when the Portuguese were full of élan and hungry for adventure is a cultural staple. It is also the standard rebuttal to foreigners' gibes about the country's modern insignificance. Through its expansion Portugal also made pioneering contributions to European scientific knowledge, bringing new insights into botany, zoology, and anthropology. ✓

The overseas expansion was, on the face of it, an unlikely development for such a small state. But in its early history lie the seeds of Portugal's later blossoming: a doughty spirit, a keen sense of identity, and leaders of rare caliber.

A Well-Armed Baker: Portuguese Origins

The Portuguese hail from the Lusitanians (hence "The Lusiads"), one of the ancient tribes that sprang from the Iberian Peninsula. It is not clear whether the tribe was made up essentially of locals or mostly of Celts, who invaded in the centuries before Christ, or was a blend of both. Either way, the Lusitanians were known, according to historian José Hermano Saraiva, as the most ferocious tribe on the peninsula. They were led by Viriathus, a revered historical figure who provided the first flush of "Portuguese-ness."

Under this lionhearted warrior chief, the embryonic Portuguese distinguished themselves with brio and delivered stinging defeats to their confounded Roman rulers. Perhaps only a people with that kind of temperament could sail into the unknown and come back rich. The Portuguese are still fond of their indomitable nature which has stood them in good stead. They like to quote a wistful observation, attributed to Julius Caesar in the first century BC, that the Lusitanians "won't govern themselves, nor will they allow themselves to be governed." (Many a modern politician would nod in sympathetic agreement.) Just as significant as the anecdote itself is the way the Portuguese tell it—with conspicuous pride. Though the rebelliousness is a treasured hallmark of the national character, it is also an attribute that can backfire. A popular gripe is *Ninguém tem mão nisto!*, an exasperated exclamation when things do not work which can be roughly translated as, "Is nobody in charge around here?"

The Lusitanians were joined by invading Swabians and Visigoths from Central Europe. Then came the North African Muslims who swept across the peninsula and settled for about 700 years in what is now Portugal.

The mixture was unleavened, however, until the advent of the man who would become Portugal's first king, Afonso Henriques. In his quest to establish a nation he displayed similar mettle to Viriathus, though he was half-French and half-Spanish by parentage. His first priority was to break away from the Spaniards, in that case the rulers of Leon and Castile, to whom his deceased father had owed allegiance and whom his mother backed. Relations with Spain would always be problematic. A defining moment was the Battle of Aljubarrota in 1385.

This was a key medieval battle because by ensuring Portuguese independence it set the stage for the Age of Discovery, which would transform Europe. On August 14, about 100 kilometers north of Lisbon, a force of about 7,000 Portuguese smashed a Castilian army of more than 30,000 in less than an hour of combat. On open land the Portuguese forces, helped by English archers, occupied a rise in the ground. They dug defensive ditches and planted spikes to halt the enemy cavalry. On each flank, brooks forced the advancing troops to funnel into the Portuguese front line where they were at the mercy of the archers. Thousands of Castilians fled in disarray. It is estimated that about 4,000 Castilians died on the battlefield and that at least the same number were killed in the following days by local people. Among these amateur soldiers was the legendary Baker Lady of Aljubarrota who came across

The Baker Lady of Aljubarrota

seven fleeing Castilians hiding inside her bakery's big clay oven. She promptly beat them to death, it is said, with her wooden bread paddle. The triumph at Aljubarrota is a milestone that still resonates with the Portuguese, for whom it is a national cultural reference.

Blessed with a series of men of action in the shape of clear-minded monarchs, and united against a common and visible enemy, Portuguese of all stripes pulled together in the *reconquista* and gradually squeezed out the Muslims. A crucial event was the Battle of Ourique, in southern Portugal, in 1139. Despite being vastly outnumbered, victory there over the joint forces of five Muslim kings proved to the Portuguese that they had what it took to shape their own future. A chronicler reported that Christ appeared in a vision to Afonso Henriques after his success, thereby granting spiritual endorsement to his bloody campaign to expel the Arabs.

The battlefield triumphs distilled a sense of patriotism and led to Afonso Henriques' declaration of independence in 1143 in Guimarães, a city known as the cradle of the nation. (Printed on the front of a popular modern T-shirt: "Portugal. Since 1143").The country's name is said to come from Portucale, the old name for nearby Porto.

The determined Portuguese dislodged the Muslims from Lisbon in 1147, though it took until the thirteenth century to clear them out of the Algarve, the country's southernmost province and the nearest to Africa. The Vatican recognized Portugal as an independent nation in 1179. All told, modern Portugal took almost 150 years to create, but centuries later it can boast the oldest fixed borders of any European nation. Afonso Henriques' reign was uncommonly long—he served as king for 46 years but before that he had ruled over the embryonic state from 1128 as a count, making his one of the longest European reigns at 57 years.

The spirit of national unity turned out to be an episodic quality, however. By nature, the Portuguese are not given to pulling together. A British friend told me how he and some other expatriates, mostly middle-aged and out of shape, were challenged to a jumpers-for-goalposts soccer game against some local Portuguese coworkers who were mostly younger and endowed with enviable Cristiano Ronaldo-style dribbling skills. The British ended up winning because they passed to each other and played as a team whereas the much more gifted Portuguese spent most of the game hogging the ball and blaming each other because things were going wrong. The Portuguese laughingly admit to this kind of thing. It is part of their endearing nature.

The nationalistic sentiment buds only when there is some galvanizing element. Salazar, who wanted to save the Portuguese from themselves, commented on their character in 1938: "The Portuguese are excessively sentimental. They abhor discipline. They are individualist, perhaps without noticing it. They lack continuity and tenacity of action."

The Portuguese ethnologist Jorge Dias said in a 1985 essay that Portugal constitutes a curious case of national unity in Europe where national bonds were usually forged by a heavy force (he cited Prussia in Germany and Castile in Spain). In Portugal, the unifying element would turn out to be the Atlantic Ocean. It was "a natural point of convergence," he wrote.

Afonso Henriques started making a country where none had existed before. The nation gelled and hardened under later kings: João I (the father of Prince Henry the Navigator), João II, and Manuel I made Portugal a flourishing enterprise by dint of the maritime discoveries. The Portuguese, without doubt, are at their best when set a clear goal by a single-minded, inspiring leader.

But it was a rare alignment of factors that paved the way for the Portuguese discoveries across the globe. First among them was geography. Portugal's L-shaped coast provides extensive access to the Atlantic. Camões, described Portugal in "The Lusiads" as being "where the land ends and the sea begins." Lisbon is a perfect port, its bottleneck mouth opening into a broad basin that shrinks even modern freighters to toy size.

The Portuguese have long been fishermen. José Hermano Saraiva recounts that in 1340 the king granted a Lisbon merchant the right to whale from the mouth of the River Guadiana on the south coast to the Minho in the northwest (essentially all the Portuguese coast) for £5,000 a year—a huge sum that offers a glimpse of how rich the coastal waters were.

The exceptional courage and seafaring skills of the Portuguese and their ancient confidence on the ocean was captured centuries later by Alan Villiers, an illustrious Australian adventurer, in his 1951 short film *The Quest of the Schooner Argus*. He went out on this four-masted Portuguese ship to witness at first hand the cod-fishing campaign in the Grand Banks by what was called the Portuguese White Fleet. Dories stacked on deck are lifted over the ship's side. One man climbs into each and is hoisted onto the high sea swell, undaunted even though the dories, like skiffs, appear as flimsy and vulnerable as the craft you might see during Sunday afternoon boating on a city lake, with water right up to the gunwale. They calmly bait their lines and spool them into the water. Heavy with their catch, the dories bob like corks alongside the rolling schooner as the men pitchfork the cod onto the ship's deck, sedately matching the rhythm of the five-meter swell. Such feats forged a tough breed, as in other Atlantic fishing countries. Villiers also wrote a piece in *National Geographic* magazine in 1952 entitled, "I Sailed with the Portuguese Brave Captains."

Political, scientific, and economic factors provided fuel for the national incandescence. Henry the Navigator was the brains and the passion behind much of the early exploration. The fifth child of King João I and England's Philippa of Lancaster, he possessed an exceptional combination of vision, pragmatism, and perseverance. At the end of the fourteenth century when he was born, the Atlantic Ocean was a wall, like an impassable mountain range. The prince imagined, conceived, and then engineered the early maritime discoveries, sometimes working by candlelight until dawn. He was also a pious and chaste man. The chronicler Gomes Eanes de Azurara, keeper of the royal library, said Henry went to his grave a virgin.

The prince, among other titles, was governor of "the Algarves," the plural being used to refer also to Portuguese possessions in North Africa. Residing on the western end of the Algarve coast near Sagres, he summoned experts on sailing and shipbuilding, nautical astronomy and navigation techniques, cartography and math. Science fascinated him. Henry collated reports from his ships' pilots about Atlantic tides, prevailing winds, and astrolabe readings, which enabled the Portuguese to speed along ocean highways. This fertile intellectual environment was the Silicon Valley of the day. Historians today broadly agree that Henry's renowned Sagres School was not, in fact, a place at all. If anything, it was a "school" in the sense of like-minded scientists coming together and devoting themselves to nautical studies.

To protect their own coastline the Portuguese first engaged the Muslim corsairs at sea. From there the sea war evolved into conquest and exploration. Though known as "the Navigator," Prince Henry never sailed farther than Morocco, which was his first target for conquest. Still, he oversaw accomplishments that were epoch-making. Fernando Pessoa wrote in a poem about Henry's contribution: "And all at once the whole earth, round, was beheld/Emerging from the deep blue." Henry the Navigator gave us the world in 3D.

The prince also had the power and the money to dispatch his ships. As well as a fervent explorer he was the head of the Order of Christ, a Portuguese military order that had replaced the Knights Templar. The Portuguese had bowed to pressure from France and the pope in the early thirteenth century and officially abolished the Knights Templar, but with typical nerve they in fact just changed the order's name and kept going. Ships' white sails bore the Order of Christ's red cross, making it the first foreign symbol natives would see when Portuguese vessels appeared off their coast. As well as furnishing some of the financial and logistical resources for the maritime endeavours, this crusading order was keen to prosecute its blessed campaign against the Muslims.

Papal sanction conferred legitimacy on the seaborne enterprise. It was a proselytizing campaign but it also upheld the sanctity of profit. The discoveries were driven by God and greed, and not necessarily in that order. The well-travelled Jesuit priest Padre António Vieira, in his *History of the Future* from 1664, explained how the symbiotic relationship worked: "Preachers take the Gospel, and trade takes the preachers."

Shipbuilding skills gave the Portuguese an edge. In the fifteenth century, the Portuguese caravels were the fastest craft on water. At first using a triangular, or lateen, sail and limited to a crew of about thirty, a Portuguese caravel could reach speeds of about nine knots—well over twice as fast as rival vessels—and could sail into the wind by zigzagging at a thirty-degree angle, much shallower than other

European ships of the time. (A jellyfish whose shape is similar to these sails came to be called a Portuguese Man o' War.) A replica of a caravel from the period is anchored on the Algarve coast in Lagos, from where these vessels set out for North and West Africa. Taking on the ocean in a wooden ship roughly the size of a bus must have provided a sometimes alarming ride. The deck is shaped like a horse's saddle to hasten water run-off.

The caravel was eventually eclipsed by the *nau*, or carrack, a bigger and slower galleon-like vessel that could carry hundreds of men and many tons of cargo from Africa, the East, and Brazil. These *naus* were the period's super-freighters, conveying spices, sugar, cloth, and jewels to Europe from distant, exotic lands. Their firepower ensured naval supremacy in the Indian Ocean, where the Portuguese carried the biggest stick and ruled the waves. Indeed, Portugal by the middle of the sixteenth century had the biggest and most powerful high seas fleet in Europe. After capturing the *Madre de Deus* the English Navy took it to Dartmouth where locals were taken aback by its staggering size. The *São João de Batista*, built in 1534, was Europe's biggest warship and was nicknamed "Botafogo" (Spitfire) because of its 366 bronze cannon. It was employed for a time to protect the entrance to Lisbon harbor. The *Padre Eterno*, launched in Brazil in the seventeenth century, was the largest ship in the world and could carry cargoes of about 2,000 tons. On way home, cargo was lashed to the deck of the *naus* and even hung over the side as those returning to Portugal itched at the prospect of the great riches it would afford them.

In crossing oceans the Portuguese juggernaut ran on potent fuel: the clergy wanted to serve God by converting savages to Christianity; nobles and merchants wanted to increase their wealth, rank, and standing; the king wanted prestige, power, and a stable realm; those lower down the pecking order wanted a better life and were ready to take a leap into the unknown to get what they did not have at home—much like the hundreds of thousands of impoverished and poorly-educated Portuguese emigrants would do in the second half of the twentieth century. Everyone who could jumped aboard. The Portuguese were brimming with energy and drive, prompting the French captain Parmentier in the sixteenth century to wrinkle his nose at their "excessive ambition." The only obvious losers were farmers, who would find themselves short of laborers until slaves started being brought back.

The traffic between the outposts of empire was not non-stop. Voyages were timed in accordance with seasonal weather conditions. An estimated half-dozen ships a year headed to the East in the sixteenth century. The carracks could carry about 800 men, but insalubrious on-board conditions meant many did not make it. The voyage from Lisbon to Goa could take eight months.

Experienced, reliable sailors were scarce, and often locally recruited ne'er-do-wells or slaves were used under the command of Portuguese captains and pilots to make up the shortfall of hands on deck. The British historian Charles Boxer recounted an anecdote of a 1505 ship having trouble steering out of the Tagus because the landlubbers they had taken on in Lisbon did not, literally, know the ropes. They kept getting mixed up between port and starboard until a string of onions was hung from one side of the ship and a plait of garlic from the other and shouted orders rang out across the Tagus: "The onion side!" "The garlic side!"

Envy grew up among those who missed out on the bonanza—sentiments that are still not far from the surface in modern Portugal. The Portuguese candidly say of themselves, "We are an envious people." It is a hallmark of countries where the gap between rich and poor is broad and deep: statistics show that in Portugal this gulf is the biggest in Western Europe. Perhaps more importantly, there is not much hope of bridging it.

The state, in the shape of powerful monarchs, was the great instigator of the Age of Discovery and most, like Camões, went abroad in the service of the Crown. That circumstance offers a clue to the unhealthy Portuguese love/hate relationship with the paternal state, which is still palpable today. They look to it adoringly as a provider, then despise it when it almost inevitably comes up short. Already during the Age of Discovery people growled that the state paid its dues "either late, only in part, or never." The same grumble can be heard today.

Gold Rush

In what Saraiva calls "a giant collective journey," Portugal led Europe out of the Mediterranean into the Atlantic and brought Asia and Europe together. The tale has a romantic flavor, but it was largely a pragmatic pursuit that lit up Portugal for almost two centuries before its brightness faded. It was a hypnotic era when industry, innovation, enterprise, and risk-taking lavished huge rewards on the youthful country.

After the taking of Ceuta in North Africa in 1415, the empire was expanded steadily. The Portuguese settled in Madeira and the Azores, then explored down Africa's west coast until they understood how to get to India by sea. They knew from intelligence gathered in North Africa that there was a sea to the east and so, the thinking went, maybe if they edged their way down the west coast they might find a way through. Their expeditions hugged the African coast and set up trading posts because tiny Portugal simply did not have the manpower to stray far inland—a shortcoming that would cost it dearly in the late nineteenth century during Europe's Scramble for Africa. A map by cartographer Lázaro Luís from 1563, kept at the Lisbon Academy of Sciences, shows the coast of West Africa and the eastern shores of South America in fascinating detail and color. Place names in blue-green ink, set off with quill-pen flourishes, are tightly-bunched along the red rim of the coastlines so that you can run your finger down them, like a telephone directory. Inland areas, however, are just filled in with drawings of jungle, lions, and camels.

Bartolomeu Dias foreshadowed the later prosperity by becoming the first European around what was aptly called the Cape of Storms (later the Cape of Good Hope). Adam Smith, the eighteenth-century political economist, judged this milestone to be one of "the two greatest and most important events recorded in the history of mankind"—along with the discovery of America. Dias crossed paths in Lisbon at end of the fifteenth century with Christopher Columbus, who was intent on probing westwards—the opposite direction—and whatever they said in the private conversation they reportedly had offers great potential for a novel or film.

Vasco da Gama went down in history as leader of the trail-blazing expedition to India, which was a prophetic event for both Portugal and

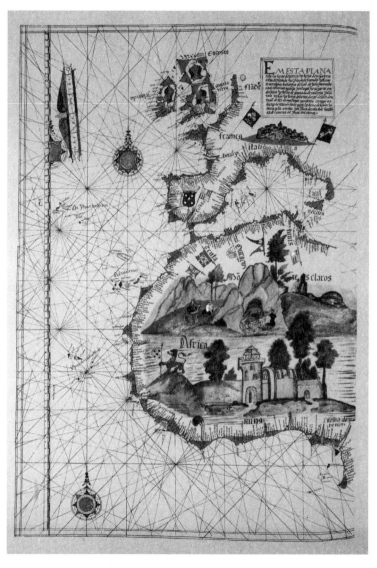

Lázaro Luís' map shows how Portuguese explorers strayed little
beyond the coast

the wider world. But the name chiseled on the monuments could just as easily have been Paulo da Gama. Vasco's older brother inherited their father's rights as a nobleman. When he was a young man, Vasco, sensing his ambitions would be thwarted by his junior status, considered an ecclesiastical career. But he elected to pursue a life at sea and became known for his quick temper. Paulo was lined up to lead the great India voyage but, in one of those great historical examples of plain bad luck, he fell ill and so King Manuel I placed his younger brother in charge of the expedition. Paulo still captained one of the ships in the fleet and his more even temperament is said to have smoothed over some of his brother's excesses, but he died during the voyage.

Vasco da Gama set sail on July 8, 1497 with four ships and crews that included many convicts being sent into exile, just as the British later did when they sent convicts to Australia. Ten months later, on May 20, Vasco da Gama anchored at Calicut, a major Indian trading port on the country's west coast. It may have been a great step for mankind but da Gama's goals were prosaic, as summed up in his famous phrase on stepping foot in the East: "We are looking for Christians and spices." The Portuguese came across a wonderful natural harbor on the Indian coast which they called *bom baim*, meaning "good little bay" in sixteenth-century Portuguese. They later gave the settlement to the English who anglicized its name, making it Bombay. ✓

The Portuguese were looking to establish an anti-Muslim alliance with Prester John, a mythical Christian king who according to medieval legend was living among heathens. They also wanted to get their hands on riches that local traders, especially the long-established Muslims, did not want to surrender. Vasco da Gama zealously conducted a terror campaign to rid the Malabar coast of Muslim ships. In one infamous episode he sank a ship carrying some 200 Muslim pilgrims. In an early episode of European gunboat diplomacy, he also bombarded coastal towns with broadsides and enacted bloody reprisals against local chiefs. Vasco da Gama is venerated in Portugal but in India is seen with cooler reflection. The Indian historian Sanjay Subramanyam published a myth-busting book in 1997 entitled *The Career and Legend of Vasco da Gama*, in which he portrayed the explorer as a volatile and violent man driven by ambition, greed, and a lust for power.

Pedro Álvares Cabral, an expert seaman from a noble seafaring family, drew up at Brazil's shores in 1500. He was ostensibly sailing to India, and it is still not clear whether he was fortuitously blown off course or whether his stated destination was a feint to throw Castile off the scent. Either way, Brazil opened a new horizon for the Portuguese, as if the one they already had in the East was not enough. They initially named the new land Terra de Vera Cruz (Land of the True Cross). The small group of Europeans who first disembarked there was overwhelmed by the magical world overflowing with natural riches they encountered. One of them, the chronicler Pero Vaz de Caminha, wrote a famous 27-page letter to King Manuel I expressing wide-eyed wonder at what they had discovered. The letter, unearthed in the national archive in 1773, expressed astonishment at the naked natives and their custom of inserting bones into their bottom lip.

Brazil presented a significant problem, however: Portugal, a tiny country of about one million people at the time, claimed a country that would end up being the size of Western Europe. The land promised plenty, but how to harvest that promise? The answer: slaves. Over three centuries the Portuguese brought hundreds of thousands of captives from West Africa to work on plantations, which sent sugar and other commodities to Europe, and to toil in gold mines. Salvador de Bahia, the first capital of Brazil, was also the site of the New World's first slave market. When gold was found, after much searching, in the late seventeenth century Brazil became a Portuguese El Dorado. Some 10,000 Portuguese a year poured in during a gold rush in the 1700s, compared with about 500 a year previously.

Before that switch in attention it was the East that for two centuries exerted the greatest pull on the Portuguese. After Vasco da Gama broke through, Afonso de Albuquerque, one of Portugal's greatest military commanders, set about establishing the foundations for a long stay. In the early sixteenth century he seized control of trade routes in the Indian Ocean and Persian Gulf, largely by capturing three strategic sites: Malacca, a major port on the eastern spice route; Hormuz, which was the key to the Persian Gulf; and Goa, strategically located halfway down India's west coast. He essentially locked up the Indian Ocean for Portugal.

Afonso de Albuquerque is a towering figure in Portuguese history. He became the second viceroy of Portuguese India as well as the Duke of Goa—the first Portuguese title pertaining to a foreign land. He was also the first duke not of royal blood. This archetypal battle-hardened sea dog had a fearsome reputation. He was known as "Lion of the Seas" and "Caesar of the East." A Portuguese chronicler said he "filled Europe with admiration and Asia with dread fear." Despite his notoriety, a particularly sweet fruit was named after him: he is believed to have brought what became known as alphonso mangoes to Goa from Africa.

The Portuguese were the first westerners to disembark in Japan and start trading there, in 1543. The Japanese termed them *namban*, meaning "barbarians from the south," the direction they had sailed in from. Words in both languages still bear witness to that long-ago contact. In Japanese, for example, there is *pan*, for bread (*pão* in Portuguese) and *shabon* (soap, *sabão*); Portuguese offers *catana* (*katana*) for a kind of machete and *biombo* (*byoobu*) for a screen. At Lisbon's National Museum of Ancient Art there are several Japanese *namban* screens depicting, in gold leaf on rice paper, late sixteenth- and early seventeenth-century scenes of Portuguese ships off the coast. The snub-nosed Japanese portrayed their visitors as having a Cyrano-esque facial feature.

The Portuguese began to appear all around the world. They planted their flag on islands that today belong to Indonesia. They established a trading post in East Timor, though only began to take real advantage of the Asian territory from the late eighteenth century when they built its capital, Dili. The Portuguese built forts in faraway places, including two dozen around the Red Sea and Persian Gulf. Some of the ruins can still be seen, including the early sixteenth-century forts at Hormuz, Keshm, and Lanak that protected the entrance to the Persian Gulf. (Other forts may be chanced upon in Ethiopia, Tanzania, or Kenya.) The Portuguese dominated the tremendously lucrative spice trade for most of the sixteenth century, conferring a new political and economic dimension on their tiny patch of the European continent.

It was no easy enterprise, though. They had to fight hard to wrest lucrative trade from the long-established Arab merchants. In 1536, it is said, António Galvão and 120 men attacked and captured a fort defended by 50,000 local warriors. Ten years later, an army of 13,000

Turks laid siege to the Portuguese fort at Diu, in India, which was defended by 250 Portuguese. The Turks blasted a hole in a wall but five Portuguese are said to have held 500 at bay. The Portuguese went out on a limb, sending a squadron of ships into the Red Sea to wreck any rival Muslim ships they encountered. Such accounts deserve to be taken with a pinch of salt. And without firm leadership the Portuguese are said to have inclined, as ever, toward indiscipline. But the country's military successes so far from home merit tribute.

Commodities such as nutmeg, mace, and cloves commanded extraordinary prices, spurring further exploration. Lisbon undercut Venice's prices and just about cornered the European spice market. The Portuguese capital became a European depot for goods from around the world. The downtown district now called the Baixa was one of Europe's busiest mercantile spots. The narrow streets contained amber and rubies from Burma, diamonds from India, pearls from Ceylon, gold from Mozambique, spices and bolts of cloth from the East. Each year 2,000 ships came into the Tagus, an average of more than five a day pulling up to the quay. Lisbon was a colorful, cosmopolitan emporium, a swanky, vibrant metropolis that invented its own architectural style called Manueline, named after King Manuel. This style was arabesque and was designed to show off the country's wealth, though the style never caught on abroad. The Portuguese also brought home Indian horses and parrots and an elephant they named Hanno. It carried a silver box containing gold coins and was taught to perform tricks. Portugal gave it as a present to the pope in 1514. The following year Lisbon took delivery of a rhinoceros, a gift from an Indian sultan. The king set up a fight in Lisbon between the rhino and one of his elephants, but the elephant is said to have run away. These were enthralling times indeed.

Spain initially lagged behind Portugal in its expansion but in 1494 the Iberian neighbors signed the Treaty of Tordesillas, carving up between them the spoils of the newly discovered—and to-be-discovered—world. The Portuguese savor the possibility that the scope of the treaty was a clever ruse on their part. At a time when geographical knowledge was limited and precious, the land that would become Brazil fell inside the Tordesillas demarcation of Portugal's domain.

Certainly there is room to speculate that the Portuguese were unforth-coming, to put it politely, in their dealings with their bigger peninsular rival. Portuguese seafarers on their way back from the East tacked close to the South American continent to avoid the east Atlantic doldrums and there is a suspicion that they had already happened across what would become Brazil. Also, there is an intriguing ten-year gap between the 1488 voyage around the Cape of Good Hope by Bartolomeu Dias and Vasco da Gama's journey on to India. Were there other reconnais-sance trips between those dates that the Portuguese did not let on about? Were they really sitting on their hands during the white-hot period of maritime exploration that they had started and led? And why did the Portuguese king turn down Columbus's offer to try to find a way to the Orient by sailing west? Did the king already know it was a wasted effort? While Columbus went one way, the king ordered a fleet of *naus* to be built and sent his expedition south. Without doubt, there was plenty of skulduggery. Maps, especially, were hugely valuable and jealously guarded. And the Portuguese, staking out land masses with their astrolabes, possessed some of the best available.

What is for sure is the glee the Portuguese still feel at the prospect of outsmarting Spain—a possibility always guaranteed to bring joy to a Portuguese heart. Cunning is also a valued attribute. The Portuguese have had little choice in this respect: throughout history, as a small country, Portugal has been at the mercy of more powerful nations. In 1749, the Marquis of Alorna wrote from Goa to King João V with a report that Dutch vessels were seizing Portuguese *naus*. He observed that against such a daunting rival the outnumbered Portuguese "must, perforce, rely more on guile than on strength." Hoodwinking a bigger adversary is, even now, deemed with quiet pride to be testimony to national acumen.

Not only were the noble seafarers bent on getting rich, they were also driven by religious prejudice against Islam. Like others, they saw themselves as agents of a biased God. There was pillage, plunder, and slaughter in the name of Christianity and the king—and wealth. Success in the overseas enterprise required an uncompromising attitude, a killer instinct. It was the *sine qua non* of medieval empire-building and a national attribute. António José Saraiva, a twentieth-century writer, commented about his countrymen: "The surface is soft, the core is hard." Boxer, the British historian, described the adventurers as being animated by motives that "ran the gamut from high-minded and self-sacrificing idealism to the most sordid lust for material gain." Their actions were sometimes unscrupulous, sometimes consummated on the back of bloody rampages.

Spend, Spend, Spend

While a romantic spirit alloyed with toughness of character led the Portuguese to conquer the merciless surf, their maritime endeavors also begat, or encouraged, unhelpful national characteristics that portended their demise. There were specters at the feast, and the Portuguese would eventually be left behind by the momentum they themselves had created.

Camões did not shrink from enunciating the dangers in *The Lusiads*. His character O Velho do Restelo (the old man of Restelo, a Lisbon neighborhood with a view over the quays from where the ships set off), was a Cassandra-like figure who voiced fears that the noble exploration was at risk because of naked personal ambition and self-interest. It was a prescient view, as the Portuguese became drunk on wealth and success. According to the portrayals of Gil Vicente, a popular dramatist of the time, and the sixteenth-century chronicler Diogo do Couto, the Portuguese were ostentatious, immoral, and corrupt and lorded it over the locals in distant lands.

The voyages became a get-rich-quick scheme. Diligence and conscientiousness were shunned as the easy money flowed. While England and the Netherlands invested the money they made from the spice trade—fetching commodities from Lisbon and selling them on—the Portuguese frittered it away. Gil Vicente depicted elegantly dressed nobles without enough money to eat. An erudite Flemish traveller called Nicolas Cleynaert was staggered in the sixteenth century by the way *escudeiros* (trainee knights) wasted their cash. Cleynaert, who was a royal tutor in Portugal, commented that "in Portugal we are all nobles, and having any kind of job is frowned upon."

The pillars of the Lisbon aqueduct punctuate the city

Brazil, which at first had yielded only quality timber, became the scene of a gold rush when after more than a hundred years of searching the Portuguese found gold at the end of seventeenth century. The first load, of 500 kilos, arrived in Lisbon in the 1690s. By 1720, the annual supply of gold delivered to the capital of the empire was up to 25 tonnes. What did they do with it? King João V decided to throw caution to the wind with the grandiose palace and convent at Mafra, and the Portuguese economy almost crashed because of it. It was a celebration of purchasing power, of ostentatious wealth. On the other hand, and much to his credit, he also had the giant Lisbon aqueduct built. This fourteen-kilometer-long architectural marvel, part of a 58-kilometer water catchment network, was a tremendously valuable addition that largely resolved the capital's chronic water shortages. Today traffic weaves between its fat stone pillars.

The Age of Discovery was a time of plenty, a cue to spend, spend, spend. Antero de Quental, a nineteenth-century writer, remarked, "Never has a people soaked up so much treasure and remained so poor." And it is tempting to draw a parallel with the cash-rich days of the early years of Portugal's EEC membership when fantastic—and politically profitable—construction projects were the order of the day while deeper, harder effort, as it turned out, was neglected. Eduardo Lourenço, an essayist, wrote in 1982: "It's a pity Freud never got to know us. He'd have found... a people who exemplify the sublime triumph of the pleasure principle over the reality principle." ✓

The Age of Discovery also brought complacency. In that sense, the Portuguese were the architects of their own decline. The historian Guilherme D'Oliveira Martins ruefully said of his people: "We're good at adapting, it's true, but we give up too easily and place too much faith in luck and fate... At the end of the day, we need more balance and organization." Silva Cordeiro, a philosophy professor, made a similar point in his 1896 book *The Crisis*: "The Portuguese character never wanted for energy or the audacity to hurl themselves into the hardest tasks... What we have almost always lacked are less poetic qualities and methodical action, gradual and persevering effort."

Portugal also reeled under a series of setbacks that sapped its strength. The expulsion of the Jews in 1492 robbed it of expertise, and the battlefield death in 1578 of King Sebastian at Ksar el-Kebir in North Africa brought a crisis of royal succession that led to a period of Spanish rule—and a different set of priorities—from 1580 to 1640, during which the Portuguese lost some of their Southeast Asian outposts to the late-arriving Dutch.

At the same time, after it had opened the gates of the East, Portugal was trampled under foot in the European rush to get at the riches. Though resourceful, the Portuguese were spread thinly across their possessions and had difficulty hanging on to their initial advantage. They maintained a profitable slave trade until the nineteenth century but the best was over by the mid-eighteenth century. Also, while the British and Dutch relentlessly improved the design of their ocean-going vessels, the Portuguese stuck with their old, tried-and-trusted ones instead of moving with the times—a national shortcoming that would be echoed in the late twentieth century. Having failed to invest the riches in productive capacity at home, Portugal's economy gradually fell behind the rest. It was a spent force. The wealth dried up, and the country's fortunes have been at a low ebb ever since. The writer Teixeira de Pascoães remarked in 1920: "The Discoveries were the start... Since then, we've been asleep." Another author, Almeida Faria, echoed the sentiment in 1980 with the observation that the Portuguese were a people "unemployed since Vasco da Gama."

Undoubtedly, Portugal burned brightly during the Age of Discovery. Bursting out of a small country that offered them few opportunities, the Portuguese demonstrated audacity and mettle as they grabbed their chance and made the most of it before the door closed. Their achievements were staggering. Eduardo Lourenço claims that apart from Rome and Macedonia, few countries accomplished so much from so little. A map of the country's trade routes of the time resembles bunting strung between the continents, from Lisbon across to Brazil, around Africa, across to India, China, and Japan.

Naturally there is a certain nostalgia for that period, just as the British once had for their empire. King Pedro V wrote in the nineteenth century that Portugal was "a society deeply demoralized by memories of its past greatness and by the sight of its forfeiture." It is a nostalgia that is translated into music in *fado*, the national genre.

Mention of the Age of Discovery can evoke opposing ideas: in the nineteenth century the period was cited as evidence of how far Portugal had fallen; in the twentieth Salazar held it up as an example of Portuguese greatness. Padre António Vieira, the seventeenth-century Jesuit priest considered one of the country's best ever prose writers, classified the Portuguese world as the "Fifth Empire"—after the Assyrian, Persian, Greek, and Roman empires. But when on occasion he was vexed by his countrymen's boorishness and mediocrity, he referred to the Portuguese as "the kaffirs of Europe."

Fernando Pessoa contemplated the Then and Now and drew a gloomy conclusion. Portugal is nowadays, he said, "a drop of dry ink on the hand that wrote an Empire." ✓

Chapter Three
Echoes of Empire
The Portuguese-Speaking World

Lisbon's second most-spoken language, it is reckoned, is creole. It is the ✓ vernacular of people who came from West Africa's equatorial regions, from Cape Verde, Guinea-Bissau, and São Tomé & Príncipe—lands the Portuguese named and settled five centuries ago when they sailed over the horizon. Portugal founded territories and enclaves in Africa, Asia, and South America, and their peoples and the former masters bear features of that colonial ancestry. Brazil has a large black population because the Portuguese took some four million slaves there from Africa in what has been described, no less, as the largest forced migration in history. In Angola, burned out wrecks of military vehicles still scar the country's southeastern plain where in 1987—just over a decade after Portugal, with unwise abruptness, quit Africa—the Cuban and South African armies engaged in the continent's biggest battle since the Second World War. In Macau, in the Pearl River delta near Hong Kong, the old downtown area, a clearing amid a forest of skyscrapers, has the same pretty

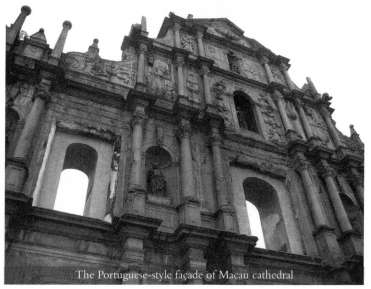

The Portuguese-style façade of Macau cathedral

streets and low buildings that can be encountered in just about any Portuguese town. East Timor, a tiny, half-island territory on the other side of the world between Australia and Indonesia, picked Portuguese as its official language when it became the world's newest sovereign nation in 2002. In Goa province on India's west coast, a schoolchildren's ditty has it that Vasco da Gama "took off his pajama and showed his ✓ banana." Black blood courses in the veins of some one million Portuguese, the legacy of generations of unabashed ethnic intermingling: "God created blacks and whites. The Portuguese created the mulatto," they used to say.

These are layers of imperial residue in the *mundo lusófono*—the Portuguese-speaking world. Portugal, which was dwarfed by its giant overseas possessions, left its footprint where it went and came home with soil on its shoes. The at times enigmatic likenesses between the metropole and its former colonies are evidence of an enriching cultural overlap during half a millennium of colonial rule. Yet there is also a darker side to the account of Portugal's overseas adventures, and the question of to what extent the Portuguese were saints or sinners has gone largely unaddressed.

The Portuguese were the first Europeans to arrive in sub-Saharan Africa and they were the last to leave. They built that continent's first European fort and its first European slaving depot. Of all the colonial domains, Africa arguably has left the biggest imprint on Portugal itself. Traces at home of the stay in Goa, by contrast, are modest if discernible, most evidently in Lisbon's Indian restaurants: when India sent its army to wrest Goa from the Portuguese in 1961 some Portugal-friendly Indians fled to Mozambique and when that African country gained its independence, and a civil war, in 1975 many upped stakes again and moved on to Portugal. Signs of the Portuguese colonial adventure further east, meanwhile, are slight; Lisbon's Museum of the Orient opened only in 2008. Brazil's visibility sharpened in the late twentieth century—almost two hundred years after it became an independent country—with the sudden arrival in Portugal of tens of thousands of Brazilian immigrant workers.

Those from the former African colonies who made Lisbon their home have endowed the city with an ethnically mixed, cosmopolitan feel. It recalls the time in the sixteenth century when, as the poet Miguel Torga wrote, Lisbon was "a world crossroads." Snatches of Portuguese-based creole can often be heard on rush-hour trains, buses, and trams as weary construction workers and office cleaners make their way back to the suburbs after another long, low-paid day of work. Africa has made a contribution that has more depth than the relatively recent introduction of modern European trappings such as fast-food outlets and international chain stores. African music, nightclubs, and food are a Lisbon hallmark. When after joining the European Economic Community in 1986 Lisbon drew a new wave of curious tourists, its African flourishes were one of the things that set the city apart, that made it special in Europe.

Groups of African men habitually gather on weekdays in the Rossio central square, in front of the thick stone columns of the Dona Maria II National Theatre. Dozens of them mill around in small groups as if they were attending an all-male village meeting on another continent. Some wear traditional African dress; some chat and others just watch the traffic swirl around the central fountains. The French writer and anthropologist Jean-Yves Loude marvelled at these scenes. In his 2003 book *Lisbon: In the Black Town*, which celebrates the city's Africanness, he likened the square to "an open-air office" where Africans who cannot afford downtown real estate prices conduct their business.

Fliers handed out at Lisbon underground stations and the classified sections of free newspapers advertise African mediums who offer "all occult work." These self-proclaimed shamans with names such as Professor Mamadu ("endowed with hereditary gifts"), Professor Fofana ("specialist in love"), and Great Professor Guirassy ("clairvoyant and healer") claim the ability to solve problems in love and business, end drug addiction, counter envy and any difficulty stemming from "the evil eye." Intriguingly, they say they charge only if their advice works.

Mandioca, or cassava root, a staple at open-air street markets in the tropics, often sits among the boxes of vegetables outside Lisbon grocers though this tuber, resembling a big, woody carrot, does not grow in Europe. It is not hard to find an African restaurant serving up *cachupa*, a traditional Cape Verde dish featuring sweet potato, boiled banana, beans, and corn with the Portuguese additions of garlic and sausage. As in Cape Verde, *cachupa rica* (rich cachupa) comes with pork, chicken, or goat while *cachupa pobre* (poor cachupa) has fish—Cape Verde being made up of nine islands. Another popular dish is the delicious Angolan stew called *moamba*, usually served with chicken. Both come with the devilishly hot African chili peppers the Portuguese call *piri-piri*.

Near Parliament, in the São Bento district of Lisbon, there is a so-called "Creole triangle" formed by three streets where Cape Verdean culture has been particularly conspicuous. One of the streets is called Rua Poço dos Negros, which translates as Negro Pit Street or Black Well Street. There are two explanations for this name: either it refers to a pit that King Manuel I in 1515 asked the city authorities to dig for the disposal of dead slaves because they were being randomly discarded on open land, or it was the water well used by a nearby abbey whose monks were recognized by their dyed black habits.

"A Silent Presence"

Black Africans have been one of Lisbon's distinguishing features for more than 500 years, from when they were first shipped back home as slaves. Their numbers quickly grew as the powerful Portuguese empire swelled to occupy new lands and its wealth mounted, and by the 1550s black slaves were a common sight, giving Lisbon an African flavor even then. It was estimated in 1551 that there were about 10,000 slaves in the capital, a remarkable proportion for a city of around 100,000 people at the time. Visitors from northern Europe, such as Nicolas Cleynaert and Hieronymus Münzer, were astonished that blacks seemed to be doing all the work—all the menial, back-breaking work, anyway. A 1657 painting by Filipe Lobo of Lisbon's Jerónimos Monastery, which hangs in Lisbon's Museum of Ancient Art, depicts in its bottom right-hand corner a woman slave in a long skirt with a basket on her head—a rare early nod to social authenticity.

With the prohibition of slavery, Lisbon's African population faded in the nineteenth century. By 1930 there were just about 5,000 Africans in the city of some 600,000 inhabitants. In the 1960s, however, they started returning to work in Portugal, this time for a proper wage. They took up the slack left by Portuguese men who were away on national service or who had emigrated to avoid conscription and find better-paying work elsewhere in Europe. Initially, thousands of creole-speaking Cape Verdean men came over—so many, in fact, that they began referring to Lisbon as their archipelago's tenth island. After the 1974 Carnation Revolution in Portugal brought independence for the African colonies, the Cape Verdeans were joined by many Angolans and Mozambicans fleeing their countries' civil wars. With the capital short of housing and the immigrants short of capital, most of these African construction workers and their families grouped together and built their own dwellings around Lisbon using whatever they could lay their hands on: spare bricks, odd planks of wood, sheets of corrugated iron. These *bairros de lata* (shantytowns) had no running water or electricity. They were slums, and some were notorious no-go areas, but for all the hardship they had a sense of community and vitality. With their bare earth streets, barefoot children, and women walking with buckets of water on their heads, these shantytowns were like little islands of Africa in Europe.

There is little racial friction in Portugal—at least of the most conspicuous sort. Portuguese who lived there in colonial times express a wistful, nostalgic fondness for Africa. And as a tolerant people, the Portuguese recoil from the idea of discrimination. In 2007 a survey of 27 EU countries and Canada by the Brussels-based Migration Policy Group placed Portugal second-best, after Sweden, at integrating immi- ✓ grants. So when that same year a Lisbon councilor suggested that, because of the proliferation of Chinese shops in the city, it might be an idea to create a Chinatown like the ones in other western capitals, there was a great hue and cry. That is how ghettos start, some said. Others argued that it amounted to herding people together by their skin color and nationality. It would be the opposite of hoped-for integration and was to be opposed on principle. The proposal was hastily shelved, though the local Chinese shopkeepers said that, actually, they would not have minded.

While Africans are comfortably integrated into Portuguese society, they have had to settle for a lowly rung on the social and professional ladder. Brazilian researcher José Ramos Tinhorão, in a 1988 book on

Eusébio, in mid-shot

blacks in Portugal, dubbed them "a silent presence." They mostly remain in humble jobs, though construction laborers had a vital hand in Lisbon's major rebuilding project at the end of the last century when tens of thousands of them helped lay the new roads and build the shopping centers and apartment blocks so appreci- ated by the Portuguese. They won no recognition for their efforts. Indeed, the only statue to a black person is that of Eusébio, the leg- endary soccer player who became known as the Black Panther for his outstanding performances in the 1960s for Benfica and Portugal. The statue, on a little grass circle outside Benfica's Stadium of Light, captures him in a dynamic pose, about to kick a ball at his feet. Born in the Mozambique capital Maputo, known then by its colonial name Lourenço Marques, Eusébio da Silva Ferreira's main concern about playing in Portugal as a teenager was that he might freeze to death. He became a national hero after Portugal's 2-1 semi-final defeat in the 1966 World Cup against host country England when he left the field in tears, broken-hearted. He won 64 caps and scored 41 goals for Portugal. In 1998, a panel of 100 experts gathered by soccer's world governing body FIFA inducted him into an International Football Hall of Fame as one of the sport's ten all-time greats. "Look," Eusébio remarked, "there are only two black people on the list: me and Pelé."

Other African contributions have been largely forgotten. Hans Christian Andersen, on a mid-nineteenth-century trip to Lisbon, was informed by his Portuguese hosts that they were going to build a statue to Camões. The Dane asked, cheekily perhaps, whether the representation would include the poet's slave, who had gone begging on the streets to sustain his down-and-out master. He was told that that would not do at all—it would suggest that Portugal had not cared for its great writer.

The Salazar dictatorship trumpeted Portugal's intercontinental empire as a single nation, "one and indivisible, from the Minho [the northern Portuguese province] to Timor" near Indonesia and bound together by a common denominator: rule from Lisbon. East Timor's tallest mountain was dubbed "Portugal's highest peak." Though they have now split up, the members of that old imperial family still show a certain resemblance, with a common language spoken by more than 200 million people at the top of the list. Much is made of this in Portugal, but the reality, however, is that Portuguese is the least consequential of the major tongues. As the internationally acclaimed Mozambican novelist Mia Couto baldly expressed it, "The Portuguese language is down at the bottom. I only exist because I'm translated into French."

Portuguese business people take to Africa easily. Unlike other western companies, whose disciplined, methodical approaches often encounter a cultural impasse, Portuguese firms know how to operate there. Their personnel are familiar with the sleepy rhythms of places such as São Tomé & Príncipe, whose people describe the lifestyle in their twin-island nation with a twin adjective: *leve-leve* (gentle-gentle, or soft-soft). The Portuguese are also familiar with the daily African aggravations of bureaucracy and the schemes to short-circuit it because it is a great deal the way Portugal was thirty years ago (and still is to an extent today). It is an instinctive, empathetic response rooted in a common lineage. They speak the same language in a metaphorical sense. Portuguese novelist António Lobo Antunes recounts that when he served in the army fighting insurgents in Angola in the early 1970s the guns fell silent whenever a Benfica game being played in Portugal was broadcast live on public radio. Both the defending Portuguese and the attacking Angolans tuned in and sat back to follow the game. The shooting resumed after the final whistle.

Deep-Felt Kinship

When Portugal's post-Carnation Revolution leaders handed Africans the keys to their own countries, the new owners obtained no automatic freedom or justice. In fact, the former colonies paid a high price for Portugal's scramble to get out of Africa. The sudden exit created a power vacuum that coincided with the Cold War's ideological antagonism. Those African countries' new political leaders took sides and became proxies as East and West confronted each other on African soil. Angola suffered the most, because its huge oil reserves made it a tempting prize—and proved to be a curse. (It is said that when Portuguese colonial engineers informed Salazar in the 1950s that they had found oil in Angola the intuitive dictator put his head in his hands and groaned, "Oh no!") Cuban soldiers and Moscow money backed Angola's Marxist government while South African troops and the CIA did their best to bring it down by helping the opposition with weapons and cash. The two sides clashed most famously at Cuito Cuanavale in southeastern Angola, when South Africa and Cuba threw their air force and infantry into a weeks-long battle. Angola's civil war became Africa's longest post-colonial conflict. It killed hundreds of thousands of civilians before its end in 2002, by which time it was known in diplomatic circles as "an orphan of the Cold War." Mozambique also succumbed to civil war, which lasted until 1992. All the former African colonies became saddled with single-party Marxist governments for more than a decade, arresting their development. Angola's red-and-black flag still bears a cogwheel crossed with a machete in imitation of the hammer-and-sickle emblem of the former Soviet Union.

Unproductive political feuding and other ills have dogged these countries ever since. The presentation of a 2009 Oxford University workshop on Portuguese-speaking nations put it thus: "Features present in the politics of all countries, patronage and corruption are perhaps of greater public concern and more fundamental to the working of politics in the Lusophone countries than in some other states." Angola, with its giant oil and diamond reserves, is guilty of corruption on a spectacular scale, human rights groups say.

East Timor fared even worse. While the Africans turned on each other after the Portuguese departure, the Timorese were invaded and subjected to a brutal occupation by Indonesia, which annexed the nearby territory of about one million mostly impoverished people. Thousands were jailed, tortured, and murdered as the world mostly turned a blind eye. Portugal did not possess enough diplomatic strength to do much about it, and the major protagonists in the strategic equation—Australia and the United States—blamed Portugal for creating the problem in the first place by leaving so hastily. The Indonesian atrocities continued until a particularly appalling massacre in 1991 grabbed the world's attention. The outcry led, eventually, to a United Nations-sponsored referendum on independence, which the Timorese finally gained in 2002.

The Portuguese felt terribly guilty about the Timorese suffering. Leaving Africans to fight each other over the post-colonial spoils was one thing; throwing a helpless former colony to the wolves was another. When the East Timorese voted in the 1999 referendum, Indonesia's supporters ran amok. Confronted with the carnage on their evening television news, and trying somehow to make amends, the Portuguese staged mass protests not seen since the 1974 Revolution. Traffic in towns and cities across the country stopped at a designated time, people climbing out of their vehicles and standing in the road to observe a one-minute silence. Tens of thousands of people used a free number provided by Portugal Telecom to send faxes of protest to the United Nations in New York. A similar number of people lined the streets of Lisbon and waved white handkerchiefs to welcome East Timor Bishop Carlos Belo, by then a refugee and soon to be a Nobel peace laureate, as he drove through the city from the airport. It was a sign of deep-felt kinship that would be hard to fathom without knowing the back-story that stretched 10,000 kilometers and 500 years.

In the aftermath of the struggle, East Timor's first independent government adopted Portuguese as its official language—a gesture that suggested a certain sentimentality, since that region's major languages are Indonesian and English and fewer than ten percent of East Timorese speak Portuguese fluently. It also picked Portugal to help set up its civil service, even though the Portuguese civil service was, and still is to an important extent, annoyingly inefficient.

It is a curiosity of the former African colonies that so many of their buildings, streets, and other infrastructure—their urban landscape—remains so very Portuguese. Especially in Africa, towns and cities still look markedly colonial, almost frozen in time but eerily overgrown by the tropical vegetation, and decrepit. I recall standing in the street in Huambo, the main city in Angola's central highlands, in front of the former headquarters of Angolan rebel leader Jonas Savimbi. The roomy, two-story house, known as the UNITA chief's *Casa Branca* (White House), would not have looked out of place among the older villas of the Algarve. The big difference was that the marks of machine-gun fire snaked across the cement and bombs had blown down some walls.

Civil strife and poor government have conspired to keep this group of African nations among the world's poorest countries. I was speaking in 2006 to a local businessman in São Tomé & Príncipe who, angry at his country's stalled development, exasperatedly pointed out of his office window at the pot-holed tarmac road. "Look out there," he said. "The Portuguese built that!" On the other hand, the development lag could pay dividends. Dense tropical jungle coats São Tomé & Príncipe, and from the air it looks unspoiled, a suitable destination for the European ecotourism that has been sweeping Africa—if only the local authorities could stop squabbling and abandon corruption as a way of life.

Goa, too, still possesses reminders of its Portuguese bloodline, even though its colonial zenith was in the sixteenth century when it had a

Rome of the East: the façade of the Goa cathedral

population rivaling Lisbon's and was nicknamed "the Rome of the East," due to the generous number of Catholic churches the Portuguese built in the jungle. Some two dozen churches and an imposing and well-kept Portuguese cathedral still stand. At the Basilica of Bom Jesus the mummified body of St. Francis Xavier, Goa's patron saint, is put on public display every ten years in its glass-sided silver casket. There are still annual religious processions, just as in Portugal. Goa has also preserved the house where Vasco da Gama lived and possesses other easily identifiable colonial buildings. This well-off, pleasant province has attracted many western tourists, starting in the 1960s with hippies captivated by its mellow way of life. Some among the locals still have Portuguese surnames such as Fernandes, Pereira, and Gonçalves, though few speak ✓ Portuguese.

Macau, where the Portuguese began to put down roots in the mid-sixteenth century, was one of the rare European toeholds in China. It was also the first and the longest-lasting (as with sub-Saharan Africa and India, the Portuguese were the first Europeans to settle and the last to depart). Macau spent 442 years under Portuguese rule though largely overshadowed during that time by nearby Hong Kong and Singapore. Chinese and Portuguese, Asian and western culture, mixed cheek-by-jowl in an unlikely blend, and still do: the downtown area is a UNESCO World Heritage site because of its Portuguese architecture. China and its language, however, were long dominant before 1999 when the Portuguese flag was run down and power handed over, two years after Hong Kong had done the same. Still, amid Macau's Las Vegas-style casinos to which mainland Chinese enthusiastically flock there remain Portuguese street names and shop signs and pavements just like those in Portugal, with *calçada portuguesa*. There is also the first western-style lighthouse in China, courtesy of the Portuguese.

Portugal's colonial genealogy allows it to claim the broadest global spread of UNESCO world heritage sites of any country. Its most common physical legacy in its former possessions are forts and religious buildings, those symbols of the Cross and the Crown. Portuguese-built monuments crop up in the oddest places, unless you are familiar with Portuguese history. There is a sixteenth-century Portuguese church, ✓ called Santa Cruz, in Bangkok, for instance: the Portuguese were the first Europeans to reach what is now Thailand. In 2009 the Portuguese voted for the "Seven Wonders of the World of Portuguese Origin" for a national television program. The candidates were 27 monuments in sixteen countries across Africa, South America, and Asia. The winners were Diu Fort and Bom Jesus Church in India; Morocco's Mazagão Fortress; the Old City of Santiago in Cape Verde; São Paulo Church in Macau; and the St Francis of Assisi church and the Ordem Terceira Convent, both in Brazil.

Brazil is perhaps the most estranged of the Portuguese offspring. It went its own way almost two centuries ago, long before the other colonies got to stand on their own two feet. Even so, Brazil was part of the empire for more than 300 years, and the kinship is evident. Salvador da Bahia, Brazil's first capital, has cobbled streets, houses painted pink, yellow, and red with white trim around the shuttered windows that make it look, as with Macau's downtown, like a little bit of Portugal stranded on another continent, more than 6,000 kilometers across the ocean. Portuguese who go there today are astonished by the patent similarities. They, like the tourists who marvel at the Monument to the Discoveries in Lisbon, stare in disbelief at how far the empire extended.

A seminal event set Brazil apart. The Portuguese royal family, the court, senior officials, and soldiers—more than 10,000 people in all—fled there en masse in 1807 to escape a French army invading Portugal. Their arrival dictated an elevation in the colony's status. Portugal's capital was switched to Brazil, the territory essentially became self-governing, and public buildings of appropriate distinction had to be put up. In 1822, chafing at Lisbon's insistent meddling, Brazil unilaterally declared independence, an occasion synthesized in the moment when Pedro the Prince Regent, by the Ipiranga river near São Paulo, is said to have shouted, "Independence or death!" In modern Portuguese, when someone is rebelling against unbearable circumstances, they are metaphorically said to be expressing "the cry of Ipiranga."

Lisbon was stung by the loss of its economic mainstay and turned hostile. It took Portugal three years to come to terms with it and officially accept that Brazil had left the fold. It is today the orthodoxy of the countries' ruling elites that Portugal and Brazil are siblings—not former colony and former colonial power. The Portuguese refer to Brazil as their *Grande Nação Irmã* (Great Sister Nation) and *segunda pátria* (second homeland). When the first ever southern Atlantic crossing by plane was made in 1922, by Portuguese Navy officers Sacadura Cabral and Gago Coutinho, they flew, naturally, to Brazil, where they were received enthusiastically. During the Salazar dictatorship Brazil gave shelter to political opponents of the regime, and after the 1974 Revolution it was an escape hatch for the ousted regime's officials and supporters. In the late 1980s, as Brazil rid itself of its military dictatorship and Portugal joined the European Economic Community, the temperature of relations grew warmer.

There have been less endearing episodes, and they suggest a distance that is not just geographical. On the 500th anniversary of the discovery in 2000, for instance, an opinion poll by the Brazilian media company Folha asked Brazilians to name the first famous person who came to mind when they thought of Portugal. Almost half of those questioned replied: "Nobody." In Portugal there have been "taking-our-jobs" controversies over Brazilian dentists and disquiet over the spread of Brazilian evangelical churches with allegedly dubious money-raising schemes. In 2009, 74 percent of Brazilian immigrants surveyed in Portugal said they had felt discrimination.

The popular Brazilian actress Maité Proença poked fun at the Portuguese in a video made during a recent visit to Portugal and decided the locals were "odd." The Portuguese blogosphere hummed with indignation. Part of the problem on this occasion was that Brazil, one of the world's vibrant emerging economies, had grown strong and confident while Portugal had waned and was feeling insecure. There were howls in Lisbon over a linguistic agreement between the governments of Portuguese-speaking countries to standardize the spelling of words. The idea was to eliminate regional linguistic variations that caused difficulties with legal contracts, Web searches, and the like. Though it was the cradle of the language, Portugal (pop. 10.6 million) ended up adopting more versions used in Brazil (pop. 190 million) than vice-versa. In fact, three-quarters of the changes fell to Portugal. The tail, it seemed to many, was wagging the dog.

Dictator's Doctrine

Brazil features prominently in one of the unflattering threads of Portuguese history. A joint documentary by the BBC and the History Channel in 2000, coinciding with the 500th anniversary of Brazil's discovery, was entitled "Brazil: An Inconvenient History." It cast light on a dark fact that many have been reluctant to confront: slavery. The documentary recounted how the Portuguese transported to South America at least four million African captives—some ten times more than the number taken to North America by other European countries.

The Portuguese do not dwell on this aspect. School textbooks divulge pages and pages about the feats of the Discoveries but cover just the bare bones of the country's almost four centuries of slavery. The city of Liverpool has a slave museum; the country of Portugal has none. A temporary 1988 exhibition on slavery at Lisbon's National Library, which gathered slaving documents from around the country, was a rare exception to the general silence. Angola's Museum of Slavery is housed in a seventeenth-century chapel on the outskirts of the capital Luanda, where slaves were forcibly baptized before being stuffed into ships and taken to other colonies.

The first black, or at least dark-skinned, slaves are believed to have arrived in Portugal in 1441. They were enemies captured in North Africa who were placed in servitude—a custom the Portuguese learned from the Arabs. The first slave auction was held three years later, in Lagos in the Algarve (its former slave market still stands), selling prisoners brought home by the caravels sent by Henry the Navigator to what are now Senegal, Gambia, and Guinea. The enterprise won top-level sanction: Pope Nicholas V, in a papal bull of 1452, formally granted the Portuguese the right to enslave pagans after the Portuguese had argued they needed to find extra hands and generate funds for their proselytizing campaign. Colloquial Portuguese echoed with this allocation of tasks: dull, repetitive labor was said to be *para o preto* ("for blacks").

Surprisingly for a country viewed at the time as lagging behind progress made in the European Enlightenment, Portugal in 1761 became the first Western European country to ban slaving, at least partly. The Marquis of Pombal, a sometime modernizer then running the government for King José I, outlawed slaving in mainland Portugal and its possessions in India. It was an enlightened ruling, even if the slaves already in Portugal and their children were to stay under the yoke. Abolition in Portugal was a piecemeal affair. Attempts to stop slavery met with ambivalence about obeying rules and were always opposed by vocal economic interests. In 1836 Portugal banned the transatlantic slave trade but only more than three decades later, in 1869, capitulated to international pressure and abolished slavery in its African colonies. Still, it went on, covertly, for years. And a question lingered over whether black workers in indentured servitude, who lived in ghastly conditions and with few if any rights, could be considered slaves—a bone of contention deftly examined by the author Miguel Sousa Tavares in his 2003 novel *Equator*.

The first words of Portugal's national anthem are, "Heroes of the sea, noble people, valiant nation." But the Portuguese are largely unburdened by recollections of the more disagreeable aspects of the Age of Discovery and the ensuing colonial empire. They barely mention them, and are broadly unaware of them because they are absent from the school syllabus and general cultural discourse. The boilerplate version of history dates from the twentieth-century dictatorship. Salazar and his propagandists cynically crafted a political artifice that was so neat, so flattering, that it has endured. Their doctrine drew on the Brazilian anthropologist Gilberto Freyre's theory of "luso-tropicalism," which viewed Portuguese colonization worldwide as benign. With that supposition as the central ingredient, Salazar's New State fabricated the myth that the Portuguese empire was benevolent and laudable. Salazar eulogized what he said was a multiracial society, even though in point of fact there were few non-white people in Portugal during his rule. This cultural currency was kept in circulation by his censors, who banished dissenting arguments. It has continued amid an apparent lack of interest in raking over the past.

Ask just about any Portuguese and they will tell you: Portuguese colonialism was kindly and beneficial. Mention, for instance, the massacres perpetrated by the Portuguese at Batepá in São Tomé in 1953, or at Wiriyamu in Mozambique in 1972 (which the local Portuguese archbishop described as "the only way to defend the Gospel on Africa"), and people do not know about them. When once I brought up these episodes a Portuguese expressed disbelief and responded, only half in jest, that they had been made up by the British. The French have owned up to torture in Algeria; Britain has acknowledged the concentration camps it set up for the Mau-Mau in Kenya; and Belgium has been shocked by evidence of the brutal exploitation of the former Congo by King Leopold II in the nineteenth century. In Portugal, however, a reluctance to examine pre-1974 Revolution colonialism has remained in place.

It does not require much effort, it must be said, to imagine the Portuguese as relatively congenial colonialists. They are by nature so affable, so willing to get along with anybody, that their colonies were bound to be different in style from those of others. Pope John Paul II, on a trip to Angola in 1992, observed: "The Portuguese settlers lived with Africans; other settlers lived among Africans." Their tolerant disposition probably also helps explain how they lasted so long in Macau, despite being harassed by British and Dutch forces looking for weaknesses in the Portuguese empire. Lisbon's National Archive holds a 1753 letter from Chinese Emperor Qianlong to King José I that is almost effusive in its diplomatic warmth. Written in Chinese, Portuguese, and Manchu on a roll of yellow silk almost four meters long, the letter exalts the kindly manner of the Portuguese in their dealings with the emperor's father and grandfather. The British historian Charles Boxer, an expert on Portuguese and Dutch expansion, conceded in his Raleigh Lecture at the British Academy in 1961 that the Portuguese "had, as a rule, less colour prejudice" than other western colonizers and "often earned themselves a friendly feeling," which the clipped coolness of their European rivals was unable to match.

But, crucially, Boxer contested the Portuguese claim that they were color-blind and tackled the luso-tropicalism doctrine head-on. He and other scholars, working from original texts, have weeded out falsehoods and demolished conceits. The Portuguese historian Manuel Heleno produced a mammoth work on slavery in Portugal. The first volume, covering the period from the birth of the nation to the fifteenth century—a time when most slavery involved whites or Arabs—was published in the 1950s. His second volume, picking up from the date of the first slave auction in Lagos, was banned by the dictatorship. Boxer's exceptionally well-researched 1969 book, *The Portuguese Seaborne Empire*, was also banned by Salazar. Like Heleno's work it was factual and, consequently, ideologically suspect.

Boxer assessed the "brute force" dimension of the conquests. They were brutish times, and all sides committed atrocities. Colonizers always regard the colonized as inferior. And they exercise their *droit du seigneur*. Boxer referred to a famous decree of December 4, 1567, which ordered the demolition of "heathen" places of worship in Portuguese territories, the expulsion of non-Christian holy men, and the seizure and destruction of the Koran. At the same time, natives were compelled to convert. Portuguese bishops expressed horror at the brutality of some of the forced conversions, as laymen who had gone out to the distant lands threw themselves into the task with righteous cruelty. "Beyond the equator," a sixteenth-century Portuguese proverb said, "anything goes." Colonial officials in places such as Goa and Cape Verde for centuries complained to Lisbon about the ignorant, thuggish type of colonizer being sent out to populate the new lands.

Further evidence of what actually went on in those distant, romanticized days was compiled by the journalist Ana Barradas for her 1991 *Black Book of the Portuguese Discoveries*. Acknowledging that the period is a "sacred" subject in Portugal, she insisted that the common view of those accomplishments as "a triumph of civilization" is mere propaganda. She assembled original texts, including letters, official reports, and personal diaries, to prove her point. These are some of the episodes and comments she listed.

Gomes Eanes de Zurara, in a 1453 account of activities he witnessed in Guinea, told how groups of Portuguese raided coastal villages in pursuit of natives to enslave, sometimes swooping in at night—presumably by the light of flaming torches and with drawn swords. Zurara recorded how terrified villagers scampered from their huts and dived into the jungle, with mothers desperately trying to hide their small children in the dark and others drowning as they tried to get away by crossing rivers. Zurara said the Portuguese mostly captured women and children who could not run as fast as the men.

Gaspar Correia's chronicle of events in India in the early years of the sixteenth century includes a tale of how Vasco da Gama ordered his men to cut off the hands, ears, and noses of prisoners and send the body parts to the local tribal chief with instructions for him to make a curry out of them.

Ruthlessness and brutality also occurred in Morocco. Rodrigo de Castro, staying in the town of Safi, wrote a letter to King João III in 1541 in which he reported of an attack: "We took them completely by surprise and killed about 400 people, most of them women and children. The troops didn't spare anyone and only when they grew tired did they take about 80 prisoners."

Fernão de Queirós, writing in 1688 about the conquest of what was then called Ceylon, recorded of André Furtado—a school textbook India hero for his military victories over Arab pirates and Dutch rivals—that he "ordered the throats of 800 Muslims to be slit because he didn't want any foreigners and avowed enemies staying in the realm."

In a blow to the theory of Portugal's supposed "civilizing" influence, an administrative report (the devil is in the detail) from 1917 about slaves in Mozambique candidly commented: "Few speak Portuguese and rare are the ones who have drawn benefit from our civilization." José Norton de Matos, a famous general, politician, and colonial governor, wrote in his memoirs published in the 1940s that slavery—"concealed, disguised, deceptive"—was still functioning in Angola and other Portuguese African colonies in the early twentieth century.

Barradas commented of this evidence about Portugal's past: "The spell has been broken." Her book, however, is hard to find.

Others, too, have taken the trouble to dig out the truth about the colonial past. Diana Andringa, a journalist, was born in Dundo, a main town in northern Angola's diamond-producing region, in 1947 and spent her childhood there. Her memory, like those of many Portuguese settlers, was of a peaceful idyll. Black-and-white photographs and film from the time showed ample Portuguese houses with gardens, a whites-only social club with reclining chairs and a swimming pool, and a church choir of young Africans dressed in pressed white shirts and dark trousers. Like other European colonials, the Portuguese tried to recreate their homes in the tropics, complete with hearths, silver cutlery, and glazed plates. More than half a century later, wanting to corroborate her recollections with local people, Andringa returned there and made a documentary, *Dundo, Colonial Memory*, which came out in 2009. People she grew up with painted her a different picture of her youth. They recalled segregation, with one Mass for blacks and another for whites, medical appointments in separate rooms, separate school classes for blacks and whites, and separate living quarters. Some described it as a *de facto* apartheid, though not a *de jure* one. They also remembered humiliating treatment at the hands of the Portuguese, ranging from what was termed a "civilizing slap around the head" to more violent punishments. Andringa recalled her family's cook who, as she fried a steak for their pet cat, muttered, "My daughter has never eaten steak."

The former colonies' view of their one-time ruler is not always flattering. While some Brazilians regard Portugal as their cultural fountainhead, others—especially Amerindians and blacks—perceive the Portuguese arrival as an event heralding the inequality and injustice that has continued ever since. On the 500th anniversary of discovery some Indian groups refused to take part in the commemorations and staged protest marches that brought dozens of arrests. In an open letter, one indigenous group accused the "European invasion" of bringing with it "lethal, organized brutality."

The 500th anniversary of Vasco da Gama's landfall in Goa also created controversy. Portugal put on a big celebration to mark the national hero Gama's breakthrough. But some in India, and especially Goan nationalists, were outraged. Many of them had risked their lives in uniform in 1961 to take by force what Indian Prime Minister Jawaharlal Nehru reportedly called "the Portuguese pimple on the face of India." For them, Gama was a cruel and rapacious intruder and a harbinger of 450 years of colonial oppression. They even accused him of genocide. Several Goan political parties united to form the Deshpremi Nagrik Samiti (Patriotic Citizens' Committee), whose supporters marched in protest and burned an effigy of Vasco da Gama at a rally. The Indian government, embarrassed, had to tell the Portuguese that it was pulling out of the commemorations.

Even accounting for the Portuguese fraternal disposition, there was never any doubt about who was in charge in the colonies. Social status and legal rights under the colonial administration were formally indexed: there were Portuguese nationals, African natives and, in between, natives who were "assimilated" through education and allowed to join imperial institutions as clerks and the like. Natives were second-class citizens because of their skin color, and the colonial elite worked them hard. In remote areas bosses administered on-the-spot justice and used forced labor and beatings *pour encourager les autres*. As the British historian Edward Gibbon remarked (and he was not only thinking of the Portuguese empire), "The history of empires is the history of human misery."

One Angolan who worked on a plantation in the 1950s described the relationship between the Portuguese master and the native as being like that between a horseman and his horse: the horseman may look after his horse, but he still sits on the beast and gives it orders and punishes it if it misbehaves. Salazar articulated commonplace colonial attitudes in a 1935 speech: "We must organize better and more efficiently," he sermonized, "the protection of inferior races whose summons to our Christian civilization is one of the boldest concepts and greatest deeds of Portuguese colonization."

Mixed Blood

The outbreak of wars of independence in the some of the African colonies in the 1960s was hard for the Portuguese to digest because it challenged their assumptions. They had been at peace for centuries and, like other Europeans, devoutly believed in their civilizing mission. A groundbreaking documentary series aired in 2008 by public broadcaster Radiotelevisão Portuguesa helped remove the rose-tinted glasses by confronting Portugal with unsettling aspects of the colonial war and the country's colonial history in general. It set out unpalatable truths, such as the use of napalm, that had been swept under the carpet. Hundreds of first-hand accounts, old photographs, and archive film footage lifted the lid on what had gone on, including atrocities and obvious racial discrimination. For the Portuguese, this was less history than news. Many were astonished because the fresh and factual look at events collided with the Portuguese version of their history, long rendered as the chronicle of a small country of "gentle ways" bullied by bigger European powers, a narrative of national victimhood. "We think of our colonization as having been soft, or mild, compared to other European countries. But it wasn't, it was just the same," the anthropologist Luis Quintais says. "We like to portray ourselves as victims, not victimizers." He adds: "There is a clear rubbing-out of history of this issue. It has been submerged in a huge silence." For some, especially veterans, contributing to the program was a cathartic experience. They gave touching accounts of their experiences on blogs, on radio call-ins, and elsewhere. There was a sense that now that they were growing old, they wanted to get it off their chest.

The broad contemporary reticence in Portugal about considering the bad old days contributed to the neglect of the country's war veterans. About 9,000 soldiers were killed and at least 12,000 wounded on the African battlefield. Like many armies, they were cheered when they left but forgotten when they returned. A national Soldiers' Day was not instituted until 1987. Only in 1994 was a monument to the fallen, listing the names of the dead on a semi-circular wall around a shallow pond, erected at a riverside fort in Lisbon, near where the troops had left for the war. And post-traumatic stress disorder was officially recognized as a medical condition only in 1999.

A Portuguese soldier in Africa

The colonial war's end in 1974 led swiftly to African independence. After centuries handcuffed to Lisbon, the colonies were set free. In the Mozambican capital Maputo a sign declaring *Isto é Portugal* ("This is Portugal") on the façade of the governor's residence was torn down and trampled on with heady joy by the emancipated crowd. There was general rejoicing—giving the lie, it would seem, to Portugal's claim that its colonies prized its presence.

The former colonies remain—literally—in Portuguese blood. In the fifteenth century, Afonso de Albuquerque, viceroy of India, encouraged his compatriots to take local women as wives as a way of dominating the territory. The Portuguese also slept with the slaves they kept. There was no repugnance at this *política de mestiçagem* (policy of racial intermingling), and it should be noted that settlers were almost exclusively young single men, including exiled convicts, who were far from home, and no white women travelled with them. Camões, the epic poet, wrote a eulogy for a beautiful black slave. In Brazil, the racial intermingling was vigorous, even to the point of polygamy. The English and other European settlers frowned on this custom, regarding it as decadent. Some famous Portuguese, such as the Marquis of Pombal, the seventeenth-century priest and chronicler Father António Vieira, the twentieth-century artist Almada Negreiros, and other renowned figures, could point to black blood in their family tree. Footballer Cristiano Ronaldo's local paper in the Madeira islands claimed he has African heritage—a great-grandmother from Cape Verde three generations earlier—and the family did not deny it. It is not uncommon for a white Portuguese over forty to declare, with some pride, "I was born in Africa."

Partly due to this easy mixing the Portuguese have long viewed racism as the province of other European colonizers. But ask a black person in Lisbon whether they think the Portuguese are racist and chances are the answer will be along the lines of, "No, not really, but..." Some 60 percent of sub-Saharan Africans surveyed in 2009 said they felt at a disadvantage because of their skin color.

The popular Brazilian musician Caetano Veloso commented in 2007 that "the Portuguese are amateur racists." He meant, I think, that their racism is unsophisticated, uncalculated, informal. They do not deliberately, or consciously, pursue a policy of discrimination; there is no malice aforethought. On the other hand, it has to be asked why there are almost no black doctors, members of parliament, lawyers, or school teachers in Portugal. It may just be a question of time: whereas colonial immigrants arrived in Britain in the 1950s, they began disembarking in Portugal in large numbers from the late 1970s on and perhaps need another generation before they start to rise up the ladder in any great number.

Though still knitted together by blood and shared experience, the relationship between Portugal and its former colonies has loosened. In exiting its overseas possessions Portugal did not make a virtue out of necessity as, say, the British did with the Commonwealth. In recent times, spurred by globalization's promises, a diplomatic effort has been made to extend hands back across the ocean. It took politicians until 1996 to finally establish a collaborative framework, though, and at a glitzy ceremony at the Belém Cultural Center in Lisbon they launched the Community of Portuguese Language Countries, known by its acronym CPLP. Apart from Portugal, it includes Brazil, Angola, Mozambique, Guinea-Bissau, Cape Verde, São Tomé & Príncipe, and East Timor. The potential benefits of this marshalling of forces were evident as the countries together might be greater than the sum of their parts. Yet after ten years of spending taxpayers' money, the nine-strong grouping had not harnessed any telling influence in international affairs. With each member country distracted by its own continental concerns, they have been out of sync and other interests have shouted louder. In 1995, in a major diplomatic embarrassment for Portugal, Mozambique—struggling to find impetus for its development—defected and joined the British Commonwealth. With a healthy dose of dark humor, the joke in Lisbon was that maybe Portugal should ask to join, too.

Portugal largely turned its back on Africa after the 1974 Revolution. It was immersed in its own problems and also wanted to put firmly behind it the decades of dictatorship and everything smacking of it. That is why Cesária Évora needed French attentiveness to become an internationally famous singer. This plump, chain-smoking grandmother from Cape Verde, known as the Barefoot Diva because of her custom of appearing on stage without shoes, is the most prominent performer of *morna*—a style of music not a million miles from Portugal's *fado*. The Portuguese paid her little attention, however. Paris was where she first made her name after a French producer recognized her talent. She won a world music Grammy in 2004 and France's Légion d'honneur, its highest civilian tribute, in 2007. At her modest home in Mindelo, Cape Verde's second-largest city on São Vicente island, in 2000 I settled onto her sofa for an interview but before I could begin she snapped, "I don't speak Portuguese!" She said it in Portuguese. In fact, she said it in very good Portuguese. But, she later explained, she was voicing her bitterness, her lingering annoyance that the Portuguese had paid her no attention.

Chapter Four
In Whom Do We Trust?
Spain, England and Portugal's Destiny

Portugal has two neighbors: the Atlantic Ocean and Spain. One of them was long viewed as a risky prospect, treacherous and dangerous; the other was wet.

Iberian history is largely a chronicle of two nations separated by their shared geography, a case of so near yet so far. Iberia's configuration invites comparisons between the Portuguese and the Spanish, and the similarities are obvious. But the differences, too, are pronounced.

Spain is roughly four times bigger, in area and population, and shunts Portugal into a remote corner, constituting a buffer between the Portuguese and the rest of Europe and engendering what the writer António José Saraiva called "a kind of island mentality" among the Portuguese. Spain was traditionally Portugal's great adversary. Encroachment or even annexation by Castile, the expansionist kingdom that grew into the Spanish state, was ever a menace. In Portuguese foreign policy, this was for centuries "the Spanish Question." In the choreography of their relationship with Spain, the Portuguese trod warily around their pugnacious neighbor. And when they needed a powerful friend to help keep Spain at arm's length they turned to England, their oldest ally. Those two countries have played a key part in shaping Portugal's fortunes.

Against the odds, Portugal throughout history mostly resisted the gravitational pull of Madrid. Agostinho da Silva, a Portuguese philosopher of the last century, observed, "Portugal's most remarkable feat in the world wasn't the maritime explorations nor the Christian *reconquista* nor the establishment of overseas territories. It was resisting Castile." ✓ The consequence was that the two countries turned their backs on each other and went their separate ways. Spain was, in important aspects, a Mediterranean country within France's orbit; Portugal went unshackled into the Atlantic while keeping a wary eye on its neighbor. Claudio Sanchez Albornoz, a Spanish historian and a former ambassador in Lisbon, concludes that the two nations have been kept apart by "cen-

João IV reclaims the Portuguese throne from Spain, 1640

turies of hostility, centuries of apprehension, centuries of incomprehension, centuries of ambitions and fears."

Their different—to an unexpected degree—national characters led them into a quirky and complex relationship. You need look no further, for instance, than the contrast between the passionate, foot-stamping power of *flamenco* and the static woefulness of *fado*, Portugal's traditional music, to grasp cultural dissimilarities. The Portuguese do not on the whole possess the spontaneous vitality and vigor of their neighbors. Spanish brio, self-confidence, and self-regard are largely absent from their collective character. Where Spaniards are aggressive, self-assertive people, the Portuguese are reserved and more attuned to indignation and humility.

Bullfighting provides another telling symbolic contrast between the tenor of the two peoples. In Portugal bullfights not only do not end with the slaying of the bull as in Spain but the sharp ends of its horns are also clipped and cushioned with a leather sheath, blunting any contact with the bullfighter on horseback or the bull-wrestling *forcados* (though against the Portuguese *toureiro* who performs on foot the horns are left *au naturel*). After the 1974 military coup, which stood Portuguese society on its head overnight but cost only a handful of lives (compared with the Spanish civil war, which slaughtered hundreds of thousands), Spaniards wondered out loud whether blood or water ran in Portuguese veins. Just as unkindly, the Spanish dictator General Franco reportedly commented that so few people were killed in that Carnation Revolution because the Portuguese were cowards. This is laughably untrue: a Portuguese can be as spirited and ferocious as the next person—when given no other option. And the macho Franco never wrestled a bull with his bare hands.

Just as revealing about national temperament, and its small size notwithstanding, Portugal is one of the few countries where the Ministry of Defense can be said to be just that: Portugal has not launched an unprovoked military attack on anyone since the sixteenth century. That was during the Age of Discovery, when the two Iberian countries so spectacularly spread their wings. While Spain bragged about its *conquistas* (conquests) of that period, the Portuguese celebrated their *descobrimentos* (discoveries): they are a people who could be cruel but never matched the scale of Spanish bloodletting in Latin America.

The Portuguese tend to have a deeply hospitable nature. In a Porto restaurant once, a waitress said to me, "You speak good Portuguese." My English friend, who worked in Spain, was astonished. Spaniards would never utter such a thing, he said. It just would not occur to them. The Portuguese, meanwhile, feel flattered—and surprised—that a foreigner would take the trouble to learn their language.

The Portuguese deride what they regard as greasy and inferior Spanish cuisine; Spaniards, when talking about Portuguese women, might slyly rub a finger across their upper lip to suggest a moustache. This is part of the inevitable game of peninsular one-upmanship. When Portugal won the right to host the 2004 European football championship the glee was all the greater because it beat a rival bid from Spain, which had assumed that it had the event in the bag and had dismissively waved away the possibility of a joint bid.

The Portuguese are perfectly conscious of the chip on their shoulder when it comes to their mighty neighbor. A joke tells how three Portuguese counterterrorism experts went to Washington, DC to inform President George W. Bush they had detected an al-Qaeda cell in Portugal. "That's terrible! We'll bomb them back to the Stone Age!" Bush told them in the Oval Office, then asking (not surprisingly), "What's the name of your capital?" The three Portuguese gulped. They glanced at each other, turned back to Bush, and replied in unison: "Madrid."

The Portuguese are neither venomous nor hostile about Spain, but resent the way the Spanish ignore them. (Spain is more vigilant about its bigger neighbor, France.) Spain's centuries-old lack of interest in Portugal is so complete that it almost seems studied. Weather forecasts on Spanish television channels and in newspapers simply leave the rectangle along the left side of the peninsula blank. The Portuguese historian António Hespanha remarked: "I go to Spain a lot and what hurts most is the silence, the lack of knowledge about Portugal. They don't even say bad things." A pan-Iberian survey in 2009 found that only 1 percent of Spaniards questioned knew the name of Portugal's prime minister, while about 55 percent of Portuguese could name his Spanish opposite number.

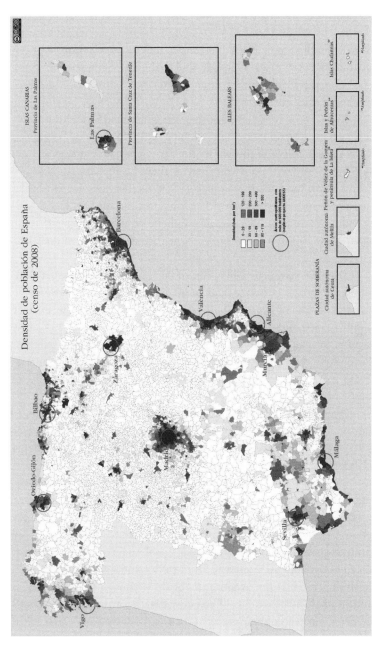

Leaving a blank: a Spanish map of the Iberian peninsula

Portugal was long the thorn in Spain's southwestern side, a nagging reminder of Madrid's inability to claim the peninsula as wholly its own, to make itself complete. (In 1940 and in 1975 Franco's Spain drew up unconsummated plans to invade Portugal.) Spaniards, it seems, have overcome this silent rebuke by putting Portugal out of their mind, pretending it does not exist.

It vexes the Portuguese that they can understand Spanish, and willingly get by in Spain by speaking a kind of Spanish-accented Portuguese with a few local words thrown in. But Spaniards come to Portugal and just speak Spanish. And if you reply to them in Portuguese, they give you a blank look. They may live next door but they are no better equipped, after all, than any other foreigners to cope with the confounding Portuguese language. It should be recalled, however, that the Portuguese harbor a secret pride about the inscrutability of their language.

Spaniards may generally disregard Portugal but at Easter they pour across the border. Easter is known as "Spanish Week" in Portugal as vacationers come over in huge numbers for a look at the historic anomaly next door. They arrive and depart in a whirlwind of noisy chatter. You can never miss a group of Spaniards in a typically subdued Portuguese restaurant. And the way Spaniards turn up for dinner at 10.55 p.m.—that is, about five minutes before the kitchen is due to shut—does little to win the affection of the staff.

Despite all such sometimes subtle considerations, foreign multinationals that do not know any better tend to establish their head office for Portugal in Madrid, ignorantly lumping the two nations together as if they were the same.

Today the two countries get along, but for centuries the relationship was frosty and punctuated with virile antagonism. Old Portuguese proverbs reveal the antipathy: "From Spain neither good winds nor good marriages come," goes one, in a reference to the hot, dry wind from the east that shrivels crops and, it is thought, to royal marriages that ill-advisedly attempted to bind the countries into one. An old Spanish proverb is just as pointed: "Strip a Spaniard of all his virtues and you have a Portuguese." Even now, the customary Portuguese reference to Spaniards being *nuestros hermanos* ("our brothers" in Spanish) is tinged with irony. If the Portuguese and Spanish are branches of the same Iberian family tree, they are estranged. The nineteenth-century writer Alexandre Herculano admitted to an incorrigible individualism among his compatriots: "We are independent because that's just the way we like it: that is the total, absolute, incontestable reason for our national individuality."

Neighbors Apart

The car journey from Lisbon to Madrid takes only four or five hours these days, thanks to new highways. There is still no high-speed train link, largely due to inveterate Portuguese quarreling among themselves—in this case, about the line's route. Planes from Lisbon to Madrid are full every weekday morning and evening with business people, laptop bags in hand. The two countries are EU partners now, and much has changed. But it was not always thus. In fact, it never was. The historian João Medina says "our relationship with Spain was always one of distrust and paranoia."

Of all the patchwork of culturally distinctive regions on the peninsula that wanted to stay out of Madrid's clutches, Portugal was the most successful—more so than independence-minded Catalonia or the Basque Country, for example. Galicia, the northwestern Spanish province that most resembles Portugal in manner and language, offers an interesting comparison. Taken over by Castile, it became a fringe region, governed from distant Madrid by people of a different temper. Portugal, left to its own initiative, blazed an independent trail that took it around the world, building an empire that enabled it to sustain itself. Catalans deem Portugal lucky for having escaped Madrid's chilly embrace: "At least there's still Portugal," they say.

Castile long rued the successes of the headstrong people on the west coast who stubbornly stood their ground. Trouble first broke out in 1127 when, after a disagreement over who owned what, Afonso VII of Castile laid siege to the northern city of Guimarães. In response, a few months later in 1128, Afonso Henriques triumphed over Castile at the Battle of São Mamede and seized the county of Portucale, the northern part of modern Portugal. In 1143, in the Treaty of Zamora, Castile begrudgingly recognized Afonso Henriques as ruler of that part of the peninsula, though Portugal's first king had to pledge allegiance and pay an annual tribute to Castile. A papal bull of 1179 gave the Vatican's blessing to Portugal's independent status.

Both ruling houses then turned their attention to expelling the North African Muslims from the peninsula but once that campaign was concluded the trouble returned. A dispute over the rightful heir to the Portuguese throne led Juan I of Castile to invade, helped by French cavalry, in an attempt to claim the crown. The Portuguese delivered him a stinging defeat at the celebrated Battle of Aljubarrota in 1385.

Another crisis of succession brought belligerent Castile back over the border and this time it recorded a rare triumph, at Alcântara in 1580. As a result, the following year Felipe I of Spain was formally recognized as King of Portugal in a lavish ceremony at the Convent of Christ in Tomar, and it is easy to imagine a scene of hissed Portuguese oaths and a general gnashing of teeth. Castile ruled for sixty years—more than a lifetime in those days. Like other foreign invaders and administrators who would arrive more than two centuries later, they are said to have treated the locals with contempt. Portuguese nobles eventually had enough and staged a revolt in 1640, placing João IV on the throne and restoring home rule in gritty defiance of Castile. The Restoration is a proud milestone in Portuguese history, and its annual anniversary on December 1 is a national holiday. Even so, there were another five major armed showdowns with Castile between 1644 and 1665 before Castile gave up and endorsed Portugal's independence in 1668—almost 500 years after the Vatican.

In an offshoot of the Seven Years' War, which engulfed all Europe's major powers, Spain made another foray over the border in 1762 (in military terms, it was almost always one-way traffic) but, with England jumping to Portugal's aid, it came to nothing. The last bilateral conflict between the two countries occurred in 1801, in an episode called the War of the Oranges because an invading Spanish army commander sent Portuguese oranges to the wife of his king, Carlos IV, during the campaign. Spain and France had demanded that Portugal line up alongside them against England, and Spain was given the dirty work of making its neighbor comply. Portugal was poorly prepared and lost. In any case, the following year England and France agreed to peace and the Iberian confrontation fizzled out. Just around the corner, though, was the Peninsular War, which darkened the start of the nineteenth century in Portugal. Three devastating French military invasions, initially supported in part by Spain, during those years brought brutality and starvation and sowed resentment.

By the 1820s a more sensible note was being sounded. A Spanish official voiced the possibility of Portugal and Spain getting together, of putting the bad blood behind them in an alliance called the Iberian Federation, but the idea did not take hold. The possibility resurfaced in the second half of that century when some prominent Portuguese thinkers, dismayed by the apparently insurmountable backwardness of their country compared with the rest of Europe, opened a debate about whether joining forces with Spain might, in fact, be a positive move. A few decades earlier, these people would have been labelled traitors. The poet Antero de Quental, identifying an Iberian breed and a shared pedigree, wrote in a pamphlet in 1868 that "under the current circumstances the only possible and logical act of patriotism would be to yield our nationality." The respected nineteenth-century historian Oliveira Martins concurred: "The union of Iberia does not at the moment feature in the manifestos of any political parties, but it's in our instinct." Once again, the idea failed to gain any purchase. The long-standing wariness of Spain was too ingrained, it was too hard to dispel so soon.

This, however, would be a recurring topic whenever Portugal's self-esteem wore thin and the thrill of independence started to pale. In the early years of this century Spain's turbo-charged economy stood as a silent reproach to Portugal, which was following behind in low gear, falling further and further behind the rest of Western Europe. The Portuguese philosopher José Gil commented: "We think, 'Why not? If we joined Spain it would all be much easier.' They would do the work we are incapable of."

Spain had done that work to merit its success. When General Franco's dictatorship fell in the mid-1970s, politicians, businessmen, and trade unions came together, decided where they wanted Spain to be and mapped a path of how to get there in the 1977 Pacts of

Moncloa, named after the seat of Spanish government. The country endured years of double-digit unemployment rates as it retooled its economy and readied itself for the new challenges. In Portugal, meanwhile, after the army coup brought democracy around the same time, the country splintered into myriad interest groups that bickered fruitlessly in an exasperating political merry-go-round. Portugal had fifteen governments in eleven years after the Carnation Revolution. European Union aid after 1986 enabled it to defer the painful but necessary economic reforms even longer. Portugal found out late that the greater pain lies in not changing with the times. Thus, when the weekly paper *Sol* conducted a poll in 2006 it found that almost a third of Portuguese were ready to ditch their independence and join up with Spain. The newspaper's editor José António Saraiva remarked: "We are envious of Spanish economic success. Spain's speed contrasts with the slowness of our economic recovery and people want to catch the same train."

There is even an abiding view among some that Portugal as a separate entity simply does not make sense. The peninsular division can seem arbitrary and implausible. Santiago Petschen, a Spanish university professor, quoted a journalist's comment from 1963: "Seldom has human insensitivity established a falser separation. Neither geography, nor ethnography nor the economy justify this brutal mutilation of a single territory."

José Saramago, the Portuguese novelist who won the Nobel literature prize in 1998 and who left to live in Spain's Canary Islands, thought that peninsular unity was inevitable. It would, he said, be a country called Iberia. (His 1986 novel *The Stone Raft* imagines the peninsula snapping off from the continent and drifting out into the Atlantic where, the suggestion is, it belongs.) Saramago, who died in 2010 at 87, argued that the Portuguese would keep their identity in the same way as the Basques, Catalans, or Galicians have preserved theirs. Such a notion gains no currency with more conservative sections of Portuguese society, however. They view the possibility as a capitulation, a betrayal of the stout-hearted Portuguese who gave their lives in the historical struggle for nationhood. A former Portuguese conservative foreign minister, who was also a former ambassador in Madrid, tartly remarked: "Mr. Saramago's vision belongs to the nineteenth century, not the twenty-first. It's very easy to hate Portugal when you're abroad. What's hard is to defend Portuguese interests abroad, and that's something which Mr. Saramago is evidently unable to do." Undoubtedly, the idea of a union does not strike a chord with a majority of Portuguese.

In between this sporadic talk of union was a half-century of apparent symmetry when the dictators Salazar and Franco ruled. Salazar, shuddering at the possibility of a communist regime on his doorstep and familiar, like all Portuguese, with the scope of Madrid's ambitions, had surreptitiously backed Franco in the Spanish Civil War, keeping on his good side by permitting an overland flow of contraband that punched a hole in the international blockade of Spain. Upon Franco's triumph in 1939, the two leaders entered into a non-aggression pact. However, some in Franco's circle were pushing behind the scenes for a swift military annexation of Portugal. The general is said to have looked favorably on the idea but differed with them on the timing. Salazar sensed this latent danger and their dealings always had something of smoke-and-mirrors about them. Meanwhile, the Spanish royal family escaped Franco and moved into exile in Portugal where the future Spanish king Juan Carlos spent his early school years, in Estoril. (Spanish tourists still go around Estoril asking—in Spanish, of course—for directions to his old house, and there is a statue of him and Queen Sofia in the middle of a busy traffic circle.)

The Second World War kept the two dictators busy with other concerns. Neither ruler was keen on seeing the forces of democracy triumph. Salazar pursued an intense diplomatic campaign to persuade Madrid to stay out of the fighting, acutely aware that Portugal would quickly be swallowed up if Spain enlisted with the Axis powers. After the Allied victory Spain became internationally isolated and suddenly needed the help of its well-connected neighbor which, through astute diplomatic maneuvering, had maintained good relations with Britain and was granted a place among the founding members of NATO. Lisbon became a Spanish conduit to, and an earpiece in, western capitals. Franco's only ever foreign trip was to Portugal, in 1949. The two dictators—Salazar was three years older than Franco, but both were children of the nineteenth century—met seven times between 1942 and 1963.

Their perceived closeness made Spanish interests a target for those bent on revenge after Salazar's dictatorship was overthrown in the 1974 Revolution. When Franco's regime sentenced five leftist militants to death in September 1975, the Spanish Embassy in Lisbon was ransacked and its contents set alight on the street outside by a local mob. King Juan Carlos, who spoke Portuguese, helped heal the wounds. On his first post-dictatorship state visit to Portugal, in 1978, he nudged the two countries closer by going to the Batalha Monastery, built to celebrate victory at the Battle of Aljubarrota, to convey the message that such antagonism was in the past and a new era was at hand.

Both countries were eyeing the potential returns of membership in the European Economic Community. Their stiff relationship was out of step with the new mood of partnership on the continent, and both were looking to consolidate relatively recent democracies. The Iberian countries (placed, as usual, in the same bag by other European nations) signed up to the bloc together as its eleventh and twelfth members, their leaders attending joint signing ceremonies in Lisbon, in the cloisters of the Jerónimos Monastery, in the morning and in Madrid in the evening on June 12, 1985. The festivities heralded a rapprochement as the European project worked its magic of overcoming old enmity, such as that between France and Germany, and Portugal and Spain began to engage economically and culturally eight centuries after they had embarked on their separate journeys.

Before they joined the bloc, bilateral trade was insignificant. Portugal did more business with Sweden and Japan than with Spain. But it was not long before Spain became Portugal's main trading partner. Those executives queuing for planes at Lisbon airport have since been doing brisk business. Today major companies dispassionately divide the peninsula up into regions, not countries, for marketing purposes. The momentum has been sustained. When the Socialist Party won Portugal's 2005 general election in a landslide, the new prime minister José Sócrates announced that his foreign policy goals were "Spain, Spain, Spain." His first foreign trip was to Madrid, as was that of new president Aníbal Cavaco Silva after his 2006 election.

The new footing of bilateral relations means that discussion about whether to join together and form a single country has become something of an anachronism and a parlor game. Portugal and Spain, once separated by their common desire to stage the 2004 European soccer championship, even agreed on a joint bid to host the 2018 World Cup.

The Spanish wear their modern clothes more easily than the Portuguese. The Portuguese come back from trips across the border enthusing about how everything works, the vitality of Spain, the opportunities, the sophistication. Portugal still feels stuck in the past, sedentary and unable to cast off its self-defeating habits. It has not seized the opportunities that have come its way, neither at an official level nor among the general public. A Portuguese friend of mine, on holiday one year, spent a week or so driving in southeastern Portugal around the rim of the huge Alqueva reservoir, which spills over the border into Spain. She and her small group toured the lakeside on the Portuguese side (paying "€15 a body," cash, for rooms in locals' houses) and encountered villages that had not changed much for decades, except now they were standing next to a huge body of water. On the Spanish side of the lake, meanwhile, the villages had built cafés at the water's edge with shady esplanades, children's playgrounds, and swimming areas—making the most of the site's potential.

A joint report in 2008 by the finance ministries of Portugal and Spain revealed that the Portuguese regions are the poorest of the peninsula in terms of GDP per capita. Only Lisbon came close to matching the poorest Spanish region. Spain's relentless entrepreneurial drive—up to the 2009 recession, anyway—still sparks some prickly nationalist sentiment among those conservative sections of society that display a residual economic patriotism that is misplaced in the EU. It offends them that powerful Spanish companies gobble up smaller Portuguese rivals in key industries such as banking, agriculture, energy, and construction. A conservative Portuguese politician, couching his grievances in the language of imperial grandeur, said—rather pointlessly: "Don't forget that Portugal was already a nation when Castile was still fighting the Moors."

The Oldest Ally

For centuries, whenever the friction with Spain reached a climax, the Portuguese turned to a hard-hitting friend: England. Portugal and England possess what is claimed to be the world's longest unbroken bilateral alliance, dating from the fourteenth century. Portuguese history is interwoven as much with England's past as it is with Spain's. For Portugal, England was always a tremendously valuable counterweight to perceived Spanish aggression; for England, Portugal provided a key strategic foothold on the continent and a proxy in its wars with France and Spain. Portugal never threatened England the way Spain did, especially in the Elizabethan age. (The Portuguese were always sailing away, towards new horizons, not sailing into European battles.) The Anglo-Portuguese ties were on the face of it mutually beneficial, but for the ✓ Portuguese the duplicitous and self-serving policies of perfidious Albion exacted an at times heavy price and strained relations.

The collaboration goes back almost 1,000 years. During the Crusades, Portugal was on the route of ships sailing from northern Europe to the Holy Land. Adventurers from England were among the military force that sided with King Afonso Henriques to dislodge the North African Arabs from Lisbon in 1147 by laying siege to the hilltop bastion where St. George's castle was later built. As a reward, they were given permission to plunder the walled city. Once the dust had settled, ✓ the first Bishop of Lisbon was an Englishman, the crusader-cum-priest Gilbert of Hastings.

Formal relations between Portugal and England were established in medieval times. They were pushed together by their clashes with Castile, confirming the old adage that the enemy of my enemy is my friend. Ferdinand of Portugal and Edward III of England entered into a makeshift Treaty of Alliance in 1373, which placed prized English archers alongside the Portuguese at the Battle of Aljubarrota. The full scope of that agreement was set out in the formal Treaty of Windsor in ✓ 1386, cemented the following year by the marriage, in Porto, of King João I and Philippa of Lancaster, daughter of John of Gaunt, the Duke of Lancaster. When John of Gaunt and an expeditionary force landed in Galicia that year to press his claim—ultimately thwarted—to the throne of Castile he was assisted by Portuguese troops. Philippa, meanwhile, turned her hand to fostering Anglo-Portuguese trade—and bearing children. She had eight and they are known to Portuguese historians as the "Illustrious Generation" because some of them played key roles in advancing overseas exploration. They included the future King Duarte, Prince Henry the Navigator, and Prince Pedro, who collected precious maps and information from across Europe.

Portugal's maritime supremacy eclipsed England in the fifteenth and sixteenth centuries. Portuguese daring and impulsiveness brought the wealth of the East within Europe's grasp. But the more pragmatic northern European countries such as England and the Netherlands used trade in those goods to their lasting advantage through artful negotiation and shrewd investment. They became increasingly rich while big-spending Portugal grew poorer.

The period of Spanish rule between 1580 and 1640 disrupted the traditional alliance. The Portuguese were press-ganged into Spain's struggle against England and their ships were summoned to join the Invincible Armada, which sailed out of Lisbon in May 1588. At the same time, Portugal's imperial constellation and conspicuous affluence kindled English covetousness. With the old alliance forgotten due to Spanish rule, Portuguese ships returning to Europe laden with goods from the East were fair game for the English Navy. English corsairs struck at Portuguese vessels, most memorably the *Madre de Deus*, an unusually large ship with a legendary cargo of riches. The English Navy boarded her in 1592 after a bloody, day-long battle near the Azores and took her to Dartmouth. Meanwhile, Sir Francis Drake was given *carte blanche* to make a nuisance of himself and assailed Spanish—and, by default, Portuguese—interests. In 1585 he attacked the Cape Verde islands off Africa, which were part of Portugal's empire, and in 1587 he ransacked points along the Portuguese coast. He entered Lisbon, overran the fort at Sagres in the Algarve and mapped the battlements before leaving. He also called in at Faro, accompanied by the Earl of Essex who carried away the famous private book collection of the city's bishop and donated its contents to the establishment of the Bodleian Library in Oxford. (Portugal has apparently never asked for restitution.)

87

FRANCISCVS DRAECK NOBILISSIMVS EQVES ANGLIÆ ANᵒ ÆT SVE43

Sir Francis Drake, a thorn in Portugal's side

In the seventeenth century the Portuguese once more needed help to fend off the overbearing Spanish and French and again they turned to England, which pledged to defend Portugal and its overseas possessions but in turn demanded favorable trading ties. The deal was sealed with another royal wedding, in 1662, this time between Charles II of England and Portugal's Princess Catherine of Bragança. As well as a generous amount of money her fabulous dowry—said to be one of the biggest on record—included the Portuguese possessions of Tangier and Bombay. She introduced tea and quince jelly, or marmalade, to England, while Piccadilly, in London, was once called Portugal Street in commemoration of their marriage. The name Queens, the largest of New York's five boroughs, is also said to have been inspired by her. Although she never produced an heir, Charles was deeply fond of her. Plans to erect a statue to her in Queens in 1998 ran into difficulty when protesters objected to her associations, as a Portuguese royal, with the slave trade. However, a bronze bust on the pavement outside the Military Academy in Lisbon shows a cherubic young woman with pigtails.

At the start of the eighteenth century, when France declared war on England, Paris tried to bully Portugal into closing its ports to English ships, denying England its valued naval havens. Portugal snubbed France and threw in its lot with England. The pair signed the Methuen Treaty of 1703, which granted favorable terms to Portuguese wine exports to England, marking the start of a lucrative port wine trade established by British men such as Cockburn, Warre, Taylor, and Croft, and removed restrictions on the importation of English goods, especially textiles. England profited handsomely from those commercial privileges as exports to Portugal soared by more than 100 percent, far outstripping the growth in Portuguese exports the other way. Only Brazilian gold enabled Portugal to withstand the trade imbalance.

The British historian V. G. Kiernan has noted that despite the closeness of the two countries England exerted no liberalizing influence in Portugal. Indeed, it was in England's interest not to, as it viewed Portugal as backward and preferred it that way. The Portuguese monarchy was despotic and concerned above all with adding to its own considerable wealth, not with spreading it among the peasantry. Forfeiting commercial advantages as the price of military protection, the Portuguese

Crown granted concessions to England which, as Kiernan observes, more discerning rulers would probably never have contemplated. For many years English merchants and financiers made a fine living out of Portugal.

That is part of the reason why Britain went to such lengths, a century later, to take a central role in what proved to be a watershed in Portuguese history: the Portuguese were able to check three overland invasions by Napoleon's armies, in 1807, 1809, and 1810, only with British help. Even so, Portugal was occupied by French forces for a brief time during the Peninsular War.

British troops under Sir Arthur Wellesley, the future Duke of Wellington, landed in Portugal in 1809. One of Wellesley's master-strokes was to order the building—in secret—of a string of 152 fortifications north of Lisbon, spanning from the Atlantic to the Tagus, which enters the capital from the northeast. Unlike the similarly-intended Maginot Line in France the following century, the structure kept the enemy at bay. The ridge-top forts, trenches, and earthworks took almost a year to build and were known as the Lines of Torres Vedras, after a local town. The mutually-supporting defenses blocked valleys and were defended by crossfire from artillery and thousands of troops. The fortifications unnerved the French, who turned back without attacking. It was a feat of engineering that provided a milestone in the Napoleonic wars: its success announced the beginning of Napoleon's eventual end at Waterloo. The defenses have not, on the whole, been properly preserved (Wellington's headquarters is partially occupied by an infant school) but can still be identified on the landscape.

The British commander William Beresford was given the task of forging the Portuguese forces, whose successful guerrilla warfare had weakened the French invaders, into efficient, disciplined army units. He was soon frustrated, quickly grasping that the Portuguese were not inclined to follow. Guerrilla warfare suits them better; their instinct is for small, individual acts of rebellion rather than marching in step. John Stanhope, who wrote a chronicle of the time, underlined the impossible nature of Beresford's task, recounting that the Portuguese army... was conspicuous for a lack of discipline which in these days would hardly be credited. To say that it was the worst in Europe would hardly give any idea of its degradation. The Portuguese soldiers were a weak, worthless rabble, without pluck or organisation, and practically useless for the campaign. Nor was the Government of the country in a much better state; a long series of misgovernment had introduced every species of corruption and deteriorated the character of the people.

After the flight of the Portuguese royal family and virtually the entire ruling class to Brazil (under Royal Navy escort) to avoid capture by the French, Beresford governed Portugal for several years as a viceroy. The British rid Portugal of the French invader, but Portugal at the time amounted to little more than a *de facto* colony of Britain.

Relations soured, however, first over the slave trade, which kept Portugal's Brazilian plantations and mines profitable but flew in the face of the burgeoning British abolitionist movement. Under pressure from London, the Portuguese and British signed a compromise in 1815, which prohibited Portugal from trafficking slaves in the northern hemisphere. Two decades later British patience with unconcealed Portuguese slaving ran out. The British Parliament passed a bill outlawing slavery and unilaterally granting the Royal Navy powers to board and inspect Portuguese ships. The move unleashed expressions of indignation in Portugal, but although the slave traders were put under pressure they typically crafted a devious strategy to outwit the British. It is said that the Portuguese would load the lead ship in a slaving fleet with innocuous cargo so the Royal Navy would inspect it and wave the convoy on, but the following ships would be filled with slaves. This stratagem possibly constitutes the provenance of a Portuguese phrase still in common usage: *para inglês ver* (literally, "for an Englishman to see"). The saying is employed for anything that tries to look different from, or better than, what it actually is.

An even more vexing episode, for the Portuguese at least, came at the end of the nineteenth century in what the essayist Eduardo Lourenço called "one of the most keenly felt humiliations of our history." British and Portuguese interests clashed in Europe's Scramble for Africa. The Portuguese had long talked about settling in the lands between Mozambique on the east coast and Angola on the west, sending expeditions to explore this area. The grand plan was known in Portugal as the "Pink Map," showing—in pink—a proposed band of coast-to-coast Portuguese-occupied territory across what became Zambia and Zimbabwe. That scheme, however, collided with the grandiose British strategy of linking its territories from the Cape to Cairo. Britain duly ordered Portugal to drop its expansion plans in what became known as The Ultimatum. Such bullying by its oldest ally caused uproar in Portugal and remains a sore point. The website of the British Embassy in Lisbon diplomatically omits reference to it in the history section.

Insurrections by natives in Mozambique using British-made weapons further fueled resentment. Portugal's national anthem is adapted from a popular song from that time that assailed the British. The song was reworded in 1957, with the original line "Against the Britons, march on, march on," for example, being altered to the current "Against the cannon, march on, march on." Marcello Caetano, who was a university professor and historian before he replaced Salazar at the tail end of the dictatorship, took a philosophical view, lucidly remarking that "no matter how close and old alliances are, there's no pact of friendship that can make powerful nations give up their interests or moderate their covetousness for a small nation if the latter doesn't first have the awareness, the intelligence and the enthusiasm for its own affairs."

Disabused of any notion that a long friendship might outweigh Britain's self-interest, the Portuguese realized halfway through the First World War that they ought to ignore the Foreign Office's request for them to remain neutral. The Portuguese government recognized that the outcome of the conflict would dictate the post-war architecture of power on at least two continents. It sensed, too, that to have any hope of holding onto its African territories it would need a seat at the post-war negotiating table. And to achieve that, it would need to be a combatant. Portugal provoked Germany into declaring war in 1916 by seizing German and Austrian vessels it had impounded, at Britain's request, in the Lisbon harbor. Portugal then deployed two infantry divisions, amounting to 55,000 poorly-equipped men, to the Western Front trenches in 1917. British commanders, just like Beresford a century earlier, were reportedly exasperated by the Portuguese soldiers' lack of organization and discipline. Historians calculate that roughly 2,000 Portuguese soldiers were killed in the war—about 300 of them when they were routed at the little-remembered Battle of Lys in 1918. The last instance of a Portuguese being executed for treason was recorded there. Reluctant to shed blood if it can be avoided, the Portuguese were among the first in the world to abolish the death penalty, in 1867, for all but military crimes.

In the Second World War neutral Portugal played a canny double game. Salazar—in a landmark demonstration of guile—engineered a foreign policy that kept his country close to Britain and simultaneously avoided causing offense to the Axis powers. Hitler wanted Portugal's tungsten, used to make steel alloy, and Churchill wanted use of the mid-Atlantic Azores islands to help win the Battle of the Atlantic. When the Allies started looking likely to win the war, and Britain increased the diplomatic pressure, Portugal accepted London's request in 1943 to use the Azores' ports—a move that risked a Nazi invasion. At the same time Lisbon kept its options open by resisting until the following year Allied pressure to stop selling tungsten to Germany. Lisbon was paid for that trade, at least in part, in Nazi gold believed to have been looted from Holocaust victims. Portugal returned almost four tons of it in 1953 through the Allied Tripartite Commission.

The Azores continued to give Portugal an unanticipated edge in international affairs during the Cold War. Despite being an unfashionable right-wing dictatorship and an unrepentant colonial ruler, on a par with pariahs like Rhodesia and South Africa, the geostrategic importance of the Azores as an ocean naval base led Britain and the United States to invite Portugal into the international community. It was a diplomatic *quid pro quo*: use of the Azores in return for an invitation to the top table. The deal gave Portugal entry into NATO.

The Azores agreement, as well as Salazar's visceral opposition to communism, was of such value that the dictatorship even merited a state visit by Queen Elizabeth II and the Duke of Edinburgh in 1957. By all accounts, the visit was a resounding success. *Life* magazine ran a big photo spread of the reunion in Lisbon between the young queen and her husband who had been away on national service. The duke, apparently swept up by the buoyant atmosphere in the streets packed with flag-waving Portuguese, at one point shunned a Rolls Royce that was the official car and climbed aboard a fire engine instead. According to a Portuguese newspaper, Buckingham Palace made it known to Lisbon through diplomatic channels that Her Majesty had a particular weakness for "your Portuguese tinned sardines."

Despite the occasionally tense moments within their overlapping narratives the Portuguese entertain a fondness for the British, though they reserve their real affection for the Irish, whose ability to prevail against the odds strikes a chord with them. The Portuguese admire British pragmatism, organization, and efficiency, their tautness and world prominence—in short, all the attributes they feel they lack themselves. It is an example of opposites attracting. The United Kingdom is Portugal's biggest source of vacationers. It sends over more than two million people a year, mostly to the Algarve.

The Portuguese refer to Brits as *bifes*, a reference to beef, that traditional British staple, and similar to the French nickname, *les rosbifs*. It is a term of endearment but I suspect it is also contains a bit of a gibe (like the irony of *nuestros hermanos*). Just as the British chafe at perceived Portuguese laxity, so the Portuguese wrinkle their noses at British rigidity. On a visit to England my youngest daughter, who is Portuguese by birth, became thoroughly fed up with the well-oiled organization, the clarity, and the order. "I feel like grabbing it all in my hands and scrunching it up and making a mess," she said.

Chapter Five
A Broken Homeland
Portugal's Long Decline and Fall

One Saturday evening in the spring of 1871 the illustrious poet and polemicist Antero de Quental stood up to address a public meeting in a tall-windowed, first-floor room in Lisbon's bohemian Chiado district. He proceeded to deliver a brilliant address that would go down as one of the most famous speeches in Portuguese history. He and other intellectuals had organized the conference to debate the miserable depths to which their country, in their view, had sunk. Four centuries earlier Portugal had reconfigured the world. Now it was a decidedly second-rank nation that was watching the world go by. Portugal had fallen far and hard, and Quental gave an unflinching diagnosis of how it had happened. He identified the wrong turns and bad choices that set the country on the path to demoralizing decline. In so doing he dissected the Portuguese anatomy, and it is almost eerie how some of the threads he picked out a century-and-a-half ago are still discernible.

The thrust of Quental's critique was that three key factors were ✓ behind his country's decline: firstly, the religious conservatism installed by the Counter-Reformation of the sixteenth and seventeenth centuries, which suffocated inventive thought in Catholic countries like Portugal; secondly, the political centralization imposed by recurring periods of absolute rule, which encouraged submissiveness and resignation; and, thirdly, the economic system spawned by the Age of Discovery whose intoxicating bounty disinclined the Portuguese towards prudent financial management and honest toil. These historical features are intrinsic to the structure of Portuguese society.

After the Council of Trent between 1545 and 1563, Quental recalled, the Catholic Church became intolerant and uncompromising. It fettered the Portuguese, as it did others, and shut them off from intellectual advances in Protestant Europe. With the arrival of the Inquisition, established in Lisbon in 1536, the Church in Portugal, which had hitherto shown tolerance towards Muslims and Jews, hardened into a dogmatic and unyielding institution. The Inquisition quickly exerted its

The bare bones of Carmo Convent, reminder of the 1755 earthquake

grip, and such was its pressure that the Portuguese ended up policing themselves. An off-the-cuff curse could lead to a careless individual being reported. Faced with the circling violence and censorship of the Inquisition, Quental said, "hypocrisy became a national and necessary vice." He labeled the Inquisition "the nation's grave" because of its hostility to critical reason, expressed so sincerely in its *Index Librorum Prohibitorum* (List of Forbidden Books). The Inquisition was where new ideas went to die. That kind of religious education, Quental went on, "sterilized intelligence." Where were the Portuguese equivalents of Newton, Descartes, or Leibniz?

Damião de Góis could have answered that question. Góis was a gifted Portuguese historian, composer, and thinker, a recognized figure of the European Renaissance who sat down with Erasmus and Luther to exchange ideas and was painted by Dürer. Despite being protected by his patron King João III he never managed to shake off the dogged Inquisition, and it caught up with him in his later years. He was tried for heresy after Jesuits accused him of, among other things, describing some past popes as tyrants. He escaped being burned at the stake but was imprisoned for life, at the age of seventy, in the Batalha Monastery. He died two years later, in 1574, in mysterious circumstances. He was found prostrate, part of his body lying in a fireplace, and was judged to have collapsed. When his remains were exhumed in 1941, however, his skull was found to have a large hole, which was unlikely to be explained by a fall.

Portugal largely missed the Enlightenment. By standing defiantly in the way of modern science, Quental said, the Church fathered "obedient imbeciles." Absolutism also engaged his ire. In the Middle Ages, he noted, representative assemblies, called *cortes*, had ensured that all social classes had a say in their lives in what amounted to "a triumph of local interests and energy over crushing and artificial uniformity." An absolute monarchy, on the other hand, shuts people off from their own destiny. Such a political system, Quental remarked, makes people expect that what they need will be handed down to them. By disqualifying people from taking any responsibility for their own fate, it leads to inertia and discourages initiative. Thus indifference set in while other European countries forged ahead. "The modern soul died inside us," Quental said.

Quental also took aim at the sacred Golden Age of Empire. "They sent us to sleep with these stories. To attack them is almost sacrilegious," he acknowledged. But he insisted that the almost two centuries of warring plunder that drove the Age of Discovery and brought comfort and plenty also had a nefarious side-effect in that the experience encouraged idleness and imprudence. Quental approvingly quoted Adam Smith's view that capital gained through war should be wisely invested to develop trade in a nation's own production. But in Portugal manual labour was not highly prized. Nothing was manufactured nor produced—just gold from Brazil, Quental said. That gold was used to pay for the work of others—that is, foreign manufacturers. The rot set in, and then came the dog days of the nineteenth century.

After shooting to world prominence, the aggregate effect of the factors Quental listed was that heroism was snuffed out, passion abated, and a dispirited and passive acceptance took their place. Portugal slumbered through the innovations of the nineteenth century. Quental judged that after three hundred years of decline his country during his lifetime offered a "painful contrast" with its former greatness. He concluded:

> From the monarch of bygone days to the "people of influence" of today, there's not such a big difference. For the people, it's the same servitude. We were ordered, now we're governed... From the warring spirit of the conquering nation, we have inherited an unbeatable aversion to work and an intimate contempt of industry... We are a decadent people because we snubbed the modern spirit.

As Mark Twain said, history rhymes, and these historical milestones and Quental's observations on them resonate to the present day. Talk of the Inquisition brings to mind Salazar's secret police and his censor's blue pencil; the detrimental effects of absolutism evoke the modern Portuguese relationship with the overbearing state and the concentration of power in Lisbon; and the failure to apply fruitfully the staggering proceeds from the maritime discoveries hints at later disappointment with the superficial legacy of exceedingly generous European Union development funds.

Quental enumerated what he saw as the main factors in Portugal's degeneration, but there were other turns of events he did not mention—some due to misfortune, others of their own making—that knocked the Portuguese off their stride.

Quental referred in passing to the expulsion of Jews from Portugal in the late fifteenth century as "virtually a national calamity." It was a short-sighted move that put another obstacle in the way of Portugal's progress, depriving it of an important pool of talent, including cartographers and other educated citizens. Jews from the diaspora had lived in Portugal for centuries, despite a degree of discrimination, and there was a huge new influx when Spain expelled them in 1492. King João II allowed them to stay, for a price. His successor Manuel I used the Jews to advance his political ambitions. He saw a chance of ruling the whole Iberian Peninsula by marrying Spain's Princess Isabella. Her parents Ferdinand and Isabella, the fervent "Catholic monarchs" as the pope termed them, would bless the marriage only if Manuel followed their lead and deported the Jews. Manuel, loath to cast out a community that could serve his plans for maritime expansion, dreamed up a clever compromise: the Jews would be allowed to stay if they converted to Christianity by being baptized. Some did, not always willingly, and the so-called "New Christians" adopted new names, inter-married and even ate pork in public to prove their devotion to Catholicism. In fact, they took their religion underground. They secretly observed the Sabbath at home then went to Mass on Sunday. They circumcised their sons and surreptitiously observed Yom Kippur, calling it in Portuguese the *dia puro*, or pure day. ✓

Such painful compromises did not always help, however. Antisemitism and persecution continued. The Inquisition tortured Jews and burned them at the stake in gruesome public spectacles known as *autos-da-fé* (acts of faith, in Portuguese). In the 143 years up to 1684, historian José Hermano Saraiva calculates, 1,379 people met their deaths ✓ in this way.

The New Christians were popularly nicknamed *marranos*, contemporary slang for pigs. Such discrimination made possible the infamous Easter Massacre of 1506. Portugal was at the time in crisis, reeling from years of plague and drought, and hungry for some good news. During an Easter Mass at Lisbon's São Domingos church someone suddenly shouted out that they beheld the face of Christ on an altar. The worshippers gasped. But then another voice was heard saying, "No, it's not, it's the reflection of the sun." The impertinent doubter was swiftly identified as a New Christian who was dragged outside and beaten to death. The commotion lit a powder trail and for three days New Christians throughout the city were hunted down, murdered, raped, and burned to death. The houses of up to 4,000 New Christians in Lisbon were ransacked by mobs.

Some Jews fled to the hills. One group established a community that still exists today in Belmonte, a small town in a mountainous region in the north, close to the Spanish border and probably as far from the Inquisition as they could comfortably get. Jews had settled there long before, as attested by the foundation stone of a local synagogue dating from 1297. Complying with the royal decree that they must convert, they took Christian names and attended Mass. But they were just covering their tracks. In their homes they performed private Jewish ceremonies. A deeply-embedded tradition of secrecy—a matter of survival—settled over Belmonte's Jews and persists to this day as they frown on curious visitors. They are now more open and relaxed than during those bloody medieval times, however. A new Belmonte synagogue opened in 1997, and in 2005 a Jewish museum was opened by the minister for parliamentary affairs.

The Portuguese have since sought atonement for the sixteenth-century horrors. In 1988 then-President Mário Soares apologized to Jews for centuries of persecution by the Inquisition. In 1996 his successor Jorge Sampaio admitted that the expulsion of the Jews was an "iniquitous act with deep and disastrous consequences." And in 2008 a plaque was unveiled outside the São Domingos church where the Easter Massacre began, stating that "the Catholic Church recognizes the deep stain those gestures and words left on its memory."

It is certain that stigmatizing Jews made little sense in Portugal, where their blood had for generations mingled with that of other people. Even today, a genetic study published in 2008 found that on average 36 percent of people in southern Portugal, for example, have Jewish ancestry. It is said that in the eighteenth century King José I instructed his first minister, the Marquis of Pombal, to take measures to ensure the public identification of Jews. He proposed that Pombal have special caps made that Jews would have to wear at all times. The next day Pombal, who did not like the idea, turned up with the first three caps. "One," he said to the king, "is for Your Majesty. One is for me, and the other one is for the Chief Inquisitor."

Before the sixteenth century was over there was another national catastrophe. Portugal's heirless King Sebastião and its military elite were slaughtered in an overseas campaign against Muslim forces. The result was that jubilant Spaniards claimed the throne by royal lineage and grasped the reins of power for the following six decades. It was a rude blow, one that twentieth-century writer Francisco da Cunha Leal considered "the worst in our history."

King Sebastião was 24 when he gamely elected to spread Christianity by the sword in North Africa. Despite having little to gain and much to lose, and defying the advice of his own war veterans, he made a foolhardy inland incursion with all the forces he could muster— about 15,000 troops. Weighed down by armor and heavy weapons in an African August, the monarch led his men in 1578 to Ksar el-Kebir in

The Battle of the Three Kings at Ksar el-Kebir

Morocco for a fight against a much bigger local army. The site of the battle lies just off the Marrakesh-Tangier highway, and anyone who has been there in the mid-summer heat will have an idea of the physical challenge of a medieval fight in such conditions. The Battle of the Three Kings, as it became known, was an unmitigated, traumatic disaster for the Portuguese. Quental drily remarked that the Portuguese nation was buried with its defeated king.

The monarch vanished. Nobles who fought in the battle with him said that they had not witnessed his death, giving rise to a collective superstition back home that he had miraculously escaped and would one day come home, emerging as if by magic out of a mist. This legend became known as "Sebastianism," and what a heavy noun that is, loaded with cultural baggage. Conveying the Portuguese longing for a savior to appear and rescue them from all their troubles, it is an abiding myth and one that is telling because it depicts a collective frame of mind—that something good will happen without any effort and without any responsibility for having to make it happen. In any case, as the historian José Hermano Saraiva points out, the mystery about what happened to the monarch probably has a prosaic explanation: it would have been a great dishonor for the surviving nobles to admit they had seen him killed because it would have begged the question: why had they not given their own lives to prevent it?

Spain's King Felipe I took the Portuguese throne in 1581. The new masters in faraway Castile essentially left Portugal to its own devices, allowing it to keep its administrative autonomy, and the local nobles to keep the privileges to which they had become accustomed. But taxation, as a form of tribute, became punitive and many left the country. Quental noted that in the fifteenth century Portugal's population was close to three million, but by 1640, the end of Spanish rule, it had collapsed to just over one million.

Under the Spanish Felipe II and Felipe III in the early seventeenth century, Portugal's decline picked up speed. The Iberian union placed it in the sights of Spain's enemies. The English, the French, and the Dutch—bent on winning an advantage over each other by adding Portuguese assets to their wealth—increased the pressure on Portuguese seafarers and encroached on Portugal's overseas possessions. The Dutch invaded Salvador, Brazil's first capital, in 1624 and occupied it for a year, then snatched the sugar-rich area of Recife and held it between 1630 and 1654. Portugal thus fell foul of bigger countries' power games. When the Portuguese were not being bullied by their own leaders they were being intimidated by larger rival countries. Ultimately, Portugal was too small to hold on to an intercontinental empire. Quental admitted that the early seventeenth century heralded its new status as an "insignificant and powerless" nation.

Earthquake and Invasion

A deadly natural disaster on All Saints' Day in 1755 added fresh momentum to the erosion of Portugal's rank. The Lisbon earthquake was the greatest calamity ever to befall the country and one of the strongest quakes ever to strike Western Europe. It reduced much of the elegant city—and one of the continent's biggest, with some 250,000 inhabitants—to a pile of debris. The papal nuncio, in a letter to Rome, commented gloomily: "The scale of the damage is so great that Lisbon won't become again what it was for a hundred years." A tsunami, which hours later also washed up more weakly on the shores of the Caribbean, and a six-day fire that engulfed the city finished what the quake had left undone. The death toll is believed to have been at least 10,000, with many more injured. A British merchant living in Lisbon at the time recounted, in an unsigned letter published in 1985 by the British Historical Society of Portugal, "a scene of utmost horror and desolation." Making his way down narrow, rubble-strewn streets he reported: "I could hardly take a step without treading on the dead or dying... This extensive and opulent city is now nothing but a vast heap of ruins."

The Lisbon earthquake, like the American and French revolutions of the same century, was a pivotal event that helped reshape European thought and the way people of the time perceived the world. The disaster was a rich subject for debate because it threw up important questions about the nature of God and faith at a time when scientific discoveries and reasoning were increasingly challenging religious assumptions. The Rev. John Wesley, one of the eighteenth-century founders of Methodism, detected God's hand. A member of the British parliament urged a return to the teachings of Moses to prevent a similar punishment befalling London. Voltaire, though, dismissed talk of retribution. "What crime, what sin did these children commit/On the mangled and bloody maternal breast?" he wrote in a poem. In his tale *Candide*, which features fictionalized accounts of the Lisbon earthquake, Voltaire mocked Leibniz's philosophy of optimism, that this is "the best of all possible worlds" under a benign God.

As the earth split it also gave rise to a great leader, of sorts. The king granted his first minister Sebastião José de Carvalho e Melo, better known as the Marquis of Pombal, who had previously been ambassador in London and Vienna, overriding powers to clean up the mess. An implacable and occasionally callous man unencumbered by the checks and balances of a democratic society, Pombal was one of those rare people who could knock his countrymen into shape. Like other notable Portuguese leaders, he had to possess a good measure of ruthlessness—and absolute power—to get things done. At more than six feet tall he literally looked down on his compatriots, and was also fifteen years older than his king. "I know their interests better than they do," he said, employing a tone and a turn of phrase that would sit well with António Salazar almost two centuries later. Though clever and decisive, Pombal also was tyrannical. He tightened censorship (banning Voltaire's works, for example) and threw political opponents in jail. He tarnished his reputation with bloody reprisals against nobles and Jesuits who had opposed him. He put down a street protest in Porto by having the demonstrators' heads chopped off and put on public display.

In what is widely regarded as the first example of modern disaster management because it amounted to a centralized state response, Pombal deployed army units to crack down mercilessly on widespread looting after the earthquake. He requisitioned judges from outlying towns and introduced summary verbal trials and public executions at hastily erected gallows. Soldiers oversaw emergency food distribution and swift burials to prevent disease. Modern relief experts express admiration for Pombal's response (his ruthlessness notwithstanding).

A bust of the Marquis of Pombal

The extent of the damage and the necessary reconstruction was intimidating. Three months after the quake the nuncio reported that rebuilding was "extraordinarily slow" (anyone employing modern builders might think how little has changed). He said the royal family spent the winter in tents in freezing mud. They were still there three months later while wooden shelters were being put up on their palace grounds.

Pombal, in the end, accomplished quite a feat. Once the rebuilding plan was approved in May 1758, the city became the recipient of Europe's first quake-proof construction. Pombal, who was in many respects un-Portuguese, adopted a gridiron pattern for the downtown streets, lending it a prim uniformity that cannot be found anywhere else in the country. Today, the roofless ruins of the fourteenth-century Carmo Convent that rise out of downtown Lisbon's skyline are the only evidence of the damage caused by the quake. Pombal, who after the disaster became one of the city's biggest private property developers and lived to the age of 83, was honored by a statue on a very high pedestal in the middle of modern Lisbon's biggest traffic circle.

The earthquake's consequences rumbled far beyond the Saturday morning when it struck. It hobbled Portugal, which for years forfeited any chance of keeping up with its European rivals. While the British statesman Edmund Burke could remark in 1777 that "the great map of mankind is unrolled at once" amid swift global expansion, Portugal was reduced to a crawl. And Pombal's enlightened and promising reforms in areas such as education, agriculture, and Church influence were revoked when he fell out of favor following his king's death.

Fifty years later another episode of great moment came with the advance of Napoleon's armies across the border. After the three French military invasions between 1807 and 1810 Portugal lurched in a markedly different direction from its previous 400 years. The brutal conflict, in which the peninsula acted as a proxy battlefield for a broader French-British conflict and became a grand theater of war, rent large holes in Portugal's economic and social fabric. They were years of social upheaval, political instability, and economic crisis. The Peninsular War, which contributed to a sea change in Europe's balance of power, left in its wake ruin, starvation, and poverty, led to the independence of Brazil and pushed Portugal close to collapse.

The French occupiers' boots trampled over local sentiment. They confiscated food from virtually destitute families, commandeered whatever else they wanted, stole art and other valuables, and levied punitive taxes. In the rural town of Abrantes, French officers ordered locals to make them 12,000 pairs of shoes. The oppressed inhabitants, many of them barefoot, worked around the clock to comply. Not surprisingly, many country folk fled to the cities to escape the violence and hunger. At the Entrecampos traffic circle in Lisbon a statue called Monument to the People and Heroes of the Peninsular War, inaugurated in the early twentieth century on the centenary of the departure of the French invaders, offers a dramatic depiction of a people caught up in brutality. In Porto a 45-meter-high column features a lion (denoting the Portuguese) sitting on an eagle (Napoleon).

The French were no more successful than others in controlling the Portuguese, who initially must have appeared vulnerable prey. Stoked by resentment and dispossession, spontaneous revolts erupted across the country and gradually wore down the French for whom the fight was seemingly unwinnable. The Portuguese reaction was characteristically piecemeal, quixotic, spontaneous, and individualistic.

With the French bearing down on the capital in 1807, the royal family decided to escape, hatching a plan to take refuge in Brazil and acting on it swiftly. Historical accounts relate that they emptied their great palaces at Mafra and Queluz in three days. The royal wealth was packed into hundreds of boxes that were carted to the Lisbon docks. Some 60,000 books from the library of the Ajuda palace in Lisbon went, too, as did about half the coins in circulation. João, the prince regent who reigned due to the incapacity of his mad mother Queen Maria I, and his entourage sailed away the day before General Jean-Andoche Junot marched into Lisbon. It was not just the court that fled, moreover. Anybody who was anybody went with them, packing into a fleet of ships assembled in the River Tagus for a transatlantic voyage under a British escort commanded by Sir William Sidney Smith.

The essayist Eduardo Lourenço likened the Brazil-bound fleet to a Noah's Ark that took the Old World to the New. It was a wretched months-long trip, by all accounts. The Portuguese ships were old and there were not enough sleeping quarters to go around. An outbreak of lice forced powdered wigs to be thrown overboard, and women had to shave their heads. Rough November seas caused general seasickness among the landlubbers, and the inclement weather kept them cold and wet. In all, more than 10,000 people—essentially the country's ruling elite plus soldiers—clambered aboard the ships and deserted their tormented homeland in the space of hours. It is said that the Portuguese royal family were the first European monarchs to visit, however unintentionally, a colony. The nineteenth-century historian Oliveira Martins found it degrading, an "embarrassing episode" whose consequences he compared to a second Lisbon earthquake. It orphaned the Portuguese and would soon draw a line under the South American part of their empire. In the aftermath, the British stepped into the vacuum and governed the country that could not govern itself.

After three months at sea, the royal party landed in Brazil and established the new capital of the Portuguese kingdom in Rio de Janeiro. Back in Europe, the French eventually went home but the chaos that had stopped Portugal in its tracks was to continue. With the royal family thousands of miles away across the Atlantic, liberal groups opposing the monarchy blossomed. They demanded freedom for people to control their own destinies, unyoked from a hereditary paramount ruler. In 1820 a liberal-inspired military insurrection in Porto brought the installation of a ruling junta. Portugal's British allies were alarmed and sent William Beresford on a ship to Brazil to persuade João VI (who had become king after his mother died in 1816) to come home. The king concurred and sailed to Lisbon in 1821, leaving his son Pedro in charge of Brazil. At the time, independence struggles in Brazil's neighboring Spanish colonies were spreading and Pedro bowed to the new mood. He unilaterally proclaimed Brazil independent in 1822 and became its first emperor.

Portugal's 1822 Constitution, consented to by the king and liberals alike, gave the country a constitutional monarchy. Hard-core royalists, however, were reluctant to give up their absolutist dream and a string of armed rebellions kept unrest in the air. João VI's death in 1826 brought a dispute over succession between his sons Pedro, who was ruling Brazil, and Miguel, who was living in exile at the Austrian court. Miguel returned and seized the throne, generously granting himself absolute power. But then a civil war between Miguel and Pedro, known as the War of the Two Brothers, raged from 1831 to 1834. This conflict just about bankrupted the already debilitated country. Amid the pernicious in-fighting, the writer Almeida Garrett issued an ardent appeal—from London—for a sober reappraisal of where his country was heading. Portugal, after decades of strife, stood bereft. "May it please God that, with one pitch, with one common agreement and a united effort, all Portuguese may set aside their differences, forget their hatred, forgive insult and injury, gird ourselves and get to work on the difficult but not impossible task of saving, of rebuilding, our forsaken and broken homeland—to restore it to its proper weight on the European scales," Garrett wrote. His plea fell on deaf ears.

Left Behind

The turmoil died out only in the mid-1800s. After that inauspicious start to the nineteenth century Portugal was doomed to lag behind in Europe's Industrial Revolution. It faced severe handicaps: an illiterate and backward rural population; a weak middle class; a shortage of capital; little technological know-how; and few raw materials, especially coal. By 1870 there were only about 200 steam engines in the country, though the 1870s were that century's best decade. Portuguese industry was too weak to compete with foreign imports. British merchants and manufactured goods became dominant. Britain had preferential trade ties with Portugal and it also had the mechanical production and cheap labor that could provide large volumes at low prices. Portugal's trade balance was unsustainable. So was the government's spending, which rose vertiginously as it spent on public works to prevent the economy from seizing up. Foreign loans, which kept the country from sinking, dried up. The Portuguese financial system, both public and private, collapsed in the 1891 crisis. And while Europe spurted ahead, stagnation and economic depression took root in Portugal.

Foreign visitors also laid some of the blame for Portugal's despondent state at the door of the man-in-the-street. Princess Maria Rattazzi, a cousin of Napoleon III and an irreverent, opinionated woman, visited the country and published a book of her cultural observations in 1880. "The people's nature can be understood and summed up with two expressions they commonly use," the French princess explained to her readers. "You make a remark about misery, vexations, abuses. Same response every time: Don't worry about it! You say a decision needs to be taken, something needs to be done, you have to stand up for your rights. Irreplaceable answer: Tomorrow." Her book caused a stir among Lisbon's social and cultural elite, who hated it. The prominent writer Camilo Castelo Branco even took time to pen a formal, pointed rebuttal in which he described her notions as "superficial." While generalizations like those voiced by the princess are inevitably unfair, even the most patriotic Portuguese would probably concede, with good grace, that there were nuggets of truth in her comments.

The Portuguese are more critical of themselves than foreigners are. They mock themselves well. Eça de Queirós, one of the most perceptive Portuguese—and European—writers of the nineteenth century, saved some of his most barbed criticism for his own country. He spent many years abroad as a diplomat and a journalist, living in Egypt, Newcastle, Bristol, and Paris and also travelling through the United States. The distance he went from Portugal afforded him a lucid and detached view of his homeland and plenty to compare it with. Queirós introduced realism to Portuguese literature and is bracketed with Zola, Dickens, and Flaubert. Such is his stature that he has his own literary adjective—*queirosiano* ("queirosian"). Eduardo Lourenço, the critic and essayist, said that Queirós' novels represented the "cruelest" portrait ever drawn of Portugal. While it can be hard for a foreign reader to appreciate the weight of the satire and irony in his pointed criticism, which requires a familiarity with Portuguese mores, some of it is blunt enough. In his novel *The Maias*, about the eponymous family, Lisbon people are described as *beata, suja, e feroz* ("devout, dirty, and vicious").

Queirós, some of whose observations still hold true, ridiculed his country as decadent and far behind civilized Europe, crippled by old-fashioned customs, an outdated economy, corrupt and lazy politicians, an exaggerated emphasis on Lisbon, and a passive and blinkered bourgeoisie who simply aped France and Britain. His bleak view chimed with that of his roughly contemporaneous King Carlos I, in whose royal view Portugal was "a dump." However, while the character of Jacinto in the Queirós novel *The City and the Mountains* sniffily dismisses Portugal as a backwater, he in the end is won over by its simple charms—as so many foreigners have been.

Portugal dug itself deep into foreign debt. When the Scramble for Africa began late in the nineteenth century, Britain and Germany were sorely tempted to call in Portugal's loans and divide Angola and Mozambique between them. The British Ultimatum of 1890, when London told the Portuguese to get out of its way in Africa, was a distillation of their predicament. It brought home the fact that, having failed to grasp the opportunities afforded by the Industrial Revolution, having forfeited the fabulous wealth of its Brazilian colony and the hugely profitable slave trade, and now humiliated by its most valued ally,

A EÇA DE
QVEIROZ

1845 - 1900

Portugal at the end of the nineteenth century was perhaps more vulnerable than ever before.

Another storm broke over Portuguese heads with the assassination of King Carlos I in a Lisbon street in February 1908. That act led to the establishment of Portugal's first republican government, which took office in 1911. Left to their own devices, politicians became locked in fruitless squabbling, splintered into various interest groups and paralyzed the country, delivering 45 governments in 16 years. The First World War's shortages compounded the problems. In 1917, in order to save flour, a ban was introduced on the baking of cakes. The economic nosedive took Portugal into hyper-inflation and forced a moratorium on the servicing of external debt. In 1919 a pound sterling cost 7.5 escudos; by 1924, it cost more than 127 escudos. Portugal started to unravel. There were assassinations, murders, kidnappings, strikes and violent street demonstrations. Finally the army had seen enough and in 1926 a coup—the first of two in the twentieth century—removed power from the hands of elected leaders and handed it to a military dictatorship. The crippling unrest turned out to be a drum roll for four decades of rule by António Salazar.

Chapter Six
A Dictator's Walled Garden
The Salazar Years

In the early 1960s the Coca-Cola company tried to prise open the closed Portuguese market. The head of its Europe division pestered António Salazar, by then in his seventies, to let the company set up a factory in Portugal. After some to-ing and fro-ing the uncompromising dictator, in power by then for three decades, drew the discussion to a close by sending the executive a letter of pointed refusal. With defiant candor it set out in black and white what his regime was all about. "Portugal is conservative, paternalist and, bless God, 'backward'—a term I consider flattering, not pejorative," Salazar wrote:

> You are attempting to bring into Portugal something which I detest above all—that is, modernism and your famed efficiency. I shudder to think of your lorries going flat-out down the streets of our old cities and, as they pass through, quickening the rhythm of our centuries-old customs.

As a succinct summary of Salazar's thinking, this letter is hard to beat. He insisted that Portugal look backward, not forward, and that it remain uncontaminated by progress. It was an apparently quixotic goal but one the obliging Portuguese went along with. Their atavistic inclination to apathy and resignation provided him with a malleable clay to work with. He gave a wide berth to what he judged to be harmful distractions, such as Coca-Cola—and parliamentary democracy.

The letter was posted in 1962, the year that the world's first commercial communications satellite was fired into orbit, a Nobel Prize went to the scientists who had discovered the structure of DNA, and the Beatles cut their first single. In repressed Portugal, meanwhile, people still had to request a government license to own a cigarette lighter, women needed their husbands' written permission to open a bank account, and censorship was so tight that newspapers could not even criticize soccer referees because it amounted to questioning authority.

António Salazar (bending, center) casts his eye over a new bridge

That is what Portugal was like barely two generations ago. The "garden by the sea" celebrated by the poet Camões became a walled enclosure where authoritarianism triumphed.

The 1960s were the end of what the Portuguese call *salazarismo*, which eventually crumbled midway through the following decade— four years after Salazar's death—after more than thirty years of autocracy. When it departed it left some significant questions hanging in the air. How had Portugal weathered Western Europe's longest dictatorship? How was Salazar able to resist the tide of democratic sentiment after the Second World War? How did Portugal defy the "winds of change" that blew through Africa and ended other countries' colonial rule? How did Salazar, the son of peasants, hold out against the transcontinental influences of 1960s liberalism? How did the dictatorship continue into the mid-1970s when Portugal, like Spain, was an astonishing European anachronism?

It is not hard to comprehend how the Portuguese initially fell under Salazar's spell. The chaotic early years of the twentieth century had nourished a craving for order. Democracy and its political manifestations were woefully unable to address the protracted crisis whose roots were so deep that superficial reform was no help. The early years of the Republic, with its long series of hapless and helpless governments, discredited politicians and the democratic process. The people had had enough of it, for the time being. A benign dictatorship seemed like a good idea, even to the poet Fernando Pessoa who imagined and advocated an "aristocratic republic." Two years before the 1933 Constitution created Salazar's New State, Admiral Luís Magalhães Correia, then head of the Navy, voiced a keenly-felt frustration about the Portuguese anarchic streak: "Portugal once and for all has to stop giving the world the impression that it is a great big madhouse," he said.

Salazar was a product of those turbulent times. Born in 1889 into a family of small landowners, he was a nationalist who took it upon himself to save the Portuguese from themselves and administered a dose of unpalatable medicine. Something of a cold fish, he was also a highly motivated individual who escaped his rustic background through academic toil. As an iron-fisted finance minister between 1928 and 1932 (he had previously been an economics lecturer at Coimbra University), he made the figures add up without so much as a sideways glance at the human sum. He raised taxes and slashed spending as the military dictatorship, established in 1926, stood guard, ready to snuff out inconvenient protests. "I know very well what I want and where I am going," Salazar said. Portugal had recorded a budget deficit in 68 of the 70 years before he pulled the ledgers onto his desk and ruthlessly set about balancing them. He also brought order—a valued commodity at a time when children were being kept home from school for fear of trouble in the streets. His success won him prestige and an invitation from the president to take the prime minister's chair in 1932, at the age of forty-three. Unburdened by self-doubt, Salazar put his plan into action.

The essayist Eduardo Lourenço remarks that Salazar was "the heavy price Portugal had to pay" to correct its course. The problem was, however, that he outstayed his welcome by decades and was so entrenched in power that he was hard to remove. Other western countries indulged Salazar, viewing him as a lesser evil in the Cold War struggle against communism.

Salazar's cool, distant demeanor lent him a sort of charisma. He was thin-lipped with sharp features that did not suggest much in the way of tenderness, and he never married, though some who got to know him at private functions, especially women, insist that he was quite charming. He had a somber, flinty public image, a forbidding blend of finger-wagging schoolteacher and finger-pointing priest. Watching black-and-white footage of his sometimes hectoring speeches it is disconcerting that his voice is surprisingly squeaky, not the self-assured, and reassuring, baritone one might expect. He made no attempt to construct a cult of personality. He shunned goose-stepping military parades and was averse to flag-waving crowds. In fact, he was a reserved, conscientious man who was uncomfortable with public eulogies and displays of affection. He perhaps most resembled a devoted and austere parent who is unable to trust his growing children, who knows better than they do what is best for them.

Salazar encouraged the popular view of his role as *salvador da pátria* ("savior of the homeland") which fed off Sebastianism, that Messianic disposition. The dictatorship's iconography appropriated the medieval heraldry of bygone heroes—swords and shields and coats of arms—to help establish a glorious image. Salazar's project for Portugal required him to distill a sense of patriotism and duty among the people. He flattered the Portuguese, insisting that their history was exceptional, and he put on the celebratory 1940 Exhibition of the Portuguese World to prove it. He championed a romantic myth of Portugal and made June 10, the anniversary of Camões' death, a national holiday, and magnified its appeal by making it a celebration of the prowess of what he unscientifically termed "the Portuguese race." Such blandishments helped win popular support. On the August 14 anniversary of the Battle of Aljubarrota in 1935 he ordered special commemorations and personally penned an essay that exalted Portugal and that had to be read out in all the schools in the land. Aljubarrota, Salazar wrote, should be a place of pilgrimage, especially for the country's youth, who there might "bring to life and fortify, in the crucible of a heroic past, their patriotic devotion."

The 1933 Constitution consolidated Salazar's grip on power. From then on, he would look after the Portuguese as their absolute ruler. The document was submitted to a popular vote, but like other expressions of democracy that took place under Salazar it was a sham. Official figures showed that more than 700,000 voted in favor and about 6,000 against. Close to half-a-million abstentions were blithely added to the "in favor" column. (Portugal had a population of about 6.8 million at the time, but voting privileges were largely limited to people who could be trusted to tick the correct box.) Salazar wanted to exorcize the country's past troubles and his adoption of the designation *Estado Novo* (New State) for his regime conveyed the idea of a fresh start.

Salazar's intentions were unambiguous and he was skilled in the dark arts of dictatorship. His National Union embraced power under a one-party system. He removed counterweights and moderating influences, even while pretending they existed. Elections were held for a National Assembly every four years and for a figurehead president every seven, but Salazar alone issued the fiats. He added the posts of foreign and defense minister to his portfolio and built a massive state apparatus that meddled in all areas of public and private life. Individual rights were submerged under the greater interests of the state. "Everything for the nation, nothing against the nation," he insisted.

The ruthless, menacing face of the regime was embodied in a sinister secret police force known initially by its acronym PVDE, which stood for Police for Vigilance and Defense of the State—an appropriately Orwellian body. Its job was to keep an eye out for, and swiftly crush, any subversive activities. Like the Inquisition, it employed a web of spies and informers to trap dissenters. It could undertake house searches, install phone taps, and open private letters without a warrant. Its officers would turn up at homes and intimidate suspects who could be hauled away, denied access to legal counsel and tortured in police cells. Special military tribunals, not unlike kangaroo courts, heard political crimes.

The secret police agents employed crude methods to terrorize anyone who stepped out of line. The American jazz great Charlie Haden had a taste of how these enforcers functioned in 1971 after he gave a concert in Cascais, near Lisbon. On stage he dedicated a song to independence movements who at the time were fighting Portugal's rule in Africa. At Lisbon airport the next day he was about to board his plane when plain-clothed political police, by then known by their new acronym PIDE (International Police for the Defence of the State) dragged him away in the face of the other band members' protests. Salazar's henchmen threw him in a cell, interrogated and intimidated him until the US Embassy got wind of it and secured his release. Haden recounted the alarming episode to the broadcaster *Democracy Now!* in 2006:

> And the next thing I know, I'm in a car, and we're travelling to a prison. And I'm thrown into a dark room with no lights, and I stay there for I don't know how long. A long, long time. And finally— I mean, I was traumatized. You know, I thought I'd never get to see my kids. I thought it was over. I didn't know what they were going to do.

It was a glimpse of life in Portugal. Convicted political opponents regarded as particularly dangerous were sent into exile or banished to a harsh prison called Tarrafal in the Cape Verde islands. Other dissenters fled the country of their own account.

Censorship tightened the stranglehold and deepened an insular mentality. It gagged public protest and muzzled the media, shutting the windows to the world and denying the Portuguese the chance of comparing their country with others. "Men, groups, classes see, observe things, look at events with their own interests in mind," Salazar maintained. "Only one institution, out of duty and standing, has to look at everything with everyone's interests in mind." And that was the state. The censors used a blue pencil as they combed newspapers, magazines, and books before publication, crossing out bothersome references to freedom and rights and anything else judged untoward. The government propaganda machine, meanwhile, relentlessly spread Salazar's message.

It is said that the censorship departments had problems finding staff because in the 1930s the illiteracy rate stood at over 60 percent. Education, or rather the lack of it, was indeed another important factor in keeping the Portuguese under Salazar's thumb. In 1960 just one in ten fifteen-year-olds was in full-time education. In the clearly stratified society that Salazar built, there was no middle class as such. There was a well-off elite ready to occupy positions of authority across society and a massive underclass of poor, and poorly-educated, people. Salazar commented in 1933 that to his mind it was "more pressing to build an extensive elite than to teach everybody how to read."

This calibration of society, divided between a mostly urban elite and the rural masses, prompted the perceptive observation by the American writer Mary McCarthy, during a visit in the 1950s, that upper-class Portuguese appeared to live in exile in their own country and look down on their compatriots as colonially-run natives—a description not far removed from those of Eça de Queirós in his nineteenth-century novels. It is a long-standing circumstance that bred feelings of envy—a national trait. In one excruciating example, poor locals were said to be astounded by the ostentatious display of wealth when in 1968 two ultra-chic, glitzy parties for international high society were thrown by foreign multimillionaires. Antenor Patiño, the Bolivian "Tin King," and Franco-American oil millionaire Pierre Schlumberger invited more than 1,000 guests to their parties near Sintra, west of Lisbon. They included Gina Lollobrigida, Audrey Hepburn, Zsa Zsa Gabor, Douglas Fairbanks Junior,

Henry Ford II, European nobles, and wealthy industrialists. *Time* magazine and Portuguese newspapers reported that curious bystanders crowded around the venues for a closer look and watched open-mouthed as limousines delivered the Beautiful People.

If rising in the social scale was unthinkable, immobility—accepting your lot—was a virtue. Salazar discouraged ideas of betterment and doused any enthusiasm for personal initiative. The cover of a 1930s school textbook for seven- and eight-year-olds shows the interior of a humble, rural home. Mother is busy at the stove in her apron and the table is set for dinner. The son is studying and the daughter is playing with dolls. The father is coming through the front door with a hoe over his shoulder and a radiant smile as the sun sets in the background after a satisfying day's work in the fields. On the wall, there is a crucifix. It is a picture of harmony and contentment, a pastoral idyll. Outside school hours the *Mocidade Portuguesa* (Portuguese Youth), a kind of Hitler Youth movement created in 1936, cemented the indoctrination from the age of seven.

Salazar insisted on a moral code rooted in what he perceived as traditional values of the kind he had grown up with in late nineteenth-century rural society. Invoking the shared traditions and common ancestry of the Portuguese, he advocated primitive virtues. Puritanism was valued as rules stipulated that swimsuits could not bare too much flesh, and kissing in public invited a reprimand. Salazar would rather his country be poor than dependent on others, and faithful to its traditions rather than tainted by modernity.

The domestic life consecrated by Salazar's moral crusade placed women at a disadvantage. The acclaimed Portuguese painter Paula Rego says that in the 1950s, when she was seventeen, her father gave her some sound advice: "'Leave Portugal,' he said. 'This is no country for a woman.'" She moved to London, where she has remained and built up an international reputation. Portugal and its history peep through her work, which is markedly biographical, even confessional. "A lot of it is in my pictures," she once said of the country of her birth, "quite a lot of it." Rego expressed her loathing for the regime in *Salazar Vomiting the Homeland*, a semi-abstract oil painting from 1960 that now hangs on the walls of the Gulbenkian Foundation in Lisbon.

In the New State, women were expected to dedicate themselves to husband, hearth, and home. The 1933 Constitution denied women certain rights due to their "naturally inherent differences and the interests of the family." Among numerous humiliations, they needed written permission from their husband to leave the country. "It was a fascist state for everyone but it was especially hard for women. They got a raw deal," recalls Rego. Women's magazines from the time offer some colorful examples of the prevailing machismo. The magazine *Querida* in 1955 toed the government line: "A woman's place is in the home; work outside makes a woman masculine," it remarked. Two years later *Jornal das Moças* listed some recommendations for its readers: "Don't annoy your husband with jealousy and doubts;" "An untidy bathroom makes husbands want to have a bath elsewhere;" "Always looking good for your husband is essential." And in 1962—the year Britain witnessed its first woman judge and its first woman ambassador—*Claudia*'s tips were: "If a wife suspects her husband of being unfaithful, she should redouble her efforts to be kind and caring;" "A woman should be aware that a man would find it hard to accept a woman who was unable to resist pre-nuptial experiences. She should reveal herself to be perfect and unique, conforming exactly to his ideal."

It was not until 1972, with Salazar gone and a successor in place, that women's liberation finally made an advance. Three women writers—Maria Isabel Barreno, Maria Teresa Horta, and Maria Velho da Costa—wrote a book called *New Portuguese Letters* containing free-thinking reflections on women's role in society. The regime proclaimed the work "immoral," banned it and prohibited the so-called "Three Marias" from leaving the country. The cultural conditioning was so ingrained, however, that it spilled over the Revolution's watershed. In post-coup January 1975, the same three Marias and a handful of others who were part of the Women's Liberation Movement, created the previous year to lobby for equal rights, staged a minor demonstration in a Lisbon park. Announced in the press, it drew a crowd of angry men who surrounded the group, physically harassed them, and shouted indelicate slogans such as "Women should stay in the kitchen" and "Women are only good in bed." Though the laws had been changed, the prejudice was slower to evaporate (some would say it still exists). In 1979

Portugal's only ever woman prime minister Maria de Lourdes Pintasilgo, who took office a few months after Margaret Thatcher in Britain, gave her debut address to Parliament and is said to have been subjected to mocking abuse by some MPs, including phrases such as "Go home and darn some socks." Like the rest of Europe, Portugal is still far from achieving parity between the number of male and female MPs.

God, Homeland, Family

Salazarism depicted Portugal in a cultural triptych featuring the so-called "Three Fs": *fado* (traditional Portuguese music), football (soccer), and Fátima. His regime co-opted the traditional *fado* genre as something authentically Portuguese, unsoiled by outside influences. Soccer, as a sort of opium of the masses, also warranted Salazar's attention. Eusébio, Benfica's star player of the 1960s, appeared set to be poached by big Italian and Spanish clubs that offered the Lisbon club phenomenal sums for him. Salazar, sensing that Eusébio's departure could arouse discontent, stepped in and designated the player a "national treasure," meaning that he could not be sold abroad.

Fátima is the small rural town north of Lisbon where three shepherd children claimed that the Virgin Mary appeared to them in 1917. The town's shrine is a potent symbol of the Church's enduring influence in Portugal. Even now, no visitor to Lisbon can fail to spot the huge statue of Christ the King, which overlooks the capital from the south bank of the River Tagus, its arms outstretched in a come-hither gesture. Inspired by the statue on Sugar Loaf Mountain in Rio de Janeiro, it was built as thanks for keeping Portugal out of the Second World War and inaugurated in 1959.

Pope Paul VI visited Fátima for the fiftieth anniversary of the apparitions in 1967. The pontiff's visit, coming at a time when the country was under strong international pressure over political repression at home and in its African colonies, merited rare live television coverage in Portugal. Even though the pope, in a discreet nod to the protests, avoided Lisbon and Salazar had to go to meet him at the Air Force base where he landed, the visit was an honor and a respite for a regime engaged in a diplomatic rearguard action at the United Nations and elsewhere. During his stay the pope notably made no mention of civil rights in Portugal nor of the military campaign against African independence movements. The Cross and the Crown have mostly been united since the birth of the nation. The Catholic Church had played a key role in ensuring public support during the *reconquista* and was rewarded with wealth and influence. It was affiliated with the voyages of discovery in the fifteenth and sixteenth centuries when fleets set out from the riverside suburb of Belém (Portuguese for Bethlehem). The historical heroes crowding onto Belém's Monument to the Discoveries clasp swords and crosses. Apart from brief periods when it was in crisis—during the rise of liberalism in the early nineteenth century and when the Republic arrived in the early twentieth, though some clergy were simply banished rather than shot, as many were during the Spanish Civil War—the Catholic Church has held a central role in Portuguese society. At the time of the Second World War, Portugal had twice as many priests as doctors. In a speech in Porto in 1949, Salazar proclaimed:

> Portugal was born in the shadow of the Church, and from the outset the Catholic religion has been a formative element of the nation's soul and a predominant trait in the character of the Portuguese people. In our journeys across the globe—discovering, trading, spreading the faith—it was easy to deduce: they are Portuguese, so they are Catholic.

One of Salazar's rallying slogans for his New State was *Deus, Pátria, Família* (God, Homeland, Family). From the age of eleven he had studied at a rural seminary, where he is said to have been a diligent pupil. His mother (who looked much fiercer than he did) called him "the little priest" and during his rule a popular proverb ran, "God in Heaven, Salazar on earth." One of Salazar's closest friends during his student days was Manuel Gonçalves Cerejeira, appointed Cardinal of Lisbon by the Vatican and the highest-ranking member of the Church in Portugal from 1929 to 1971, largely coinciding with Salazar's rule. In his prime minister's office Salazar kept a framed picture of Pope Pius XII and a

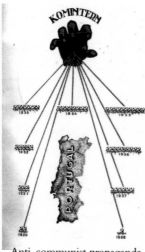

Anti-communist propaganda,
Salazar-style

statuette of the Virgin of Fátima. Each day before work he attended Mass. With the Church, he shared an intense opposition to godless communists and an insistence on obedience to conservative values.

Though the Church might be thought of as Salazar's natural constituency, he preferred to keep the Catholic Establishment at arm's length while at the same time co-opting it. He never demonstrated the presumption of General Franco, who had coins minted showing his image and beneath it the phrase, "By the Grace of God, the leader of Spain." Salazar maintained the policy introduced by the Republican regime of keeping Church and state separate. Even so, he reached a Concordat with the Vatican in 1940 to grant special privileges to the Church such as exemption from taxes and the imposition of mandatory Christian teaching in state schools. In return, the Church stayed out of politics. In the African colonies, some Catholic missionaries told natives that desiring independence was a sin, and the Church prized its presence in those territories where the red cross of the Order of Christ had arrived on the sails of seafaring explorers.

Eventually, though, the dictatorship and its consequences, especially widespread poverty, became too much to stomach for some Catholics who were familiar with what was happening in the rest of world. The venerable Bishop of Porto, António Ferreira Gomes, was the first major figure publicly to break ranks. In 1958, with the regime showing signs of mounting unpopularity, he wrote what became a celebrated letter to Salazar. The bishop eloquently explained that after wrestling with his conscience he had decided he could no longer stay silent in face of the dictatorship's evident rottenness. He offered praise, noting that Salazar had brought hope and inspired enthusiasm during his early years in charge. He recalled that on a visit to the Vatican before

Salazar took over, a major bank in Rome had refused to change his Portuguese currency because it was virtually worthless. The benefits had ebbed, however, and now, the bishop said, he witnessed a "tremendous national crisis" that had brought dangerous social and political tension. As he travelled through Europe, he continued, he found that the Portuguese were viewed as barefoot, backward "ragamuffins." The Church was compromised and was losing the trust of the people, and he feared that it was becoming a spiritual ghetto. At the same time, he complained, it was being intimidated by supporters of the regime to stand firm beside Salazar. The bishop urged the country's leader to ensure a fairer division of wealth. He questioned the value of nationalism as an overriding government policy and appealed for the "respect, liberty and non-discrimination which is owed to any honest citizen in any civil society."

Salazar was incensed. The bishop had overstepped the mark and was sent into exile for eleven years, with the blessing of the Vatican. There were other prominent Catholics who endorsed the bishop's views but, especially after witnessing his fate, they kept a low profile. Some—so-called "progressive Catholics"—still dared to organize literacy campaigns among the poor, engaging in a kind of muted activism despite the severe punishment reserved for subversive acts. In 1972 there was an eye-catching protest from this quarter when on December 30 a group of educated, distinguished, and upright worshippers—the kind of people on whose support the regime had once counted—attended Mass at the Rato chapel in Lisbon on World Peace Day. Once it was over they informed the priest they were staying inside to protest against Portugal's war in Africa. Riot police moved in the next day and carted about sixty of them off to jail.

In the political and social tumult after the 1974 Revolution, which ended the dictatorship, the Catholic Church backed conservative groups against dominant left-of-center parties. It organized well-attended marches for "freedom." Radio Vatican, taking aim at the communists, urged the Portuguese not to support parties that were "incompatible" with Christian teaching, while the Church looked kindly on right-of-center counter-revolutionary groups in the north of the country where there were violent clashes.

In recent times the Church's influence has faded. A 2005 report
✓ stated that for every two priests who die only one is ordained.
Portuguese bishops were summoned in 2007 by the pope, who
expressed concern that cultural changes had eroded church attendances.
The secretary of the Portuguese Episcopal Conference, Carlos Azevedo,
acknowledged the Church was out of step. "To use an economic
analogy, we are still selling products that have gone out of fashion and
that bear no relation to the people we are dealing with," he conceded.
When the country's first two private TV channels were launched in the
early 1990s, the Church was granted one of the licenses. However, when
a monk wearing a habit introduced the channel's inaugural broadcast
with a preaching presentation it was clearly doomed and within years
it was sold off. The Catholic Church is also feeling strong pressure from
Brazilian evangelical churches, which have proved appealing to immigrant workers from the former colonies. In 2007 it lost a mammoth
battle against the socialist government to keep abortion illegal, and three
years later the same government pushed through a law allowing gay
marriage.

Faith remains a bedrock inspiration, however, and the Catholic
Church still maintains significant influence. Every May 13 and October
13, the date of the first and last apparitions, upwards of half a million
people gather at the Fátima shrine for a candlelight vigil. Some give
thanks to the Virgin by shuffling hundreds of meters on their knees
along a marble path towards the shrine, which despite knee-pads is
reported to be very painful.

The Church's strength also manifests itself more subtly. Portugal is,
tellingly, the only European country where there are no soccer league
games on Easter Sunday. When José Manuel Barroso, later president of
the European Commission, was prime minister between 2002 and 2004
he tried to shift bank holidays to the nearest Monday, as is the practice
in Britain. He was trying to put an end to what the Portuguese call
"bridges"—taking, say, Friday off when a holiday falls on a Thursday to
make a four-day weekend—because it was hurting national productivity. The Church nipped the plan in the bud with a simple remark to the
effect that religious commemorations could not be relegated below
economic interests.

Nobel literature laureate José Saramago also felt the shadowy power of the Catholic Church. The government once withdrew his name from Portugal's nominees for the European Literature Prize because, it said, his 1991 novel *O Evangelho Segundo Jesus Cristo* (The Gospel According to Jesus Christ)—in which Christ lives with Mary Magdalene and tries to back out of his crucifixion—offended Portuguese religious convictions. Saramago, who was still resentful of the snub decades later, said that it amounted to censorship.

Saramago was to gain his revenge when in 1998 he became the first Portuguese writer to win the Nobel Prize for literature. The award was a tribute to his novels' themes of compassion and anxiety and the skewing of priorities in modern society. Those themes also provide a clue to his enduring sympathy for the Communist Party, as do his humble beginnings in a small farming town in the fertile Tagus Valley, north of Lisbon. From a poor family, he never finished university but continued to study part-time while supporting himself as a metalworker. His first novel, published in 1947, *Terra do Pecado* (*Country of Sin*), was a tale of peasants in moral crisis. It sold badly but won Saramago enough recognition to allow him to jump from the welder's shop to a job on a literary magazine. For the next eighteen years, however, he published only a few travel and poetry books while he worked as a journalist. "I suppose I had nothing to say," he conceded about that barren period. A gaunt, outspoken and sometimes prickly man, Saramago's novels are not to all readers' tastes, especially due to their elongated sentences, which are at times testing, and his Nobel triumph raised a few eyebrows in Portugal. The irony of his sudden popularity late in his life (he was 76 when he won) was not lost on Saramago. "'People used to say about me, 'He's good but he's a communist.' Now they say, 'He's a communist but he's good,'" he remarked. And when the president commented that the Nobel Prize was for all Portugal, the old communist quipped: "You keep the prize, I'll keep the money."

The Church remains deeply embedded in Portuguese society partly by virtue of the more than 2,000 social institutions it runs, caring for the elderly, orphans, and handicapped people whom the state cannot afford to take care of. The Patriarch of Lisbon, José Policarpo, noted in 2007: "The Church is, after the state, the most organized and most present structure in society as a whole." This has not exempted it from some sharp criticism. The We Are Church movement protested in 2008 that the Church was alienating many because it is "extremely rigid." It cited the head of the Fátima shrine who said that year that a woman should not leave her husband if he hits her only occasionally.

Foreign Complicity

Salazar faced few real difficulties during the 1930s as he methodically fashioned Portugal in his own image. The arrival of the Spanish Civil War and the Second World War ended the period of stability as the small and vulnerable country had to seek an accommodation with bigger powers. Salazar showed impressive acumen—that familiar national guile—in playing the Great Game.

Mindful that Portugal had no chance of stopping a Spanish army pouring across the border, Salazar sought to avoid conflict with Franco's Spain. He deftly negotiated the non-aggression pact with the *Generalísimo*, his circumspect approach perhaps convincing Franco that Portugal feared a fight and prompting him to dismiss the Portuguese as, to his mind, cowards. Anxious to keep Spain at arm's length, one of Salazar's populist slogans was *Contra o Iberismo* ("Down with Iberianism"), referring to political and cultural suggestions that the two should unite.

Salazar walked a perilous line during the Second World War but successfully pulled off his strategy of "neutral collaboration." It was obvious, however, where his ideological preferences lay: "Our century is a fascist century," he announced, prematurely, and the extended-arm salute was adopted at official ceremonies in the late 1930s but quietly dropped before the end of the conflict when the Nazis looked to be on the losing side.

Even so, his careful plans were almost upended by Portugal's consul general in Bordeaux. When Germany invaded France in 1940 Aristides Sousa Mendes, a career diplomat, defied Salazar's instructions and issued visas to an estimated 10,000 Jews and 20,000 other refugees fleeing the Nazi advance. For many people the only way out by land was to head for Portugal's Atlantic coast capital and board a ship there, but a Portuguese transit visa was needed to leave France and cross Spain. Sousa Mendes and a handful of staff worked furiously to issue visas to thousands who queued around the consulate for days in what is regarded as one of the great heroic deeds of the war. But, as the Bishop of Porto found out later, Salazar was remorseless in his punishment of those who stepped out of line. Sousa Mendes was called back to Lisbon where he was stripped of his position and thrown out of the diplomatic service. Denied a pension and barred from practicing his profession as a lawyer, as well as socially shunned, he lived the remainder of his life in poverty with his wife and fourteen children and died in 1954. In 1998 Parliament approved a bill that posthumously rehabilitated Sousa Mendes, promoted him to ambassador and paid compensation to his surviving family members.

Portugal, and especially Lisbon and the nearby elegant coastal resort of Estoril, was a curiosity during the war. Spies and royal exiles, British ships and German submarines engaged in cloak-and-dagger maneuvers in the neutral territory. Graham Greene and Ian Fleming spied in Estoril. The town's casino is said to have provided the inspiration for the 007 book *Casino Royale*. Edward VIII went to Estoril after abdicating, and Humberto II, Italy's last king, and Carol II of Romania called it home.

All was not well in Portugal, however. Though state coffers profited handsomely from trade with the Allies and Axis powers, food shortages and inflated prices hurt the poor. The French writer Antoine de Saint-Exupéry, passing through Lisbon in December 1940, decided that the Portuguese were clinging to an "illusion of happiness." The spell, however, was starting to wear off. In July 1946 *Time* magazine devoted its cover to Salazar. It called him "the dean of Europe's dictators," though with an admirable lack of subtlety it pictured his face next to a rotting apple. Portugal, it noted, had emerged intact but not unscathed from the war. The magazine described "a melancholy land of impoverished, confused and frightened people." Predictably, the journalist in question was kicked out of the country, and the magazine was removed from newsstands and banned from sale for six years (why six years and not five or seven is not known).

Salazar's Cold War usefulness ensured the indulgence, not to say complicity, of other western countries with his authoritarian regime. Their geopolitical interests spoke louder than their democratic scruples. The mid-Atlantic Azores military base was Salazar's trump card and he played it to help ensure that Portugal was a NATO co-founder in 1949, admitted to the United Nations in 1955, to the European Free Trade Association in 1959 and the International Monetary Fund in 1961. At NATO and EFTA, Portugal stood in anomalous isolation as the only member that allowed no political freedom. Membership of those international institutions lent credibility to a distasteful regime and aided its longevity.

Salazar tacked closer to the victorious Allies and made some post-war political concessions at home, introducing elections for the country's president and closing the notorious Tarrafal prison in Cape Verde. The president was little more than a figurehead, however, and Tarrafal-bound prisoners were dispatched to other, no less sinister establishments. The United States trod delicately around Salazar in large part out of fear that his demise could hand Moscow the chance of a foothold in Western Europe. The best-organized underground opposition to the regime was the Portuguese Communist Party, aided and abetted by the Soviet Union. Salazar always mistrusted American motives and was wary of the consequences for Portugal of getting too close to Washington's orbit. Initially during the Second World War, he allowed British forces but not the Americans to use the Azores. He warmed to America only once he realized that he would need Washington's help to get Australia back out of East Timor at the war's end.

President Dwight Eisenhower, on an official 24-hour visit to Portugal in May 1960 after a meeting in Paris with Nikita Khrushchev, Harold Macmillan, and Charles de Gaulle, described Portugal—where workers had no right to strike and where secret police goons could drag people off the street—as "a fantastic ally and a friend." Salazar by that time was keen on recruiting American sympathy for his uncompromising policy on Africa. He picked an American company over European rivals to build the River Tagus suspension bridge and he explained away African independence movements as guerrilla groups in the pay of Moscow or Peking. The situation, he knew, was pressing. In

1960 Nigeria won its independence from Britain and de Gaulle had agreed to negotiate Algeria's future.

Politically reactionary and stubborn, Salazar refused to abandon his dogmatic stance, even though his rule had clearly started going sour in the 1950s. Outlawing opposition parties in the 1930s was one thing; in post-war Europe and into the 1960s it was scandalous. He barricaded Portugal against the world with policies that checked the cultural fermentation process, the enriching exchange of ideas. Although joining EFTA brought fresh foreign investment and generated economic growth of up to 11 percent a year in the 1960s, permitting a spurt in public infrastructure investment, there was little trickle-down of wealth. The private sector was commonly thought of as being in the grip of forty families, including the landed gentry. ✔

Salazar allowed blue-collar guilds, but only with government-vetted leaders, and white-collar confederations that benefitted from the regime's policies and supported it. The government supervised negotiations between the two parts while fostering national cartels that kept progress and development under Salazar's control. He favored protectionism, thereby undermining competitiveness. A government law of July 1937, for instance, stipulated that all typewriters used in Portugal had to have a HCESAR keyboard, not the internationally common QWERTY. The aim was to protect the national typewriter manufacturer Messa, which used the so-called Portuguese keyboard, from foreign competition. (The company is now defunct.) To the same end, licenses were required for cigarette lighters to protect national matchmakers.

The sociologist António Barreto describes his country in the 1960s thus:

> A shut-off nation. An authoritarian state. An ignorant people. Small, poor and outside the mainstream. That is how we were then. With narrow horizons, terrible schooling, bad health, little employment and no freedom. Without a welfare state, with an obscene rate of infant mortality, low life expectancy and a high mortality rate from contagious diseases related to poverty.

People looking to escape the miserable conditions at home, to avoid the conscription that would take them to fight in Africa, and to take advantage of the economic boom in the rest of Europe, absconded to France in large numbers in the 1960s. Between 1965 and 1975 up to 200,000 a year went to work there, many of them living in suburban shantytowns called *bidonvilles*—including the one at Champigny-sur-Marne, east of Paris, which was the largest slum in France—and working long hours in unskilled jobs, such as in the construction of La Défense business district and the Périphérique ring-road. The exodus to France left a manpower shortage in Portugal. Though a military coup delivered the final, fatal blow to the regime, its demise is perhaps better seen as a kind of death by a thousand cuts, of which mass emigration was just one of the wounds.

The 1958 presidential election, when a distinguished Air Force general decided he had seen enough and boldly stood as an independent candidate, contradicted the regime's claim to a popular mandate. General Humberto Delgado had a sterling military record that began at Lisbon's prestigious Military School. He had backed the 1926 military coup and supported Salazar's power-grab through the new Constitution. He became Portugal's youngest Air Force general at the age of 47 and for five years was the Portuguese military attaché in Washington, DC. But then in the 1958 election he unexpectedly became a lightning rod for widespread discontent. Asked at a Lisbon press conference what he would do about Salazar if he won, Delgado famously replied: "I shall sack him, of course." The remark set the country alight. His valiant assault on the apparently impenetrable fortress of Salazarism earned him the nickname the Fearless General. Tens of thousands of people—apparently everyday folk who had had no political voice—turned out to cheer him at an electrifying campaign rally in Porto. The occasion sent a shudder through the regime. When Delgado arrived in Lisbon for a second such rally he was met at the train station by huge, enthusiastic crowds and also by mounted riot police with swords drawn who prevented him from speaking and dispersed the crowd. The election, it is now widely accepted, was rigged, and Salazar's man was elected (the Bishop of Porto's letter was prompted by this political crisis.) Afterwards, Delgado was scorned by

The Fearless General

his superiors and hounded by the secret police to such an extent that the following year he knocked on the door of the Brazilian Embassy and was granted the political asylum he requested. He returned secretly to Portugal in 1961 and with other conspirators tried to stage a coup, which failed. He was lured back by the secret police in 1965 and assassinated by henchmen on the Spanish border near Villanueva del Fresno.

The 1958 presidential election proved to be a watershed. The regime, confronted with the massive and unexpected popular support for Delgado, was never again fully at ease. Salazar scrapped presidential elections and from then on the head of state was appointed by a panel of government trustees.

In 1961 other bizarre political events rocked the regime. Captain Henrique Galvão, also a career soldier and previously a fervent supporter of Salazar, led the capture of a Portuguese luxury cruise liner bound for Miami with almost 1,000 people on board, many of them American. Galvão had become disenchanted with Salazar's rule in the 1950s and had been imprisoned for subversive activities. He escaped and while in exile in Venezuela hatched his plan to draw international attention to the injustices of Portugal's dictatorship. His bold, swashbuckling scheme to capture a 20,000-ton ship caught the public imagination. Galvão and his two-dozen rebels boarded the cruise liner in Venezuela disguised as vacationers but secret compartments in their suitcases contained guns. *Paris Match* magazine wrote: "In the middle of the twentieth century, the world has learned with stupefaction that there are still pirates." It reported that the *Santa Maria*—the pride of the country's merchant fleet—was "a small, floating bit of freedom," describing it as a Battleship Potemkin for the nuclear age. Galvão changed the ship's course to Africa, where he planned to attack the Angolan capital Luanda, but was cornered by American warships and eventually surrendered in Brazil. The same year one of Galvão's supporters, Palma Inácio, and four others hijacked a commercial plane flying a regular route from Casablanca to Lisbon. They forced the pilot to swoop low over the capital and three other cities while they threw out of the windows thousands of leaflets calling for Salazar's overthrow.

The following year Portuguese university students took up the gauntlet of opposition. The government outlawed a plan to hold a first National Students' Day in Coimbra attended by students from around the country, but it went ahead anyway. Some of the student leaders were suspended from classes, igniting a broader revolt that included a student strike. Riot police stormed a Lisbon University canteen where students were holding a meeting. Many were beaten and arrested. The protests continued through the year. The people, however, never rose up.

It was perhaps 1961 that could best be described as Salazar's *annus horribilis*. While expressions of discontent at home chipped away at the regime's credentials, heavy blows were landed from abroad. In 1961 Angolans rose up against their colonial masters in a spasm of unanticipated and shocking violence, while milder (for the moment) unrest surfaced in Guinea-Bissau. And that year the Portuguese were ejected from Goa, on India's west coast, where they had settled 450 years earlier.

Portugal had only about 4,000 troops, armed with single-shot carbines, in Goa. When an Indian force ten times larger, carrying automatic weapons and supported by air power, gathered for an attack Salazar sent a message sent to his military commanders instructing them to hold out against greater numbers as a demonstration of "Portuguese virtues." He wrote: "It is awful to think that this might mean total sacrifice, but I recommend and expect this sacrifice as the only way we have of living up to our traditions and doing our duty for the future of our nation." The message was plain: they must fight to the death. India invaded and after two days of fighting, in which 26 Portuguese died, the local commander ran up the white flag. It was a bitter blow to Salazar's prestige and made a mockery of his romantic portrayal of the greatness of the Portuguese empire. Rubbing salt into the wound, Portugal's allies at NATO and other international organizations, though they made all the right noises by urging India to settle its claim through negotiation, pointedly did not lift a finger to help Salazar.

War Atrocities

In Africa, one of the darkest chapters in Portuguese history opened in 1961. The war there broke like a thunderclap over Salazar's head. Five hundred years after the Portuguese had dropped anchor, rebellious Africans, spurred by the successes of other independence movements, tried to send them packing. Other European colonial powers had started relinquishing their grip in the early 1950s, but Portugal would keep fighting for thirteen years. There was nothing sentimental about the refusal to leave; Salazar had not even visited Africa. He simply made a political and economic calculation: subtract the African colonies and Portugal would be just a cloistered country of fewer than nine million people. Salazar was keenly aware that the wealth and influence furnished by Portugal's possessions on the African continent were what enabled him to stand "proudly alone." They kept him afloat and other countries at bay and were evidence of Portugal's rank in the world. His prime foreign policy goal was to hold onto them.

Angola was the jewel in the crown of Portugal's empire. It was its largest African colony, its coastal capital Luanda was the third-largest Portuguese city by population, and in the first half of twentieth century, Angola was the world's third-biggest coffee producer. When the armed revolt erupted, Salazar issued the order, "To Angola, in strength!" and called on Portugal's Christian faith to prevail. Troop ships left Lisbon from a dock near where Vasco da Gama and other heroes had departed five centuries earlier. Television footage from the time shows a brass band playing the national anthem amid a scene of fanfare and imperial pomp. Mothers, wives, children, and girlfriends waved white handkerchiefs and wailed as the ships weighed anchor. A voice-over bade the troops farewell, saying "Have a good journey, boys, have a good mission, and we'll see you soon."

The state-controlled media recounted tales of heroic military deeds and kept the Portuguese at home in the dark about what was happening thousands of kilometers away. The truth was not pretty. The war began with a gruesome initial frenzy of bloodshed after Angolan rebels crossed the border from newly-independent Congo and staged surprise attacks. Armed with machetes, they butchered Portuguese settlers, including women and their small children, on remote plantations. In retaliation, and despite unrelenting pressure from the United States and the United Nations for Lisbon to concede that the colonial period was over, Portuguese militia and troops were deployed to quell the insurrection. They at first engaged in a vengeful and violent repression. The heads of dead enemy soldiers were hacked off and impaled on the branches of roadside trees. Hundreds of prisoners were tortured, killed, and tossed into mass graves. Napalm was dropped on the thick jungle where guerrillas sheltered, and grass-hut villages were razed.

In Portugal, the New State's propaganda machine went into overdrive. At beaches in the summer, loudspeakers churned out a chant of *Angola é Nossa!* ("Angola is Ours!") with the kind of thumping repetition that drowns out rational thought. In 1951 Salazar, sniffing change in the air as European countries readied for decolonization, had produced another Orwellian flourish by switching official terminology: the outposts of empire were no longer to be known as colonies but rather as "overseas provinces." The intention was to convey the impression that Portuguese-ruled lands were one and indivisible. At the United Nations, Portugal disingenuously argued that it had no colonies, hence the national stupefaction at Angola's bid for independence. Salazar claimed in a 1963 speech: "Angola is a Portuguese creation and does not exist without Portugal." A Portuguese atlas from as late as 1973 boasted about the country's presence on four continents, the land mass of its colonies together representing the equivalent of one-fifth of the area of Europe. The Portuguese and natives, geographer Amorim Girão explained in the atlas, lived together "without any racial discrimination and, therefore, in perfect moral unity" as "one people, one nation."

Within a year the Angolan rebellion dwindled to a low-intensity conflict as the army got to grips with guerrilla warfare. But parallel wars broke out in two other Portuguese African colonies—Mozambique on the southeast coast and Guinea-Bissau on the continent's western bulge. The Portuguese armed forces were in danger of overreach as war on three fronts compelled them to launch their biggest mobilization of modern times. Within a year of the conflict's start Portugal had 50,000 men in Angola; in 1974, when the war ended, there were 130,000 troops in Africa. Altogether some 800,000 went to fight in what was a bigger military effort, in relative terms, than the US undertook in Vietnam. Conscription entailed a year's training followed by a two-year tour of duty. Home leave was a very rare exception. Many conscripts were barely literate youths from rural areas who had never travelled far from their birthplace, though the draft encompassed men from all walks of life, including doctors and engineers. Everyone, it seemed, knew someone who was over there. The war also bled the Portuguese treasury. At its peak, the faraway conflict drained away more than 40 percent of the annual state budget.

Clinging to the colonies proved to be a folly. The conflict sapped Portugal's strength financially, socially, politically, diplomatically, and militarily. The outlay crippled the economy, removing resources that could have been invested in modernization. Resisting African liberation also deepened the international isolation of Portugal's unapologetic regime. The Portuguese were berated in the United Nations, where newly-independent African and Asian nations vociferously criticized them, and shrieked at in the streets of London: *The Times* broke the news of the Wiriyamu massacre, as reported by Catholic missionaries, just before an official four-day visit to Britain by Marcello Caetano, who had replaced Salazar, to mark the 600th anniversary of the Treaty of Alliance. (Portugal denied the massacre ever happened.)

The government's policy resoundingly backfired because the conflict's unpopularity among the Portuguese amplified the clamor for change. "It was always said that Portugal would never survive without its overseas colonies," António Barreto says. "In truth, by holding onto the colonies the regime would end."

Salazar died while the war was still going on. In August 1968, while staying at his summer residence in Estoril, he sat down on a deckchair on the veranda but it collapsed and he fell awkwardly, hitting his head on the floor. It was apparently a minor accident but it caused brain damage that sidelined him. Despite undergoing surgery he never recovered and died in 1970 at eighty-one. Bizarrely, for two years from mid-1968 when he was replaced due to incapacity, his advisers, government ministers, the president, and his staff all kept up the pretense for his sake that he was still in charge and leading the country. Officials would go to Salazar's residence and feign to consult the old man, who was paralyzed down his left side, unable to walk unaided, and had impaired memory and vision, about national and world affairs. He was never informed that he had been relieved of the duties he had held for the previous three decades. Salazar was given a state funeral at the Jerónimos Monastery in Lisbon but was buried, according to his wishes, in the small graveyard in his home town of Santa Comba Dão. He bequeathed a great number of problems.

The "Caetano Spring"

Salazar had not groomed a successor. It fell to President Américo Tomáz, after consultations, to appoint Marcello Caetano prime minister. The change in tone was clear. Though he was a Catholic conservative and had been a high-ranking party official and a government minister, Caetano had fallen out with Salazar and had returned to his job as a law professor. He was 62, married with four children and, compared with Salazar's angular features, had a rounder, almost cherubic, appearance. He also had a more cosmopolitan style and offered the prospect of compromise.

He began a television and radio program called "Family Chats," in which he addressed the nation, informed them of his plans and countered criticism. Responding to a reported comment that Portugal, in the colonial war, was experiencing its own Vietnam, he replied: "We didn't go to Africa ten years ago." Hemmed in politically, Caetano devised a deliciously absurd concept of "renewal through continuity," introducing some cosmetic changes such as altering the name of the secret police force and of the single party. More significantly, he relaxed censorship and allowed some political exiles back into the country. Some liberal MPs were elected to the still-tame National Assembly and a new weekly newspaper called *Expresso*, which would to a large extent be their mouthpiece, was launched.

This period became known as the "Caetano Spring." Like the Prague Spring in Czechoslovakia a few years earlier, it initiated reforms intended to loosen the state's authoritarian grip. Hopes were frustrated, however. Caetano was trying to pull off an impossible juggling act by promising conservatives continuity and liberals renewal. Nor could he end the deeply unpopular war. Stalemate had ensued in Angola and Mozambique, but in an alarming new dimension to the Guinea-Bissau campaign, rebels had obtained Soviet-made ground-to-air missiles, canceling out the vital Portuguese advantage of air power. In 1970 Pope Paul VI received at the Vatican the leaders of independence movements from Angola, Mozambique, and Guinea-Bissau. Economic difficulties at home, meanwhile, were compounded by the oil crisis of the early 1970s. Just as importantly, Caetano possessed neither the charisma nor the steeliness of Salazar.

Caetano presented the last of his "Family Chats" in March 1974, less than a month before the coup that ended his premiership. Within weeks he and his family were sent into exile in Brazil. Disgruntled army officers had already been conspiring for seven months, incensed by new rules that made militia ranks equivalent to those in the regular army and fearing that, as had happened with the Goa debacle, the military would be blamed for what evidently was an unwinnable war. Caetano's remark that he preferred military defeat in Guinea-Bissau to negotiating with the independence groups sharpened the officers' frustration. In February of that year General António de Spínola, a monocle-wearing war hero and popular deputy chief of the armed forces, embarrassed Caetano by publishing his book *Portugal and the Future* in which he proposed a negotiated end to the fighting. He refused to join older generals, dubbed the Rheumatic Brigade, in a public display of support for the regime and was sacked. Still the people were silent. But soon soldiers disaffected with the regime made the crucial move, demonstrating the danger for a dictatorship of a large standing army.

The government crumpled under an aggregate of factors that by the April 25, 1974 Carnation Revolution had reached a critical mass.

The strain between reality and the regime's fiction made the political circumstances untenable.

Barreto points to five trends that were catalysts of the Carnation Revolution: emigrants (by the 1970s more than 1.5 million Portuguese had left their country) witnessed other political options in the countries where they went to work; the advent of mass tourism, especially in the Algarve, introduced the Portuguese to other customs; conscripts from isolated rural areas gathered together in barracks and engaged in discussion; membership of EFTA brought foreign companies and new ways of work; television, launched in 1957, opened Portuguese eyes to the world despite the constraints of censorship.

Salazar is an ambivalent and uncomfortable figure for the Portuguese. When public television ran a program in 2007 called *The Great Portuguese*, in which viewers voted for figures they thought had left the biggest mark on the country's history, everyone was expecting the winner to be one of those secular saints from the Age of Discovery who line the country's hall of fame: Vasco da Gama or King João II, for example. But the winner's envelope contained Salazar's name. The dictator had not even featured on the broadcaster's initial list of possible candidates, and though the vote for Salazar was perhaps mischievous, the outraged reaction to it was illuminating.

In popular lore the Carnation Revolution was the glorious, romantic moment when Portugal cast off its shackles and joined the European mainstream. Just about every city, town, and village has an April 25 avenue or street or square. What went before is hence troubling, especially when four decades passed with no significant popular revolt, and there is a reluctance to rake over the past.

In one of the most poignant expressions of how the past has been summarily left behind, the former secret police headquarters in Lisbon's Chiado quarter, in whose notorious cells thousands of suspects were tormented, was turned into luxury apartments in 2007. During the dictatorship the wife of the Brazilian ambassador, whose official residence was across the street from the HQ, complained about the cries coming from the building. The police told her she was mistaken—the screaming noise was made by the wheels of the tram that passed outside.

Chapter Seven
A Very Portuguese Coup
The Carnation Revolution

A lone soldier strides across fallow land in grainy, black-and-white footage captured by Portugal's public broadcaster RTP in the spring of 1974. He belongs to mutinous troops who have staged a coup to bring down the chafing dictatorship and he is approaching a garrison of loyalist holdouts. Girdled by townsfolk (men with long sideburns and flares, women biting their nails, fidgeting children) and pursued by a camera crew, the soldier pleads with an emissary sent out by the loyalists. "Join us," he urges. The loyalist hesitates: "No, really, I can't," he says with a glance over his shoulder towards the garrison. "My boss will be furious." They argue good-naturedly for a while, about politics, democracy and empire, all the while watched intently by the gathered locals, until the loyalist scratches his head, gives a deep sigh, grumbles that he will probably get into big trouble, and yields—"All right, then"—to cheers from the crowd. In this fashion, Portuguese history was made.

The Portuguese world was turned upside down on that partly cloudy Thursday, April 25, when most people were anticipating another humdrum workday. Tanks, armored vehicles, artillery units and lorries carrying hundreds of fully-armed combat-ready troops, many of them veterans of the war in Africa, had under the cover of dark fanned out across the capital. In an almost perfectly synchronized assault, the army pulled off a triumphant overthrow. Everyone—the regime, the people, foreign governments—was caught napping. The dictatorship shattered at the blow, the people rejoiced, and Western Europe witnessed its first revolution since 1848.

The uprising signified more than the swift dismantling of an unpopular regime. It was also a geostrategic inflection. The Carnation Revolution announced the end of 500 years of empire as before long Portugal quit its remaining overseas possessions and threw in its lot with Europe—a continent that had always been at its back. A straight line can be drawn from that day to January 1, 1986 when Portugal and the European Economic Community embraced.

Rejoicing at the Revolution: crowds celebrate the coup

Abroad, Portugal's sudden change of direction stunned its European and NATO partners. The military overthrow and the country's subsequent lurch towards communism pitched Portugal into the heart of Cold War conflict. Foreign journalists, who for years had paid scant attention to a country deemed to be Second or even Third World, quickly formed queues at the closed border, and when they were finally let in had to recruit interpreters to help with the unintelligible language.

For all the drama of that April 25, the coup cost only four lives—and none was at the hands of the revolutionary forces. The rebellion, indeed, had a very Portuguese flavor.

The historian Rainer Daehnhardt recounted a street scene he observed that day that exposed some of Portugal's intrinsic qualities. At a strategic crossroads in downtown Lisbon, three armored cars pulled up on one side of the street and five on the other. Each was under the command of a different section of the mutineers. They immediately started arguing about who was entitled to give the orders and who out-ranked whom. Their indignant yells and threats echoed off the low buildings as the tension mounted until one soldier shouted to the other group: "Mind what you do—I've got a wife and kids at home!" The dust quickly settled. In the end they spent several hours standing around, smoking cigarettes, chatting, and waiting for orders. Daehnhardt commented: "The Portuguese don't want to kill, they want to find a way of living together peacefully, as the whole of Portuguese history demonstrates." Amid the chaos of regime change, the Portuguese—expectant, worried, and out of their depth—muddled their way through and made it work somehow. Daehnhardt, like many, was fascinated by their "fabulous ability to adapt to circumstances and find a solution."

The wholesale, overnight emancipation unleashed a wave of euphoria, like a dam bursting, across the nation. A friend of mine who worked as a translator for one of those foreign journalists described the day as "a collective orgasm," to which the American reporter replied, "I can't print that. I work for a family newspaper." As the news spread, over the radio and by word of mouth, people stayed away from work, offices closed, and schools canceled classes. People began milling in the streets, at first hesitantly but soon joyfully, spontaneously climbing onto armored cars, jumping up and down and fêting the liberating soldiers. The full-throated jubilation was like that seen on VE day in London, or in France or Italy when Allied troops rolled into town. People who lived through the coup still recall vividly what they did that day.

The gates of the notorious Caxias prison in Lisbon were flung open and dozens of political prisoners ran out and into the arms of their elated families and friends. Newspapers rushed out special editions—the first entirely uncensored papers since the 1920s—throughout the day in an attempt to keep pace with developments. In Lisbon some placed red carnations in the barrels of soldiers' guns, lending the historical moment its iconic image and its enduring name: *Revolução dos Cravos.* There are various theories as to why so many carnations suddenly appeared: that they had been intended for a wedding that day that was called off because the registry office stayed shut; that a company exporting flowers gave away a truck load because the airport was closed; that a restaurant that was going to hand out the flowers to women clients on its first anniversary did not open so the waitresses gave them to soldiers; that street vendors spontaneously showered the soldiers with them. In any event, carnations were in season and flower sellers had plenty to go around.

The military takeover was as good as bloodless, to the astonishment of Spaniards, but there were some tense episodes. Soldiers rounded up suspected secret police agents at gunpoint in the street, sometimes making them partially strip. The worst moments came when a crowd cornered members of this despised cadre at their notorious headquarters in Lisbon's Chiado district. The agents, under siege by what they perceived to be a mob bent on revenge, opened fire from the building's windows on a crowd of unarmed civilians. Four young men were killed and about 45 injured. A plaque now commemorates the victims on the wall outside.

A few streets away Marcello Caetano, Salazar's successor, was holed up at the main barracks of the loyalist National Republican Guard in Carmo Square. He went into hiding there before dawn following a telephone tip-off and refused to come out of the thick-walled, four-story building for fourteen tense hours. Carmo Square became, unexpectedly, the epicenter of the coup. Unanticipated in the battle plan, the revolution's success suddenly hinged in large part on what happened in this downtown street, located in the city's shopping district. It was like a cinematic plot twist. A captain called Salgueiro Maia, who had initially deployed with his unit at the main square called Terreiro do Paço, was ordered to go and sort it out. He recounted the scene to Coimbra University researchers:

> As we went from Terreiro do Paço to the Carmo barracks I came across the biggest celebrations I've ever seen, and which it would be hard for me ever to see again. People were weeping and holding each other... When I get there there's a company of men standing on their vehicles and I wasn't expecting it and there's a jeep at the front of the column and a captain steps out of it. I go up to him and ask him, "So what are you doing here then?" And he says, "The government sent me here but I'm with you lot," so I told him to tag along.

Caetano's bolthole was promptly sealed off by tanks and crowds of curious onlookers pushing in at the back. Soldiers took up battle positions, in a crouch or lying down in the street like snipers, their muzzles trained on the building's windows. Bizarrely, men, women, and children stood or sat next to the troops, watching. As the crowd of spectators swelled to several thousand, some civilians climbed up trees and onto telephone boxes or shinned up lampposts to get a better view, as if it were a big soccer match. Some sang the national anthem. Radio journalists reported live from the scene. Salgueiro Maia, under orders to avoid bloodshed, urged those inside to come out with their hands up. He used a megaphone, which allowed the crowd to follow each development. Caetano dug his heels in, declining the advice of his advisers to hop over the wall and sneak out through the back, saying he would leave the way he came in as he ate sausage and chips for lunch. When he realized, by early evening, that the game was up he relented and agreed to sign a transfer of power. He refused to capitulate, however, to a mere army sergeant like Salgueiro Maia and so General António Spínola had to be driven over.

The coup leaders arranged for the fallen president to be taken through the building's narrow gate in an armored personnel carrier that was shut tight as a tin can and far less comfortable than his official car. The throng erupted in cheers as he left and surged forward shouting *Vitória! Vitória!* They banged on the side of the vehicle as it slowly pulled into the square. Inside, in the dim light, it must have been frightening. But while revolutions traditionally conjure up images of machine guns fired from the hip, bodies in the street, smoke and tear gas, the overthrow in Portugal produced few fireworks. There would be no arbitrary bloodletting, no noble suicides, no mob rule, no show trials. Caetano was dropped off at the airport from where he went with his family to the Madeira Islands and from there into exile in Brazil, where he died of a heart attack in 1980 and was buried in a Rio de Janeiro cemetery.

The conspirators had been sharpening their knives for months—since the previous year, in fact, when military disenchantment with the regime reached a critical mass. There were cloak-and-dagger meetings in an Alentejo barn and in an architect's atelier in Cascais, near Lisbon, where, astonishingly, almost 200 plotters crammed into the small room without drawing attention. Caetano sensed all was not well in the army but he had no intelligence about any concrete plans for an overthrow. The regime was blindsided.

Army Captain Otelo Saraiva de Carvalho authored the coup's operational plans, which amounted to three handwritten, almost scribbled, pages in blue ink. The trigger for the uprising was pulled at about twenty minutes after midnight: three civilians who had a regular freelance show at national radio station Renascença and who were sympathetic with the coup's aims and in league with its leadership, played the folk song *Grândola, Vila Morena* (Grândola, Dusky Town.) It was the cue for the plotters to take up arms and has ever since been a tune bound up with the revolution—one of those evocative pieces of music that conjure up precise memories of a time and place. It invariably provides the soundtrack for TV documentaries about the time.

The coup drew mostly on junior officers for its initial support and its leaders would become popularly known as the *Capitães de Abril* (Captains of April). When the signal to move had come over the radio these officers ordered the men under their command out of their bunks and told them to fall in because they had some news for them. Joy, it is said, was the broad reaction among the conscripts when they learned of their superiors' plans. Almost all the important army garrisons were involved; air force and navy officers had promised to stay neutral.

As dusk fell, so did the regime. At 7:50 p.m. a military communiqué declared the dictatorship dead. A proclamation fifteen minutes later informed the people that Portugal would now enter a transitional period and that the army would return to barracks while elections were prepared. "The Armed Forces Movement thanks the people for their civic attitude and the indisputable collaboration they have shown as events have unfolded—a clear sign that our actions reflected the nation's thinking and desires," it said.

In less than 24 hours, Portugal slammed the door on almost half a century of authoritarian rule. A newspaper cartoon portrayed a grateful man in traditional Portuguese dress with his arm around a soldier and holding a placard that read, "Better late than never." The country had tolerated the intolerable for too long.

The revolution is almost always referred to simply as "the 25th of April," or even just "April." It is shorthand from something bigger, something epoch-making in the same way the fall of the Berlin Wall is. The date went down as one of those grand historical episodes, a watershed like the regicide or establishment of the Republic 64 years earlier. The day has been a national holiday ever since.

The Portuguese got their first look at the previously anonymous ringleaders when a Junta of National Salvation appeared on television in full ceremonial dress at 1:30 in the morning on April 26. In a reference to Salazar's "Three Fs" (*fado*, football, and Fátima), the self-named Armed Forces Movement, MFA in Portuguese, promised to deliver what became known as the "Three Ds": democracy, development, and decolonization.

The public glee at the demise of the dictatorship carried to the following Wednesday. As part of Portugal's falling into line with most of the world, May 1 was declared Workers' Day, a national holiday, and an estimated half-million people came together on a sunny day in Lisbon for what turned into an electric demonstration of public support for the coup. Similar displays took place across the country. In the capital, soldiers in uniform mingled with banner-waving locals who, punching the air, chanted the mantra, O povo, unido, jamais será vencido! ("The people, united, will never be defeated!") They seemed drunk on freedom as they marched in a tight mass through downtown Lisbon and squeezed into a packed stadium. Politicians who returned from exile or came out of hiding gave hours of grandiloquent speeches filled with references to liberty, fraternity, and equality. People who were there still talk about that May 1 as a magical, unforgettable moment when everything seemed possible—and when everyone was on the same side.

Yet the only thing everyone agreed on was that they wanted an end to the dictatorship and the right to choose their leaders. Beyond that common denominator the direction of the new enterprise was less clear, and some restless Portuguese demons soon reappeared. The initial consensus quickly frayed, and the country was blighted by two years of political pyrotechnics. The post-coup period was fraught with crises that threatened to drag Portugal into civil war and bankruptcy.

"A New Portugal: Extremely Fragile"

By pushing aside the dictatorship and the whole way of life it represented, even going so far as to change street names, Portugal opted to start from scratch: 1974 would be Year Zero. But the post-Salazar attempt to reinvent Portugal was all the harder because established points of reference—cultural, political, economic—were removed. On top of that, while the Portuguese had abruptly swept aside the old order, the new order was not ready to govern. And in effect, there would be no tabula rasa because the past is never easy to escape; the new regime inherited a host of problems, not least a poorly educated people and an outdated way of doing things. A 1974 newspaper advertisement recommended: "Keep your money safe. Put it in a bank."

The revolution produced charismatic leaders. The gallery features such famous names as General Spínola, who made Time magazine's cover, occupied 28 years earlier by Salazar; the coup's military architect Captain (later Brigadier) Otelo Saraiva de Carvalho; and previously exiled party leaders Mário Soares, mild-mannered head of the Socialist

Party, and Álvaro Cunhal, the stern Stalinist leader of the Portuguese Communist Party. But while they were strong on idealism they had no experience running a country.

Soares and Cunhal, especially, engaged in gladiatorial political rivalry. They had returned to heroes' welcomes in the days after April 25 and were bellwethers in the post-revolution period, but swiftly became political antagonists. The May 1 celebrations were a case in point. Whereas in 1974 Soares and Cunhal shared the soccer stadium's tribune, it was the first and last time they would appear together at a rally, as they came to personify the dueling sides and friction between their parties intensified. On May 1 twelve months later, communist zealots landed punches on Soares as he tried to speak at a Workers' Day gathering.

Cunhal was a charismatic and imposing figure with thick white hair, jet-black eyebrows, and eyes the color of anthracite. An unbudging Stalinist who was top of his law class at Lisbon University, he was lionized by the party he led until 1992, and clung to his communist ideals long after the collapse of the Soviet Union. As one of Western Europe's diehard communists, Cunhal applauded the Soviet invasion of Czechoslovakia in 1968, praised the Soviet war effort in Afghanistan,

Álvaro Cunhal (white hair, center) leads a demonstration

and disavowed Mikhail Gorbachev's *perestroika* and *glasnost*. After the revolution he passed some of the Portuguese secret police's files to Lisbon's KGB officer (Cunhal always denied this, but the truth came out when Vasili Mitrokhin defected in 1992). It emerged in 1995, ten years before his death, that Cunhal had a hidden romantic, literary side: he had published a series of novels under the pseudonym Manuel Tiago.

After the regime fell the only two functioning organizations were the Communist Party and the Catholic Church. The Portuguese would have to learn the hard way, by arguing, by trying and failing, how to live together in a democratic environment. A sculpture by Portuguese artist José Aurelio depicts Portugal at the time as a wooden crate, cut in the shape of the country, and stamped with the date 04/25/74 as if it were being sent to the future. Stenciled on the side: "Contains a new Portugal. Extremely fragile."

The first of a string of civilian governments was appointed three weeks after the coup, but a clear doctrinal split had already emerged and would prove hard to mend. Which route should the country take: towards Olaf Palme's admired "Swedish model" of democratic socialism, as Soares and his moderate Socialist Party proposed; or Moscow-allied communism, which Cunhal's well-organized disciples, including some in the military, wanted?

While Portugal prepared for the promised elections, someone had to be put in charge. The MFA designated General Spínola as president and he took office in mid-May. His maiden speech made oblique reference to the double-edged sword of sudden freedom. "We serve democracy in order to serve Portugal in one of the most tragic and most glorious moments of its history," he said. The next day an interim government was sworn in. Its members stood for the kaleidoscope of new political colors, including Soares, Cunhal, and the liberal centrist Francisco Sá Carneiro. The prime minister was the distinguished lawyer Adelino Palma Carlos, who sounded a wise note of caution: "A revolution happens in a day; a change in the social structure is a job that requires extended deliberation and reflection."

The interim government lasted less than two months. In the torrid political climate of the day, nothing much could flourish. Over almost two years, six interim governments bore Portugal, with tormented duty, to its first general election. The balance of power was delicate and easily upset, and the memory of guns in the street was fresh. New parties and new demands sprouted like daisies in the post-coup soil. At one point 32 registered parties were involved in the political brawl, most tiny and on the left of the political spectrum, comprising an alphabet soup (OCMLP, FEC, PUP, etc.) of self-described Marxists, Trotskyists, Maoists, and Stalinists. The Trotskyist Independent Communist League proclaimed, with a seductive flourish, that no other party was further left. A certain radical chic attached to all this, which is why future European Commission president José Manuel Barroso in his Lisbon student days enlisted with the Maoist MRPP, Reorganizational Movement of the Party of the Proletariat. (There is nothing strange about Barroso's membership in such a group—a generation of Portugal's political leaders was caught up in the fanatical intensity of the time.)

Spikes in tension punctuated the march towards democracy as many Portuguese grappled with their new-found freedoms. Declaring that the gains of April 25 had to be safeguarded, the interim prime minister General Vasco Gonçalves aligned himself with the Communist Party and with Saraiva de Carvalho's COPCON, the new military command structure that was set up after the revolution and that did not shrink from beatings and intimidation. Saraiva de Carvalho was dubbed by the foreign press as "Portugal's most powerful man." He at one point wondered out loud whether it might not be better to round up all the country's "fascists," herd them into the Campo Pequeno bullring in Lisbon, and shoot them.

The Revolutionary Council overseeing the transition to democracy lined up behind the government's decision to decree a wave of nationalizations. It was a momentous decision. Banks and insurance companies were the first, followed by the transportation and communications sector, then steel, cement and chemical companies. Over sixteen months, 253 companies were nationalized as the state expanded and Portugal increasingly resembled an embryonic communist country. Many captains of industry—those families who ran the country's private and public sectors under Salazar and who had decided to risk staying on after the revolution—now fled, mostly to Brazil where a military dictatorship ruled. It was a migration reminiscent of the court's departure to Brazil at the time of the French invasions insofar as people who had run things now walked away from Portugal.

The nationalizations were part of the willed eradication of the dictatorship's apparatus. Seasoned officials were declared *personae non gratae* and purged from the civil service. Future prime minister Maria de Lourdes Pintasilgo, serving as Social Affairs Minister in 1974, recalled that she was handed a list of some 500 people to purge but, arguing that they were the only ones who had experience and that the country had a limited pool of talent, refused. Common sense and ideological correctness occasionally collided.

A torrent of dangerous developments gathered momentum after the March 11 decision to nationalize, stoking the superheated atmosphere of the middle months of 1975 that would become known as Portugal's "Hot Summer."

After decades of being denied a say, the Portuguese embraced democracy almost frenetically, organizing workers' committees, student committees, residents' committees. Passionate, finger-jabbing debate was the norm for months as those who once bit their lip or hid from the secret police could now shout their opinions at the tops of their voices. A recently-arrived foreign journalist who witnessed these scenes but who struggled to follow Portuguese made a mental note to ask for an interview with a man called "Pá" he had never seen but who was repeatedly mentioned whenever people argued. It must, my colleague thought, be someone powerful, some shadowy figure pulling the strings behind the scenes—a general, perhaps, or a KGB-linked politician. He soon learned that "pá" is one of those verbal ticks that people tack onto the end of sentences, like "know what I mean?"

Despite the deafening clamor of the Hot Summer, the country's leaders made good on their promise to hold elections for a Constituent Assembly that would be charged with drawing up a new Constitution allowing for general, presidential, and municipal elections a year later. Twelve parties stood in this ballot, the country's first election with universal suffrage, on April 25, 1975. After having no choice since 1926, people were suddenly presented with an abundance of campaign promises. The fractious political climate prompted scrawls of joking graffiti on city walls: "You vote for me and I'll vote for you," offered one. And, in a reference to the cork-popping fraternity that had given way to bad-tempered quarreling, another anonymous author observed: "The effects of the injection are wearing off!"

The weekly newspaper *Expresso* had reported in 1973 that 61 percent of Portuguese had never voted. The electorate set that right in the first ballot, which produced a huge turnout of 91 percent—a figure that reflected the people's engagement and sense of hope and that has never been matched. People recall that even teenagers at the time were engaged by politics. In a startling result, moderates won the day. The Socialist Party collected almost 38 percent, while the Communist Party came in third with less than 13 percent, behind the right-of-center PPD. For all the commotion, the Portuguese were still true to their un-extreme nature. And in all elections since then they have demonstrated an uncanny ability to make a sober diagnosis of the political climate and make the most pragmatic choice.

To win an election, however, was to be handed a poisoned chalice. Democracy was unfamiliar territory. Trying to rule Portugal at the time was like shouting for order at a wild party. The falcon, to quote W. B. Yeats, could not hear the falconer.

Despite the clean election, the constant rows showed no signs of abating and a crippling stalemate took hold. The Hot Summer was rich in confrontation. There were massive, intimidating street demonstrations. At one point, 1,000 of the army's automatic weapons were found missing. COPCON mounted roadblocks on roads into Lisbon and a state of emergency was briefly imposed. In an atmosphere of political persecution, people were rounded up on the pretext that they were defiling the virtues of April 25. COPCON's Saraiva de Carvalho signed blank arrest warrants that his men could use as they saw fit. The Spanish Embassy was ransacked. Parliament was twice surrounded by protesters and its members held hostage overnight. The atmosphere deteriorated to such a point that the exasperated prime minister announced that the government was going on strike. The Portuguese were riding a tiger.

General Vasco Gonçalves, a senior member of the Armed Forces Movement who was prime minister of four of the six interim governments over the year, groaned at the political strain that was stretching Portugal to breaking point. In a 1975 interview with Germany's *Süddeutsche Zeitung* he drew a parallel with the ruinous years of political upheaval at the start of the century that had ushered Salazar into the seat of power: "I never thought I would witness such party conflict," he confided. "I thought the parties had drawn lessons from the time of the First Republic and would heed them. But unfortunately they didn't learn much." Manuel Antunes, a priest and university professor, argued that the change had to go deeper. "We need a moral revolution," he said. "So that the 'old' society doesn't return and that the 'new' one doesn't perpetuate the mixture of hate and antagonism, opportunism and factiousness, utopias and chaos it has been so far."

Amid all this impulsive feuding the Constituent Assembly, given the task of authoring a new Constitution, sat for the first time on a Monday in June 1975. President Costa Gomes addressed the inaugural session at the neoclassical parliament building in the São Bento district of Lisbon. The gallery was packed with foreign ambassadors eager for clues about which way Portugal was heading. In his speech Costa Gomes set the bar rather high: "It is the task of geniuses to draw up a Revolutionary Constitution so advanced that it cannot be overtaken, so suitable it cannot be bettered, so inspired it is redeeming, so fair that it is worthy of the workers of Portugal," he announced.

Outside on the streets, ordinary people—for so long Portugal's have-nots—were shouting loudly for their rights. Duty, the bedrock of *salazarismo*, was a word seldom heard—now it was all about rights. Often at the urging of leftist parties the have-nots walked in and simply took over houses, farms, and factories. The newly-established right to strike was seized with both hands. Builders, metalworkers, national airline staff, and farmers walked off the job and, for good measure, blocked roads. It was a period crowded with incident. With the situation repeatedly threatening to spiral out of control, political leaders barely had time to catch their breath before the next crisis, much less plan ahead. They had to address the varied demands of belligerent trade unions, student delegations, and committees of vocal squatters. These were not the countercultural punks of contemporary London or Berlin but poor middle-aged people with children who walked out of their damp and draughty shanties and settled in abandoned brick houses. In October 1975 the Labor Ministry tried to extinguish some fires with an appeal that amounted to heresy: "Socialism, for now and unfortunately, will not be about earning more and working less; it may well be, amid this acute crisis, about earning less and working more," it announced in a communiqué. The strikes continued apace.

The longstanding Portuguese taste for disorder was generously indulged. University students refused point-blank to sit exams or be evaluated. There was an anarchic mood, especially at rock concerts, as youths who had missed out on the 1960s cashed in on the new permissiveness. Their high jinks were facilitated by cheap and potent marijuana that started arriving from the African colonies and that added some fuel to the proceedings. Teenagers felt free to skip classes, and university students, like workers, fragmented into rival political groups. The Union of Student Communists was known by its acronym UEC, which when pronounced as a word sounds like the Portuguese for "quack," so conservative students would mock them with a quacking sound. The UEC, predictably, branded their adversaries as fascists.

In this revolutionary crucible, the authorities attempted a redistribution of wealth. While workers were placed in charge of the companies that employed them, farmland went to laborers who had tilled it for decades. The policy of agrarian reform (Motto: "The land belongs to those who work it") expropriated roughly 1.2 million hectares, much of it belonging to the landed gentry—those few dozen leading families. One of the country's largest farms, Herdade do Machado, covering more than 6,000 hectares and resembling a little village, even with its own medical center, was divided between about a hundred of its workers, including clerical staff and mechanics. Such spontaneous decrees presented serious challenges to the legal system and the ramifications would be felt long after. In 2007, a years-long court case over who were the Herdade de Machado's rightful owners was still going on.

A fly-on-the-wall documentary of this period by the German director Thomas Harlan, shown at the Cannes film festival in 1977, depicted in miniature what was going on more broadly in Portugal. Harlan filmed events at a 3,700-acre estate called Torre Bela in the Ribatejo province northeast of Lisbon. The film is sometimes hilarious, often poignant, and always fascinating. Torre Bela, said to be the country's largest walled estate, was a huge hunting reserve, where the dictatorship and its friends (allegedly including the CIA and the South African security service BOSS) gathered. It was owned and run by the Duke of Lafões, who could have been a caricature of the country's Old School. With a rarified accent, in an opening interview, he speaks fluent French (whereas his workers probably could not even write Portuguese), conceding that he does not actually know how many people are employed on the estate. He flees abroad as, in his view, the country is going to the dogs. A rag-tag band of local people, including the unemployed and some ne'er-do-wells (about 500 people in all, representing the clichéd *Lumpenproletariat*) move in and take it over, guided by an agitator with a silver tongue who belongs to LUAR (Unified League of Revolutionary Action), a popular radical leftist group.

While in Lisbon there was cool political plotting, in the countryside events were usually more spontaneous. The rural population had been excluded from education by Salazar's policies and was largely made up of illiterate peasants. In the documentary, unsure of how to proceed now that they are in charge, they form a workers' committee to go and consult army officers at the local barracks and are told by a commander, "You have to write your own laws." A bulky farm woman's eyes well up with tears as the momentousness of what she is doing almost overwhelms her. At meetings on the estate they are exalted and all talk at once, but there is no violence. There is rather a tragicomic mixture of hope, desire, naivety, illusion, and faith. They step hesitantly, with reverence and awe, into the vacated manor house. Gradually relaxing, they flick through heavy coffee-table books, admiring the color pictures, rifle through drawers and try on outfits. A man picks clothes from a wardrobe, puts them on over his overalls and announces to giggles, "Now I look like a duke!" There are echoes here of the chateau-stripping that occurred after the French Revolution but, revealingly, the Portuguese did not as a rule match those extremes.

Cracks appear as the workers discuss who is entitled to what in the cooperative they have set up to run the estate. One episode wonderfully debunks the inflated political theorizing as one of the elderly male workers refuses a communist organizer's pleas for him to share his spade.

The exchange goes something like this: "Put that spade with the others," says the communist organizer. The worker demurs: "This is my spade. I paid for it." Communist: "It's not yours or mine any more, it's the cooperative's, everything belongs to the cooperative now." Worker: "The rest of them left their spades at home! They're keeping theirs while mine gets given to the cooperative." Communist: "What's that spade worth?" Worker: "You'll be taking my trousers and my boots off me next! At this rate I'll end up walking around naked!" Infuriated communist: "We're working together so that you'll have more clothes than you've got now, can't you understand that?"

Almost two years later, when the country was finally approaching stability, the army surrounded the estate, arrested the workers' committee and court-martialed the officers who had encouraged them. The duke got his land back.

Giddy Change

Against this tumultuous canvas, the 250 members of the Constituent Assembly admirably kept to the task in hand and worked out a new Constitution, which still stands today, with some key amendments. It established equal rights and freedoms—egalitarianism in answer to Salazar's elitism—a pluralist democracy, and was permeated with leftist ideology: the main means of production and farmland were to be collectivized, though it permitted private enterprise. The document of 103 pages contained 312 articles confirming Portugal's break with the four preceding decades. Echoing Marx, it grandly envisioned a "classless society" and the "socialization of the means of production." In what would prove to be a source of antagonism, it also decreed that the nationalizations were "irreversible conquests of the working classes."

The 1976 general election—held, of course, on April 25—delivered power to the moderate Soares. Two months later, General António Ramalho Eanes, a 41-year-old career officer and a political moderate, was elected president. The country completed its democratic process with municipal elections in November, which the moderate socialists also won. Moderation became fashionable.

Soares, who became prime minister (the highest executive political office in Portugal, where the president is mostly a figurehead), immediately endeavored to dampen the agitation and restore order. He spoke of the "naivety and careless imprudence" of the early post-revolution days. He insisted that the Portuguese "know that only work can save us, and that that requires discipline, respect for others, professional competence and deference to the necessary professional hierarchy." During 24 months of giddy change Portugal seemed, in a single bound, to have vaulted a generation. The sociologist Maria Filomena Mónica commented, "In the space of two years, the Portuguese lived through fifty years of history."

Political instability, however, had sent the economy into hibernation. In 1975 the economy contracted by more than 5 percent. The sight of tanks in the street, communists in the Cabinet and nationalization as a central tenet of economic policy gave foreign investors and businessmen a fright. Tourism nosedived. An international economic crisis caused by soaring oil prices compounded the problems of political paralysis. Wages went unpaid and the escudo was repeatedly devalued to keep Portuguese exports competitive. Recession set in and bankruptcy beckoned. The International Monetary Fund came to the rescue, providing a $750 million bailout in 1978.

Paul Krugman, the 2008 Nobel economics laureate, was among a group of students from the Massachusetts Institute of Technology who came to Lisbon in the summer of 1976 to study the Portuguese economy. Krugman told the weekly paper *Semanário Económico* in 2004 that Portugal "looked a lot like a Latin American country" of the time—a mess. Just obtaining reliable data and understanding what was going on was a formidable challenge, he said. He encountered a country that was sliding ever deeper into debt, where the state was handing out subsidies to numerous groups in a bid to shore up the government's popularity. State help for various sectors of society surged by 50 percent in 1976 and jumped by 86 percent the following year. The Portuguese were free but poor. In 1978 in Portugal there were 113 telephones per 1,000 people (compared with 220 in Spain) and 66 television sets per 1,000 (in Spain, 174).

The Portuguese still had trouble pulling in the same direction. The shared sense of purpose, so evident immediately after the coup, went out of focus. The first elected government lasted two years but the infant democracy was fragile and the following two years brought a flurry of five different governments, disabusing the Portuguese of any notion that democracy alone was the answer to all their problems. No government would achieve the comfort of an overall majority in Parliament until 1987. Given that politics is the art of the possible, the legislative records of the string of governments were patchy. Perhaps the greatest accomplishment during the late 1970s was the establishment, finally, of a welfare state, including universal health care and a pension system. Built up piecemeal since 1977, a national health service was established in law in 1979. A minimum monthly salary was also introduced.

The other "D," decolonization, kept a prominent place on the political agenda. The Portuguese made common cause with those abroad who also wanted to cast off the yoke of unwanted rule. In July 1974 Spínola had announced in a televised speech the intention to free the colonies, starting with warring Guinea-Bissau, Angola, and Mozambique. His historic address to the nation also amounted to an apologia of the Portuguese empire: "We are essentially a peaceful people who over the ages sought through adventure an easing of our needs. Yesterday, as today, it was the search in foreign lands for a better life which motivated Portugal in the pursuit of new worlds."

But making good on the promise to grant colonies their independence added another burden to an already considerable number of problems as upwards of 500,000 Portuguese returned to the homeland from Africa in the space of a year. The population of Portugal jumped by 7 percent; after the Discoveries 500 years earlier, the Portuguese had come full circle. The essayist Eduardo Lourenço remarked that decolonization was carried out at a "fabulous speed" as in months, and in chaos, the Portuguese came home. Many of these *retornados*, like the *pieds noirs* who had returned to France from Algeria the previous decade, arrived back with no houses, no jobs, and no money. At docks in the African colonies and in Lisbon, crates and suitcases were stacked up above head height as the exodus from Africa gathered pace. Two TAP Air Portugal planes performed an unprecedented airlift, but the government had to ask the United States for more aircraft. In Lisbon, the authorities had to find the *retornados* somewhere to stay. The government commandeered hotels and used military tents for temporary shelter, while families made space in their homes for relatives. Thanks to the abiding decency of the Portuguese people, the emergency did not become a crisis.

Once they had settled down, however, many *retornados* voiced their anger. Under the dictatorship, they had been promised land and a fresh start on the African continent and many had chanced everything. There was deep bitterness and lasting resentment about the way Portugal had abruptly, and somewhat untidily, uncoupled from Africa and handed everything over. Soares took a Panglossian view of the decolonization policy he supported, frowningly concluding that it was "the best possible way, given the circumstances." The plight of those uprooted from Africa and dropped back in Europe, and the resentment and suffering attached to it, have provided moving material for Portuguese books and films.

Apart from the catalogue of political, economic, and social problems, Portugal also found itself trapped in a Cold War diplomatic pincer movement. Washington and Moscow lavished rare attention on this revolutionary experiment roughly equidistant between them. In the United States, events in Portugal crystallized fears about creeping Soviet influence in Europe. A *New York Times* editorial in February 1975 sounded the alarm, warning that "a Communist takeover of Portugal might encourage a similar trend in Italy and France, create problems in Greece and Turkey, affect the succession in Spain and Yugoslavia and send tremors throughout Western Europe."

It was also believed that NATO could start to unravel if Portugal quit the alliance, though General Costa Gomes later insisted that the coup had the full, if tacit, support of NATO countries. Also, Portugal was privy to confidential NATO documents, especially nuclear weapons secrets, which might fall into Moscow's hands. And the United States was worried, too, about losing its strategic air base in the Azores—that enduring symbol of the twentieth-century transatlantic alliance and its benefits, which is why George W. Bush, Tony Blair, José Maria Aznar, and Barroso held a pre-Iraq invasion meeting there in 2003. US President Richard Nixon had a contingency plan drawn up that foresaw the establishment of a separatist Portuguese government in the islands if Lisbon became officially communist. Nor were the Americans the only ones worried by the strength of the Portuguese Communist Party. In July 1975 the conservative French President Giscard d'Estaing vetoed EEC aid for Portugal, which was racing towards bankruptcy, because of its government's leftist sympathies.

The coup had caught the United States unprepared. It had had no ambassador in Lisbon since 1973 and the administration was embroiled in Watergate. Six weeks after April 25, Nixon, on his way home from a Middle East trip, stopped off in the Azores for talks with Spínola, becoming the first foreign head of state to step on Portuguese soil since the overthrow. During the two-hour meeting Spínola assured Nixon that Portugal had no intention of leaving NATO.

Portugal, meanwhile, was receiving an unprecedented amount of attention from foreign dignitaries. The summer after the revolution, UN Secretary-General Kurt Waldheim caught a plane to Lisbon. In October, armed forces chief General Costa Gomes and Soares joined Nixon and Henry Kissinger in the Oval office for a forty-minute meeting, and Senator Edward Kennedy visited the Portuguese capital. In parallel, prominent Portuguese officials went on official visits to Cuba, meeting Fidel Castro, and to Yugoslavia for talks with Tito. Romanian president Nicolae Ceaucescu came to Lisbon. Costa Gomes also went to Moscow to meet Leonid Brezhnev in October 1975. In a four-hour chat, Costa Gomes later disclosed, Brezhnev confided that the Soviet Union would not risk a conflict with NATO over the Iberian Peninsula.

At the October 1974 meeting in Washington, Soares said, Kissinger expressed a conviction that Portugal was doomed to communist control: "Portugal is lost." The Americans were confounded by the Portuguese willingness to countenance parties of the radical left. Kissinger predicted that Soares would be the Portuguese revolution's equivalent of Russia's Alexander Kerensky, whose post-February Revolution government was eclipsed by Lenin's Bolshevik Revolution eight months later. Kissinger had cynically commented in 1970, referring to Chile's elections, "I don't see why we have to let a country go Marxist just because its people are irresponsible." But with little Portugal he took a different tack, tempted to write it off in the belief that its conversion to communism—and its inevitable decline as a result—would "inoculate" the rest of Europe against Soviet influence. The new US ambassador to Lisbon, Frank Carlucci, felt otherwise. He was sure that moderate democratic forces, especially Soares' socialists, would prevail—and the election results proved him right.

In the late 1970s and early 1980s Portugal's former African interests were neglected as the country focused its attention on getting into the EEC. Shrunken by the loss of empire, Portugal needed something just as big to cling to and give it scale. Looking away from Africa towards Europe (in Spain, it has been argued, a similar turn of the head began after the loss of Cuba in 1898), almost all political parties, with the notable exception of the Communist Party, backed joining the European club. The chorus of a popular song by rock band GNR in 1981 went, "I want to see Portugal in the EEC."

Some view Portugal's formal request for admission to the EEC in 1977 as the point of no return on its road to democracy. The commitment locked the Portuguese into something bigger, tethered it to a stabilizing influence and discouraged further in-fighting. Crucially, acceding to the Common Market became a question of national pride, of proving the foreign skeptics wrong.

In 1984 the daily paper *Diário de Notícias* gave a bleak review of what had been achieved in the decade since the dictatorship had been felled. The people had seen "disillusionment heaped on disillusionment," it said in an editorial to mark the tenth anniversary. "The civil service, the courts, education, health care have perpetuated—expanded, even—the Salazarist tradition of bureaucracy plus inefficiency." Nevertheless, it ended on an upbeat note: "Despite all the wrong turns, the mistakes, the rifts, there are things worth commemorating: freedom, for instance."

The socialists won another general election, in 1983, but they were cornered by an unfolding economic emergency that took Portugal close to rationing. The politicians' hands were tied by twin demands: those of the International Monetary Fund, which came to the assistance of the balance of payments once more but demanded traumatic economic measures, including deeply unpopular cuts in state subsidies; and the coveted membership of the Common Market, which compelled the country's leaders to exhibit political maturity and pursue modern policies. With no cards left to play, the main parties, the socialists and the social democrats, set aside their differences and formed an alliance known as the Central Bloc. Despite the stormy political seas, they kept their hands on the rudder and in June 1985, Portugal fell, gasping, into the arms of the EEC. They had made it.

The mad, glad days of homespun revolution brought out the best and the worst in the Portuguese character. The combustible atmosphere encouraged their anarchic impulse, but when it seemed that anarchy was indeed imminent their natural robustness and common sense prevented ultimate collapse. Portugal had again buckled but, once more, it did not break. As ever, it adapted. Carlucci, the former American ambassador, later saluted the relative peacefulness of the successful transformation from dictatorship to democratic European nation. "Portugal was an example for other countries and what it achieved was in fact unique in historical terms," he said.

Others have been less impressed. The historian João Medina claims that April 25 was a "failed" revolution because, while it established a formal democracy, the Portuguese did not grow into their new clothes. It is easy to see his point: the results of the only three national referenda

which Portugal has held, two in 1998 and one in 2007, were declared null and void because not enough people turned up to vote, even though the issues (abortion and regional powers) were emotionally charged and went to the heart of people's values and how they wanted to live. It was a far cry from the activism of the 1970s and was as if a private listlessness had settled on the country, as if the revolution had exhausted the democratic fire. Some say the Portuguese feel nostalgia for the future which the revolution promised but incompletely delivered.

The older Portuguese generation that lived under the dictatorship, though, is acutely aware of the revolution's benefits. For them, April 25 is talismanic. Every bank holiday on that date they hold marches and, brandishing red carnations, chant revolutionary slogans. But they also express resentment about how the younger generation enjoys the benefits while demonstrating little or no interest in finding out what others went through to get them. This generation gap came to light in a 1999 survey of students aged between eight and eighteen at a suburban Lisbon school. Teachers were shocked when some students described General Ramalho Eanes, the first elected post-revolution president, as "the last king of Portugal." (The excellent research carried out by the Center for April 25 Studies at the University of Coimbra is doing its best to correct this.)

Despite the forgetfulness, the political legacy of the revolution can still be felt in Portugal in the same way as the May 1968 watershed can still be detected in France, where politicians remain wary of the street. The mayhem—the collapsing governments, the demonstrations, the insurrections, the fanaticism and recriminations—left scars. Politicians who lived through, or are familiar with, the post-revolution years retain a certain timidity about pushing change too hard. The revolutionary experience has distilled into a reluctance to do anything that might provoke a repeat of that turmoil and circumspection about challenging other deeply entrenched attitudes and beliefs, such as workers' rights. Political stability is a cherished commodity. The country's leaders tend to be indulgent with reactionary pressure groups whose post-revolution sense of entitlement is unquestioned.

The revolution remains part of the political vernacular. High-minded talk of "rescuing April" or "consecrating April" can still be heard. To a foreign ear, it is a peculiar political discourse. To cite just two examples of this abiding political touchstone, both from late 2008: the right-of-center Social Democrat Party leader accused the Socialist Party of browbeating voters, commenting "We didn't have the April Revolution for that," and a retired former army chief of staff publicly warned that junior officers in the armed forces were deeply unhappy about the government's reform policies and that simmering unrest could boil over, bringing "very negative effects" for Portuguese democracy.

Still, with the Carnation Revolution, the future had—finally—arrived. Coca-Cola was authorized in 1976 and, as Salazar had predicted, those trucks began changing customs and accelerating the pace of Portuguese life, for better or for worse.

Chapter Eight
The Good Times Roll
Europe and the Boom

In the classified section of a Lisbon newspaper in the early 1990s a small ad for a house for sale listed the property's most becoming features and added, in bold type, a detail the owner clearly regarded as the clincher: "With view of highway."

Consumerism came to Portugal in 1986. Signing up to the European Economic Community that year brought a bonanza. Membership in the bloc furnished the country with all the modern accoutrements that other consumer societies had, and there was a kind of Rip van Winkle fascination with the newness of it all, including with highways, which elsewhere on the continent were commonplace. The first out-of-town shopping center, featuring the country's first McDonald's, opened in Cascais near Lisbon in 1991. Inside, elderly people from the surrounding countryside delighted in playing on escalators they had never been on before, giggling as they rode up and down and waved to each other. (The story went around that these people set up barbecues in the parking lot and rustled up some grilled sardines and wine. It may be apocryphal, but it could very well be true.) Also in the early 1990s, Portugal welcomed its first two private TV channels to bring some much-needed competition for the leaden public broadcasting.

A flourish of European leaders' signatures in suitably heavy books at the Jerónimos Monastery elevated Portugal to the Big League and spawned a period of optimism as the country prospered. It was an unfamiliar sensation but one the Portuguese quickly warmed to. Brussels sent over princely sums of money to help modernize the country—financial help that would, by 2006, amount to more than €48 billion. It was a fabulous harvest for a country of about ten million people and it brought a broad and pronounced improvement in the standard of living. Economic growth surged, allowing for huge public infrastructure projects, and catapulted Portugal's GDP per capita from 52 percent of the European average in 1986 to 70 percent within nine years. Interest rates

plummeted from post-revolution highs, placing loans for new homes, cars, and domestic appliances within the reach of many. They were the fat years.

Highways are the enduring symbol of those days of plenty and are perhaps the most striking illustration of the country's physical transformation. In 1986 Portugal had fewer than 123 miles (200 km) of highway. Twenty years later, it had more than 1,243 miles (2,000 km)—in a country about 348 miles (560 km) long and 137 miles (220 km) wide. It is no exaggeration to say that for a while motorists had to buy a new roadmap every year. Now you could travel from the northern to the southern tip in about six hours and from the west coast to Spain in under two. Before the highways there were plenty of people in Portugal—a small country—who had never seen the ocean or been to the capital. In 1991 a highway between Lisbon and Porto, which had started construction thirty years earlier, was finally completed. Aníbal Cavaco Silva, the prime minister at the time, commented as he cut the ribbon at the opening: "This is the image of the new Portugal—on the move."

Yet much of the change was cosmetic. Even as they celebrated their new circumstances, the Portuguese were sowing the seeds of their later demise. As with the riches that arrived from Brazil and the East during the Age of Discovery, they preferred extravagant spending to cautious husbandry. Distracted by the bounty, people went on a credit-fueled spending spree. Growth, rather than developing out of a new manufacturing base or an export drive, too broadly sprang from credit-based internal consumption—a well-known economic pitfall. Politicians invested in eye-catching, and vote-winning, public works projects in an economic development policy that would become known as *política de betão* (roughly, "the politics of concrete") instead of restructuring Portugal for the emerging challenges of a rapidly changing world. The historian and political commentator José Pacheco Pereira observed: "We have to recognize that in recent years much of our material well-being is due to the taxes of Germans, Dutch, Britons, and isn't the product of our own work, of wealth we generated ourselves." Therein lies a story.

The errors would make the early twenty-first century a painful time. But before the hangover came the party.

All the EEC's leaders were in attendance at the Jerónimos

Monastery to witness Portugal's accession ceremony in June 1985. It was a fittingly solemn occasion as one of the continent's oldest countries committed itself to the new Europe. "In these 400-year-old cloisters, the past and the future of Portugal come together," Mário Soares, then the prime minister, said in his speech. The daily paper *Diário Popular* announced in a front-page headline: "The modern adventure has begun." *Diário de Notícias* produced the sharpest observation, remarking that the ceremony "combined the features of a baptism, an affair of state, and a wedding."

Portugal had been knocking at the bloc's door for more than seven years, having opened negotiations with Brussels back in October 1978. It was no formality, as some of the EEC's member nations harbored serious misgivings about Portugal's suitability. On the one hand, its checkered modern history raised fears that it could be a political liability. On the other, the Portuguese economy was heavily reliant on agriculture and fishing—areas already overloaded within the bloc. Portugal, it was feared, might become a dead weight; it might subtract instead of add to the EEC. Soares later acknowledged that he had encountered some resistance: "It wasn't easy negotiating with our future European partners. The bill, for them, wasn't very appealing... For Portugal, there was no other strategic alternative."

Portugal won a period of economic grace, granted protection for the traditional sectors of its economy and, in tandem, funds for its modernization. But it would have to use the time and money wisely. Soares, in his speech at the monastery, while noting that adhering to the EEC was a hopeful moment, went on: "But let us not assume that this is the easy option. It will demand a lot from the Portuguese." It was a cautionary note repeated by senior officials worried that the Portuguese might look upon EEC membership as a windfall. The deputy prime minister Rui Machete made a pointed observation to Parliament that marked him out as a soothsayer: "What Portugal has negotiated does not allow it—in fact, much to the contrary—to believe that its future is assured and that the dynamism of more developed countries will be imparted to Portugal by some kind of miraculous osmosis." Cavaco Silva, who became prime minister in late 1985, recalled the Age of Discovery and the proven abilities of the Portuguese who are "able to face up to and meet the hardest tasks." "We now face a new challenge," he said. "It's up to us now, through our work, to make the most of the opportunities placed in our path."

Nevertheless, the breathless revolutionary period was now in the past. Europe was an open road and the Portuguese conducted themselves in an exemplary manner, winning praise from the former European Commission president Jacques Delors who dubbed Portugal a "good pupil" for the way it obediently accepted the EEC's tutoring. Brussels had taken the role of disciplined, demanding leader.

Portugal had an extraordinary amount of ground to make up. When it joined the EEC, its vital statistics were like those of a Third World country. It was buried under a pile of unwanted superlatives: lowest income, lowest industrial productivity, highest percentage of people living from agriculture, highest illiteracy rate, lowest welfare coverage, highest infant mortality, lowest life expectancy.

Portugal started driving down those numbers as Brussels bankrolled the country's fast-track development program. Infant mortality, which stood at an astonishing 18 per thousand births in 1960, was down to less than 6 per thousand by the end of the century. Over roughly the same period the number of people dependent on farming went from 43 percent of the working population to around 7 percent (600,000 agricultural jobs were lost, and abandoned farms are a common sight in the Portuguese countryside). Farming changed places with the services sector, including tourism, which shot up from 27 percent of total employment to more than half. The illiteracy rate dropped from more than 30 percent of the population in 1960 to 10 percent in 1996 (still high, though, and in 1991 only 13 percent of Portuguese said they read a daily paper, against the European average of 46 percent).

Even though by the start of the 1990s more than 90 percent of homes had electricity and drains and more than 80 percent had toilets, progress was uneven: in the Western Europe of 1995 Portugal had the lowest number of dwellings without a bath, hot water, or telephone. And in 1993 entire families were still living in an estimated 43,000 slum dwellings around Lisbon and Porto—in other words, 160,000 people, in late twentieth-century Western Europe, living in the kind of squalid conditions usually associated with Africa. Many were African immigrants who constituted the first wave of arrivals from the former colonies; others were migrants from poor rural areas of Portugal. All were consigned to low-paid blue-collar jobs. A re-housing plan was launched with the help of EU funds to shift these have-nots into unlovely high-rise blocks that have, distinctively, no balconies. A census thirteen years later found 15,000 families were still waiting to be re-housed.

In a 1991 article the French newspaper *Le Monde* reported, in shocked tones, that in northern Portugal there was still a two-year waiting list for home telephones. On the whole, though, the French newspaper decided that membership in the EEC constituted a "goodbye to tears" for the Portuguese. Portugal sprang smoothly from an economy based on family savings (the absence of a welfare state meant that people had to keep a nest egg) to one fueled by galloping consumption. Between 1990 and 2004 the number of vehicles on Portuguese roads surged by 130 percent, powered by easy credit terms. As the essayist Eduardo Lourenço remarked, "We have changed, literally, and almost without noticing, our world."

The New Portugal

Portugal, not surprisingly, swooned over the EEC. Given the net gain and material improvements it provided, it was—and is—extremely popular. In 1996, ten years after joining, a poll indicated that more than 80 percent of Portuguese felt that joining the European mainstream had been "extremely beneficial" for their country.

Dissenting voices are hard to find, even in politics. Only more radical elements on the left and right sounded an alarm that Portugal would be absorbed by its bigger European partners and would forfeit its national identity (the Communist Party stayed away from the Jerónimos signing ceremony in protest, leaving empty seats). Otherwise, as Barreto observed, such broad political consensus had not been witnessed since the establishment of the constitutional monarchy in the 1820s.

After the rough-and-tumble of the post-revolution years, Portugal settled into a cosily Manichaean political system where the electorate hands power either to the Socialist Party, which is a little left of center, or to the Social Democratic Party, which is slightly right of center. Sometimes conservative or leftist parties get a glimpse of power through coalitions or parliamentary alliances. The socialists are slightly more statist while the social democrats are fonder of unfettered private enterprise, but both the main parties champion welfare capitalism, tempering free-market economic policies with social concerns, and there is not a great deal to choose between them, the varying charms of their leaders notwithstanding. A communist member of parliament once likened it to a choice between Coca-Cola and Pepsi.

A key moment arrived in 1987. The social democratic prime minister Cavaco Silva, a gaunt bureaucrat who gained his economics doctorate at York University in England, had been in power for two years when opposition parties in parliament brought down his government with a vote of no-confidence. They had miscalculated: voters were disenchanted with political ploys, did not want to go back to the turmoil of the late 1970s and did not want their new-found well-being snatched away. In an outcome anticipated by nobody, in the subsequent general election Cavaco Silva captured that Holy Grail of Portuguese politics—an overall majority in parliament, handing him the power to remake Portugal. The political stability it generated proved to be a cherished asset, and Cavaco Silva repeated his landslide win in 1991.

The result was that the Portuguese economy crackled with life. And by plugging into the EEC Portugal had become a viable proposition: the head of the Confederation of Portuguese Industry commented in 1980, with a glance over his shoulder at the post-revolution nationalizations, that businessmen viewed membership as "a kind of full-cover insurance against political risk." Foreign capital and investors were lured to Portugal by its low labor costs and prices and the opportunities afforded by a poorly developed country that was just waking up. Portuguese political leaders imagined a country rich in high-grade industry brought by foreigners, and their blueprint looked like it might work when Ford and Volkswagen set up a huge car plant south of Lisbon. AutoEuropa, as the project was called, opened in 1995 and came to account for about 10 percent of Portuguese exports. Its executive director Ralph Rosignolo was thrilled: "One of the main reasons Ford and VW came to Portugal was the workers' ability to learn and adapt to our system." It seemed like a seal of approval for the New Portugal and an indication of the country's future trajectory. But it would be the exception that proved the rule. The plan fell short and Portugal moved swiftly from a mainly rural economy under Salazar into one disproportionately based on services.

Nevertheless, growth rates outpaced the European average, stoked by declining interest rates (in 1985 they stood at around 30 percent, but by 1995 were down to single figures) and declining inflation (down to 4.1 percent in 1995, from almost 20 percent ten years earlier). The lower interest rates placed cash within easy reach of new consumers. There was a sudden glut of Opel Corsas clogging city streets, while new apartment blocks went up as Lisbon's suburbs spread along the coast and back into the countryside. Foreign restaurants appeared and thrived. International rock and pop stars began including Lisbon on their expensive-ticket world tours.

The success proved a magnet not just for foreign companies but for Portuguese who had, reluctantly, forsaken their country. In the 1950s and 1960s hundreds of thousands of mostly uneducated Portuguese emigrated in pursuit of better-paid work, mostly heading to wealthier European countries. After the Carnation Revolution many captains of industry went to do business elsewhere, often to Brazil. Now the blue-collar workers and the entrepreneurs came home. Foreigners followed them as Portugal switched from a country marked by emigration to one that drew immigrant workers. Bizarrely, there were now Ukrainians treading grapes in Douro Valley vineyards. The turnaround seemed almost complete.

António Champalimaud was one of those who had prospered under Salazar. In the 1940s and 1950s he had built up an empire of steel and cement companies in Portugal, Angola, and Mozambique. In the 1960s he added a bank and insurance companies and was considered the seventh wealthiest man in Europe. When the coup erupted he fled to France and then Brazil. In his absence his companies were nationalized. Undaunted, he began rebuilding his fortune in Brazil through farming and cement enterprises. He came back to Lisbon in 1992, gradually bought back into his banking and insurance businesses, and left a €2 billion fortune when he died in 2004. He bequeathed a quarter of that to a Lisbon-based foundation in his name dedicated to medical research.

Champalimaud's buy-back was eased by two hotly-contested government policies that represented another symbolic break with the past. Bowing to European peer pressure and defying protests from leftists who complained that the "conquests of April" were being rolled back, Cavaco Silva's government needed all the political power it possessed to slaughter a sacred cow: a law was passed to permit the re-privatization of companies that had been seized by the state. Adding insult to injury, in the view of the plan's opponents, compensation, too, was provided to those whose assets had been snatched away.

Tourism pulled out of its steep post-revolution decline and resumed the growth it had promised with the advent of mass tourism to the Algarve in the late 1960s. As the Portuguese economy gathered speed, hitting growth rates above 7 percent, curious foreigners came to look for themselves at this southern European dynamo; the number of vacationers doubled from 5.6 million in 1986 to almost 11 million in 2004. The Portuguese, too, soon began to have enough money in their pockets to go away on package holidays whereas even in the 1980s those crossing paths on roads abroad would flash their headlights at each other in greeting: it was a novelty to see compatriots touring Europe at their leisure.

As prime minister, Cavaco Silva took up Margaret Thatcher's torch of popular capitalism. A privatization drive was a tremendous success as the sell-off of blue-chip companies offered easy rewards to anyone who could afford a modest investment. By 2006 the privatizations had raked in about €24 billion, and publicly-owned businesses declined to just over 10 percent of the economy in 1995, from almost double that in 1988.

Amid the euphoria, the stock market boomed. In 1996 business on the Lisbon Stock Exchange was 35 percent up on the previous year. In 1997, it was 75 percent up and at the end of that year the Portuguese capital's stock market was upgraded from emerging market to developed, providing it with another shot in the arm. Foreign investors poured $2.5 billion into Portuguese stocks in 1997—a 50 percent rise on the previous year. Project finance flourished as did real estate speculation in this apparent land of plenty, which was gradually becoming gentrified. Capital was in abundance for new companies, delivering more choice, more jobs, more wealth. Such things had never been seen.

Mergers, reorganizations, and modernization brought a much-needed facelift for banks and placed the financial sector among the continent's most innovative. Exhibiting their proverbial adaptability as they skipped across banking generations, the Portuguese quickly took to ATMs, which appeared in large numbers along city streets and offered an unusually broad range of functions, including the payment of household bills, the purchasing of train tickets and the payment of taxes. (Despite the benefits there are few things more irritating than being stuck in the ATM line behind someone who wants to do all these together.) It is not hard to comprehend the Portuguese appetite for swift change—in the late 1980s people still endured patience-testing bureaucratic procedures whenever they went to their local bank.

The fast-paced development and membership of the EEC magnified Portugal's international status. When Cavaco Silva went on an official visit to Brazil in 1990 he was no longer the leader of a faded and shabby former empire whose people were viewed as *barrigudos, de bigode, e baixinhos* ("pot-bellied, moustached, and short"). The success seemed to go to Cavaco Silva's head, however; he once memorably remarked, "I'm never wrong and I rarely have doubts." His popularity sagged. In a 1995 general election Portugal traded this steely technocrat for a more personable socialist rival—perhaps, with hindsight, not the wisest choice for a people who confess that they benefit from a firm hand. Socialist leader António Guterres, a kindly and intelligent man with a sincere desire to position Portugal in the European mainstream, favored a red rose symbol over his party's traditional red fist and rode a wave of optimism into the São Bento palace. There was a gathering impression that while under Cavaco Silva the economy was, for the most part, making progress, there had been less success addressing some of those unwanted superlatives, a feeling that more could, and should, be done to help those being left behind. After Salazar's "3 Fs" and the Carnation Revolution's "3 Ds," the Portuguese now were promised—in a tidy alphabetical rounding-out—the new prime minister's "4 Es": education, employment, the economy, and equality. Guterres was speaking partly in jest—

equality starts with an "i" in Portuguese—but his proposals resonated with many. He declared to cheers that, within the space of a generation, he wanted to see Portugal on a par with its European partners.

The "Golden Year"

Everything seemed possible. The country's self-confidence was galvanized in 1998, which then-president Jorge Sampaio dubbed "Portugal's golden year." In those twelve months Portugal cleared the fiscal hurdles for admission to Europe's new euro currency; José Saramago became the first Portuguese-language writer to win the Nobel literature prize; and Lisbon hosted the final world fair of the century, Expo 98, which neatly coincided with the 500th anniversary of Vasco da Gama's pioneering voyage to India. These were totems that instilled a sense of triumph. "Portugal is in fashion," Prime Minister Guterres announced.

World fairs had become something of an anachronism by the late twentieth century but Expo 98 was primarily about reinforcing Portugal's credentials. "Expo 98," Guterres said, "will make the Portuguese proud of what this demonstrates about our ability to organize, to build, and to achieve." The $2.4 billion event, requiring the most ambitious urban renewal in Lisbon since it was leveled by the 1755 earthquake, was a test that the country passed with a flourish. The fair's centerpiece was the second-largest oceanarium in the world. Its American designer Peter Chermayeff declared himself impressed by local engineers and workers who got it all ready in time. He recounted a story about how a giant piece of thick glass supplied by a Japanese company turned out, when fitted into place, to be the wrong size by a few centimeters. In a panic, the engineers went back and checked the plans, only to learn that the Portuguese had got it right and that the famously efficient Japanese had erred.

The fair itself drew seven million visitors over its four months—a large number, but significantly fewer than hoped for. Poor marketing abroad, which plagues Portuguese business, was largely to blame for the shortfall in foreign visitors. Among the Portuguese themselves, modest attendance could be blamed on a national trait that survived the broad

Vasco da Gama bridge, Lisbon

modernization: the tendency to leave things until the last minute. Organizers had predicted an average of 140,000 visitors a day to the fair but for the first three months received only about 30-40,000. In the final few days, however, people woke up to the fact that Expo 98 was about to end and started pouring in. The last day brought more than 200,000 visitors, causing traffic jams that stretched across to the other side of the city.

Expo 98 was part of a wider 840-acre urban regeneration program and a major city facelift. The project included a breathtaking new bridge over the Tagus, stretching more than ten miles and named—inevitably—after Vasco da Gama. This emblem of the new Portugal (and EU money) was inaugurated with a record-setting bean stew for 15,000 people seated at tables along its length. At the same time, an expansion of the Lisbon underground system doubled the size of the network to four lines at a cost of $2 billion. The giant drilling machines that burrowed beneath Lisbon came across 2,500-year-old artifacts, including a huge Roman hippodrome where chariot races, like those portrayed in the film *Ben Hur*, were staged. New high-speed trolleys debuted on the capital's streets and new expressways ringed the city. The regeneration was called Lisbon's "Big Bang." Porto, meanwhile, resented Lisbon's development windfall, even if the northern city could not complain too much, as it was given the magnificent Contemporary Art Museum of the Serralves Foundation, by Portuguese architect Siza Vieira, and Dutch architect Rem Koolhaas' exhilarating Casa da Música concert hall, one of the world's most striking modern buildings.

Joining the euro further embellished Portugal's prestige as, with relish, it proved the doubters wrong. Foreign governments had contemplated the country's record and, Prime Minister Guterres disclosed, scoffed at the possibility of it making the grade for membership in the exclusive club. Because the endeavor was successful, the riskiness of the gambit at the time has been forgotten, but the implications of failure would have been profound. In a sense, the criteria for membership of the new currency were not especially challenging; they essentially required fiscal discipline and responsibility. Yet it was a significant test for Portugal where the public purse has often been shamelessly picked for political advancement. Somehow Guterres had to curtail the natural impulse for reckless spending and with this aim in mind recruited a professional auditor and university professor called António Sousa Franco as his finance minister to administer the financial medicine. Sousa Franco pruned state spending through strict budgeting and close financial oversight. It was not always smooth going. He came under intense pressure from politicians worried about their re-election chances, and Prime Minister Guterres famously had to take him out for tea one Sunday afternoon to the elegant Seteais Palace hotel in Sintra to talk him out of resigning.

But Portugal accomplished what Guterres had termed "our chief national goal." Inclusion in the currency project symbolically shifted Portugal from the hinterland to the heart of Europe. It confounded the skeptics and proved its mettle. A long historical tide seemed to have turned. And yet...

The positive official narrative had a dark subplot. Coimbra University sociologist Boaventura Sousa Santos accused politicians of creating the illusion that Portugal was now like the rest of Europe. "However, when you look closely... it's easy to see that reality is heading a different way from the speeches," he said. The same thought had occurred to António Barreto, another sociologist. "We are a small country going through big changes," he said in 1998. "And yes, so far we have been very successful. But while things are incomparably better than twenty years ago, Portugal is still fragile and is still very much dependent on Europe." Beneath the well-to-do exterior, all was not well.

If EU aid was supposed to act like an injection of a growth hormone, it also had the effect of a narcotic. Sated by abundance, Portugal grew fat instead of building muscle. (And, extending the metaphor further, when the twenty-first century came around Portugal was too out of shape to compete.) Core problems went unaddressed or, when they were confronted, measures for reform were blunted by an entrenched sense of entitlement. Attempts to refit Portugal, especially its traditional industries such as textiles and footwear, which were major employers, particularly in the north, advanced slowly. Productivity in the mid-1990s was languishing at 65 percent of the EU average (in

Spain, it had surged to 90 percent). Industry was slow to take up new technology that could have kept it ahead of the curve. Globalization sharpened competition and the arrival of new EU members in Eastern Europe removed much of the international attention previously lavished on Portugal.

Old problems gnawed at the nation: levels of school education, professional training and adult learning were still among the continent's lowest. Rigid labor laws dating from the immediate post-revolutionary period remained in place. The inefficient legal system was choking and the even more inefficient welfare system was creaking. The state was as bloated as ever and its red tape tripped up progress.

Political traditions also stood in the way. A time-honored convention dictated that whenever a new party took office, it replaced senior civil servants and heads of public companies with its own apparatchiks, curtailing any continuity of policies and strategies. Guterres tried to stop what many commentators view as pork-barrel politics, devoid of a broader vision, telling a meeting of Socialist Party delegates after his election, "No jobs for the boys" (he said it in English). He was met with a stunned and stony silence by an audience anticipating a spree of favoritism after years in political opposition. Guterres' creditable ambition failed and when he resigned in 2002 he grumbled something about a "political swamp."

Especially in small rural towns where relations are more personal than official, local politicians kept their hands on the EU purse-strings and indulged in rash and frivolous spending that perpetuated patronage and nepotism. Enduring wealth-generation was too often neglected. The head of the National Audit Court acknowledged in 2008 that "many infrastructures were built for no one." It was a manifestation of the bridges-to-nowhere syndrome. Barreto remarked about the squandering of EU funds: "The notion that there's free money... was an incentive for promiscuity, corruption and irresponsibility... Millions and millions were handed out uselessly." He observed that political parties had cashed in on the possibility of immediate returns—"whatever's easiest, whatever makes the biggest splash, whatever's quickest."

The EU was supposed to forge a new Portugal, as if poured into a mold, and the Portuguese undoubtedly live better today than, say, twenty years ago. In another sense, however, everything and nothing has changed. Looking back from the twenty-first century, the first decade or so of Portugal's membership in the bloc looks like an historical interlude, its success a flash in the pan. Hard times were, once again, just around the corner. After the vertiginous growth and the euphoria of 1998, several years later the Portuguese would be feeling chastened, uncertain, and even embarrassed. From "good pupil" Portugal would soon be held up as an example of what not to do.

The Portuguese, after all, did not heed the warnings that EU membership could be a mixed blessing. And payment for their mistakes would fall due the next century.

Chapter Nine
Gentle Anarchists
Portugal's Peaceful Disorder

In Portugal traffic signs say "Stop" instead of using the equivalent Portuguese word, which is *Pare*. With that in mind, a friend once told me about a white-knuckled taxi ride he survived in Lisbon. The driver, much to his passenger's alarm, went hurtling through a junction where he was supposed to give way. When my friend pointed out that it might be wiser to obey the traffic signs, the driver replied over his shoulder, "'Stop' isn't a Portuguese word!" and erupted in gales of laughter as he sped down the street. For the taxi driver, the existence of traffic signs in a foreign language was just more evidence of how bizarre life can be in Portugal. The Portuguese have a saying that offers advice on how to deal with their country's sometimes baffling irrationality: "Laughter is the best remedy." The taxi episode would barely be worth mentioning if it did not offer a glimpse of the peculiarities that run through Portuguese society.

Portugal is closer to Africa than to Brussels, and the Portuguese carry in their blood the legacy of 700 years of Arab occupation as well as the rebelliousness of that *ur*-Portuguese Viriathus. They espouse, or at least consent to, what in northern Europe would be regarded as a disorderly way of life. The twentieth-century Portuguese poet Jorge de Sena thought his compatriots were "the most anarchic people in the world."

A cavalier attitude towards the notion of order is perhaps most conspicuous in Portugal's rural clutter. Provincial towns appear to have been planned on the back of a napkin, over lunch. Even places containing remarkable architectural and historic gems, such as Tomar with its twelfth-century Convent of Christ, are disfigured by slovenly urban design. "Tomar is ugly," my (Portuguese) wife sighed as we drove through. It is an oddity captured by Daniel Blaufuks in his 2006 documentary "Slightly Smaller than Indiana," which catalogued landscapes the Portuguese director described as "adulterated." The overriding impression is one of sloppiness—a cue for that perennial question: who's

Sense of the absurd: graffiti in Lisbon

in charge around here? "We like to live in disorder," says the writer and columnist Clara Ferreira Alves.

Portugal has long had a government ministry in charge of territorial planning. In at least one sense, however, its administrative endeavors have backfired. A university professor who at the time was secretary of state for territorial planning acknowledged in 2007 that the authorities had created a monster—"a bureaucratic world nobody can figure out." He went on: "Our planning system is slow, complex, bureaucratic and not very open to scrutiny at all... The system appears to have been invented by someone who didn't want any planning in Portugal."

The authorities in 2007 confessed to another mind-boggling mystery: nobody knows who owns 20 percent of the country. That anomaly contains part of the explanation for the calamitous wildfires that have blackened large swathes of Portugal's forests during recent summers. The forests are unkempt. Many landowners do not adequately clear brush nor dead wood and seldom go to the trouble of creating fire breaks that would help control the blazes. A study by Lisbon University published in 2008 found that the apathy was a main contributory factor to the massive forest fires of 2003 and 2005, when the authorities blamed the scorching heat and lack of firefighting equipment for the devastation. "The blame for the fires lies with us, the Portuguese, because we allow this kind of disorderliness," said the professor who organized the study. "The problem wasn't caused by this or that government. It stemmed from forty years of collective negligence." The government announced in 2006 it would start updating the national land registry, but two years later the World Wildlife Fund said that at the rate the inventory was advancing it would be another fifty years before it was complete.

Official muddle opens a door to malfeasance, big and small. Some suspect that part of the explanation for the laxity in urban planning lies in the murky relationship between construction companies/real estate developers and political parties. (The biggest chunk of party financing comes from those sources.) At a lower level, Portugal has a chronic problem of dumping waste. Rare is the rural road that has no pile of builder's rubble amid the greenery. I once confronted someone dumping bits of brick, broken porcelain, and bathroom piping from a truck at the side of the road near my house and was met with the thick accent of an Eastern European immigrant laborer, doing the dirty work for his Portuguese boss, who shrugged and said, "This is Portugal."

✓ One thing most Portuguese will always be is late. In 1984, when Portugal was on the cusp of EEC membership, *Newsweek* magazine published a country guide that recommended people turn up for appointments 15-20 minutes late, to avoid long waits. And to do business in Portugal, you have to open a meeting by chatting about the weather, your family, or a surprisingly tasty meal at a little-known restaurant, for example, before getting down to brass tacks. Also, the Portuguese do not eat as late as their Spanish neighbors but, compared to northern European habits, they tend to save themselves for late evenings. Concerts and films start at 9:30 or 10 p.m. on weekdays, as do soccer games. I recall shortly after I arrived in Portugal some Portuguese friends suggested we go out. We met at my house and sat around having a few drinks. As time went by I noticed it was past midnight already so assumed we were no longer going out and kicked my shoes off under the table. About an hour later, after 1 a.m., someone sat up and said, "Right, shall we head off then?"

So much for those one-time fears that European bloc member countries would end up forfeiting their national identity. Truth be told, the cross-fertilization has been very uneven.

The Portuguese, of course, are perfectly aware of their foibles, and newspapers, magazines, and websites feature special sections for funny

photographs taken by readers called, with deliberate irony, *Portugal no seu Melhor* (Portugal at its Best). Mostly these show absurd signs along roads, such as traffic signs standing next to each other that tell you to go both ways at once. In one instance, a placard for an EU-funded construction project says, "Total cost: €4,000; EU share of cost: €5,500." One website carries hundreds of these comical photos.

The historian João Medina has described his fellow countrymen as "gentle anarchists" because this waywardness does not translate into aggression or malice or violence. The Global Peace Index for 2009 placed Portugal fourteenth in a list of 144 countries.

The Portuguese are, on the whole, a conservative people and elaborate, old-fashioned courtesies are still common. In fact, the Portuguese can be excruciatingly formal, especially the older generations. When two elderly acquaintances cross paths in the street they enact a ritualized social code of greeting that is like a dance by exotic birds. Forms of address can be archaic and are exquisitely calibrated (the Portuguese rarely pass up a chance to complicate something straightforward). There is no cover-all-contingencies word like "you." The way you are addressed depends on your intimacy with the other person, your social standing, even your demeanor. Most weirdly to foreign ears, people may address each other obliquely, in the third person, so you get someone asking someone else about their health like this: "How is Mr. Architect today?"

Driven Mad

As ever, though, there is contradictory evidence. No doubt the gloomiest by-product of this anarchic way of life is the number of lives lost on the country's roads where mild-mannered individuals mutate into fiery balls of fist-shaking, foul-mouthed fury, as if tarmac were a potion that unlocked all their simmering rage and frustrations. Someone once described behavior on the roads as a kind of "undeclared civil war." Portuguese figures for traffic deaths have for decades been among the worst in Europe. Between 1977 and 2007 more than 60,000 people died on the roads, about a fifth of them pedestrians—that in a country of 10.6 million people. In an article in 2001, the leading weekly newspaper *Expresso* suggested that the figures were even worse than they appeared because if someone is involved in a road accident and dies only later in hospital, they are not logged in the road casualty column of official statistics.

The thousands of miles of new highways built since Portugal joined the EEC in 1986 are an invitation hard to decline. The reckless streak in the Portuguese at once relished the long, smooth roads, as appetizing as race tracks. It is not at all uncommon to see cars weaving between lanes at breakneck speed or cars pulling, literally, to within inches of your rear bumper and flashing their headlights in an attempt to intimidate you into getting out of their way. The US State Department offers some advice for foreign visitors to Portugal: "Drivers should use extreme caution, as local driving habits, high speeds, and poorly marked roads pose special hazards." It is as if the Portuguese are placing their faith in a higher (divine) power to save them from themselves.

Typically, nobody accepts blame for the carnage on the roads, as everyone is a great driver and beyond reproach. As the poet Fernando Pessoa complained in a more general context about his fellow countrymen, "It's never possible to find out who's to blame: it's always the sixth person in a group of five." There is also a large degree of machismo attached to the helter-skelter driving style. Travelling with my wife at the wheel is an instructive experience. Occasionally, when she overtakes a male driver, the man will look daggers, put his foot to the floor and go flat out to get back in front, even if he is in an old beater that is shaking violently and the hub caps are flying off.

More broadly, there is something tragicomic about the chaos and the way the Portuguese blithely go on living in it. The daily school drop off is a case in point, where parking outside school gates is a free-for-all. People abandon their vehicles on the pavement, on grass verges, they double-park, they leave them in the middle of the road with the warning lights flashing, they block in the cars of other parents who are trying to get to work.

Anarchic parking is not limited to school drop offs. The annual Portuguese Cup final is held at a Lisbon stadium alongside a highway and, inevitably, fans used to park their cars on the hard shoulder for several miles and nonchalantly walk away until one year police finally stopped the practice by putting up barriers. In the city center pedestrians often have to slalom between parked cars strewn across the pavement, even on the street outside police headquarters. The Portuguese are disarmingly candid about all this. How many times have friends and family, confronted by my reluctance to park on the pavement or break the speed limit, urged, "Go on, this is Portugal!"

As crazy as all this sounds, there is something bewitching about it. The Portuguese give the impression of being unfettered, free-spirited. It is as if it is all a great lark, and it is seductive—who would not like to live a carefree life? It has captivated tens of thousands of expatriates who live and work in Portugal, even while they recognize that it is a double-edged sword. They have learned to take the rough with the smooth, and when they do the arithmetic the good points outweigh the bad. The essayist Eduardo Lourenço commented that, despite all their faults and troubles, the Portuguese remain "insolently happy"—a trait recorded by Mark Twain in his nineteenth-century Azores visit. It is a winning mentality in some ways, infuriating in others. When the 250th anniversary of the devastating 1755 earthquake came round, I asked people in the older parts of Lisbon whether they were worried about it happening again. Everyone gave the same reply: it is in God's hands, there is nothing we can do about it, so why worry? Then they gave me a broad smile. It is not hard to see why—when your destiny is out of your hands you are relieved of responsibility, you can relax. Disaster management experts are infuriated by this attitude because it obstructs their efforts to get people to prepare for the worst.

There is a general sentiment among the Portuguese that they do not have to obey, or certainly do not need to, because the law is an ass. Jorge Sampaio, when he was president between 1996 and 2006, grumbled that the country's laws were treated like rough guidelines, not rules. For many years anyone with outstanding parking fines used to keep their fingers crossed for a papal visit when, according to custom, the president granted an amnesty for misdemeanors. In truth, so much goes unsanctioned. Portugal's ombudsman admitted as much in a newspaper interview in 2007. "Portugal doesn't have a tradition of legality and the state is the first to set a bad example," he conceded.

A classic example of this ambivalence towards the law came in 1999. A small town called Barrancos on the border with Spain had for a long time deferred to a local tradition of killing the bull in bullfights, aping the Spanish custom in defiance of a 1928 Portuguese law that forbids it. Even though Barrancos flouted the law, it went on with the full knowledge of—and, indeed, in full view of—the local authorities and the police, who simply turned a blind eye. When anti-bullfight campaigners and the media protested, the government simply granted the town an exemption from the law. In essence, people there were choosing not to obey the law, so the law was altered to cater to the illegality of what was going on. It was an interesting approach to jurisprudence.

That is a circumstance that draws to the surface the Portuguese rebellious streak. It feeds a pride at being crafty enough to hoodwink bigger adversaries, including all forms of authority. During a tense semifinal soccer match at the European Championship in 2000, when Portugal was playing France and just about the whole country was watching the evening game on TV, an unscrupulous developer near Lisbon sent crews with bulldozers to tear up scores of cork trees that stood in the way of his real estate project (one needs official permission to cut down a cork tree). It is known in the vernacular as being a *chico esperto*, or smart-alec.

Rebels without a Cause

Contrariness dwells deep in the Portuguese soul. In the elevator of a Lisbon building once I overheard a group of office workers complaining about some new rule they did not like and one of them commented, "A good Portuguese always dissents." They all laughed. The nail had been hit squarely on the head, and their skepticism about authority provided a sense of complicity that is an abiding national bond. The German author Hans Magnus Enzensberger discerned in this behavior "a kind of silent sabotage which doesn't stem from rage, conviction, rancor, ideology, stubbornness, like in other countries." It is as if the Portuguese are rebels without a cause, ready to unleash the untargeted revolt of the downtrodden. And the rancor does exist. In one of the most accurate concise descriptions I have ever encountered about Portugal, the poet Miguel Torga in 1950 described his country as "a peaceful collective of outraged people." The Portuguese feel that destiny has dealt them a poor hand and they shake their fist at their lot in life, but they do not as a rule express this indignation in a constructive way. They became mavericks for whom sidestepping the law offers the thrill of successful transgression. If public services such as the legal system, schooling, and the national health service were better run, the people would feel cared-for, as if there were someone in charge making sure they were all right. Instead, they feel fooled, short-changed, and inclined to seek revenge through misbehavior. It is a tame insurrection.

Disobedience long manifested itself in chronic tax evasion, especially by small businesses. While the great majority of people abide by the law and pay what they have to, avoiding taxes has been a way of hitting back at the authorities who are conspiring to repress the ordinary citizen. João Vieira Pereira, a newspaper columnist, noted: "The taxpayer who evades the taxman in order to fill his own pockets continues to be the classic Portuguese hero." The system is so infuriatingly unfair that it is asking to be duped. Though many people live on shockingly low wages, official statistics conceal the fact that many people work on the side and do not declare their full income. When old-age pensions may be as low as €200 a month, the elderly who are officially retired keep working on the sly to make ends meet.

The writer and columnist Miguel Esteves Cardoso once commented that in Portugal "to be good is to be a revolutionary." He pointed out that because the state is "slow and stupid" there is always a temptation to skirt it whenever possible. The Portuguese need to be infinitely agile. Engaging with officialdom is burdensome and an often painful waste of time. Corruption creeps in here, though that disagreeable word is often employed for what in fact is just an informal (i.e. unofficial-cum-illegal) way of simply getting things done, an indispensable bending of the rules. A joke going around some years ago wonderfully captured the often small-time, folksy flavor of most Portuguese corruption: NASA is interviewing three candidates shortlisted for a year-long trip to Mars. They ask the British candidate how much he would want to go on the mission and he asks for $9 million. Asked to explain why, he replies that he has a family who will miss him and that his diligence merits such a reward. The French candidate also asks for $9 million, explaining that $5 million is for him and his family and the other $4 million is to be shared between his two lovers. Next the Portuguese, who also asks for $9 million. He explains why: $3 million is for him, $3 million is for the interviewer, and the other $3 million is for whoever they can get to go to Mars.

Out of sight is the more sophisticated, big-time fraud higher up the ladder. The sociologist António Barreto observed that during the late 1980s and in the 1990s, when Portugal was on a steep curve of economic growth due to its EU membership, corruption became "a burdensome reality." The shadow economy accounted for perhaps 20 percent of economic activity, he said. João Cravinho, a longtime socialist member of parliament, launched something of a crusade in 2007 to stamp out the corrosive nature of backhanders and influence-peddling involving state-awarded contracts. "The biggest corruption is state corruption," he remarked. In 2006, 48 percent of police corruption investigations focused on the local and central public administration. But it is a taboo subject. Cravinho admitted that he was "astonished" by the resistance he met in his own party against his proposed adoption of new anti-corruption rules. He described corruption as "a serious, extensive phenomenon with no mechanisms good enough to stop it." He asked, rhetorically, how many corruption convictions people could recall. He, like everybody else, knew the answer: not very many at all. The writer and commentator Miguel Sousa Tavares remarked, "Portugal is a country of impunity." A study of corruption cases in 2002-3 found that two in three police investigations into corruption were dropped due to lack of evidence; fewer than 8 percent of investigations came to trial; almost 30 percent of cases involved construction companies; and in just over a quarter of cases the alleged pay-off amounted to less than a palm-greasing €1,500.

In 2009, the Lisbon City Council, as part of a response to a string of corruption cases sullying its name, went back and checked dozens of approvals for building projects. Selecting cases at random, it found that

40 percent broke building codes and rules and should never have been allowed. Everyone has a tale to tell about the funny business that goes on. I have heard, for instance, about a foreigner who was building a two-floor house in the countryside. The local council's building inspector told him he would have to install an elevator to be granted a construction license. The owner was dismayed. What for? he asked. Well, the inspector replied, you might have handicapped people as guests and they have to be able to get upstairs. It was nonsense, of course, but the inspector was speaking in code: either slip me some cash or I will hold up your permit.

On the tax front, the demands of being part of the EU have led to tighter controls and some successes for the government. In 2006 the Finance Ministry warned about 4,000 companies that had officially recorded losses the previous year (suspiciously reporting income that was just under the threshold to make it taxable) that if they did it again the following year tax inspectors would go and audit their books. Half of the companies then miraculously showed a small profit, even though the Portuguese economy was teetering on the edge of recession. The crackdown raked in €1.5 billion in outstanding taxes—about 1 percent of the country's GDP.

The unregimented life is an atavistic national feature. Portugal's misfortunes through history taught her people forbearance, a talent for living with adversity and a reluctance to harbor great expectations. A diplomat in the early 1700s, José da Cunha Brochado, wrote from Paris about how the Portuguese were viewed in France: "It's all the same to (the Portuguese): war, peace, or neutrality... As far as the economy's concerned, they don't pay much attention: they live on what they come across without knowing whether they might have more or may live better."

Such complacency, whether trivial or serious, has tended to elicit a ho-hum response at all levels. In a 2007 party financing scandal over slush funds, a construction company was convicted of footing a bill of almost €250,000 incurred by one of the country's two main political parties during a general election campaign. The party brushed off the enormous sum as an "oversight." Astonishingly, a senior party official insisted that the state's honor had not been besmirched and reminded anybody listening that party officials were "above suspicion." One newspaper columnist was astonished that the case caused barely a ripple. "Portugal has learned to live like this. It doesn't even think it's strange any more," he wrote. The party's political adversaries, presumably squeamish about drawing attention to their own expenditure, kept their heads down.

The revelation in 2007 that a former defense minister who was in office at the time of the invasion of Iraq—which the conservative government of the time endorsed—had photocopied and taken home more than 60,000 documents when he left the job caused almost no public indignation nor, indeed, much surprise.

The hazards of a free-wheeling, laissez-faire attitude crystalized in the notorious Casa Pia case. A newspaper detonated this major scandal in 2002 when it published chilling allegations about decades-long sexual abuse at a state-run boys' home in Lisbon called Casa Pia. More than a hundred boys at the home claimed to have suffered abuse, including alleged homosexual rape and pedophile prostitution, since the late 1970s. To make it worse, there were claims of a top-level cover-up. A former secretary of state for families testified to a parliamentary committee that a former president, a former foreign minister, the police, and the home's governors knew about the abuse allegations but failed to act. (They denied it.) The episode stunned and chastened the Portuguese. One thing was paying the price themselves of their own laxness, another was passing on the cost to unprotected children. The attorney-general's office brought charges against ten people, including prominent political and entertainment figures. But by early 2010 there was still no verdict as the five-year-old trial dragged on and the case was barely mentioned any more. The daily paper *Diário de Notícias* published an editorial in 2007 lamenting the "seeds of indifference sown among us." It explained that "problems take so long to resolve and keep cropping up for so long after they first come to light that first they cause disgust and then lead to passivity. It gets to the point where instead of feeling indignant about injustice we just start shrugging."

It is perhaps in the media glare of the soccer world that the spotlight catches the worst Portuguese features. Soccer is deeply contaminated by the subversive inclinations and pervasive sense of impunity.

The sport is dominated by men who portray themselves as rather raffish but essentially down-to-earth good ol' boys. These bosses are a shameless group. Club chairmen have been simultaneously league officials in charge of refereeing—a kind of cross-pollination that infects all levels of the game. They provide some burlesque scenes, and their misplaced vanity offers plenty of unintended humour. Once, a powerful soccer boss suspected of match-fixing gave an indignant nighttime rebuttal to journalists outside his house—dressed in his pajamas and slippers to show that he was a man of the people.

Zé Povinho: Idiosyncrasy Personified

As with the "Portugal at its Best" photos, the Portuguese are perfectly aware of their shortcomings, and it is difficult be harsher about them than they are about themselves. Miguel Torga, the poet, wrote: "It really is a penance travelling the world with Portugal on your back. Not with the Portugal that could or should be, but with the one that is, for our sins." Putting aside its many positive aspects, the nineteenth-century poet Cesário Verde grimaced at his country, which he deemed to be a hotbed of "laziness and foolishness." Another famous poet from that century, António Nobre, remarked: "What misfortune to be born in Portugal!" Compare that to the phrase attributed either to Cecil Rhodes or Rudyard Kipling: "To be born English is to win first prize in the lottery of life." No matter which one is true, the point is the way the people see themselves.

The Portuguese temperament brings a yawning gap between theory and reality. Officially, for instance, the law dictates the days of the year when shops are allowed to hold sales. But for the rest of the year any shop can just advertise "price cuts" rather than sales so the theory of state control is, in truth, a fiction. The gulf between theory and practice even attaches to the agenda of weekly governmental cabinet meetings. The issues up for discussion are supposed to be confidential because they might contain privileged financial or economic information. But the morning papers on the day of the meeting routinely carry news about what the government ministers will be talking about—and nobody seems to mind. As the historian Rui Ramos says, "this is a country of theories, not facts."

It is the same with the judicial secrecy law covering ongoing police investigations. Under this law, it is forbidden for anyone to disclose information about the police's inquiries. But this is a myth. Newspapers publish transcriptions of incriminating—and classified—phone taps gathered by police in high-profile investigations. A daily paper once published an entire pull-out supplement of transcripts from the Casa Pia pedophile investigation, scorning the idea that such information was off-limits and, as usual, getting away with it. Receiving official information as a journalist in Portugal can be rather like getting your hands on state secrets in Albania, bringing with it a perilous reliance on leaks from anonymous sources which, in turn, grants plenty of room for mischief.

Foreigners had a taste of this irrationality as they followed the investigation into the 2007 disappearance of the British girl Madeleine McCann in the Algarve. To pick just a couple of examples from many, in a Portuguese television program about the case, a criminologist who used to be a detective said press reports about how the girl's mother allegedly reacted under interrogation "were not in the police file." How did he know? If he did know, was he not breaking the law by telling everyone on a nationally broadcast program? And how was it that he was not punished for doing so? The same three questions were valid when in the same program one of the McCanns' Portuguese lawyers disclosed that the police were unhappy about "slight discrepancies in the timeline" provided in statements by the McCanns and their friends about the night Madeleine vanished. And a few months after the disappearance, the head of the country's criminal investigation department said on TV that the DNA in blood spots taken from the McCanns' car was not a perfect match with Madeleine's. Even a police chief, it seemed, could get away with flouting the judicial secrecy law. No wonder the Portuguese express so little faith in their legal system and the chances of justice being done.

These are episodes in a narrative whose protagonist is Zé Povinho. He is a kind of John Bull figure, a Portuguese Everyman created in the nineteenth century by the illustrator and journalist Rafael Bordalo

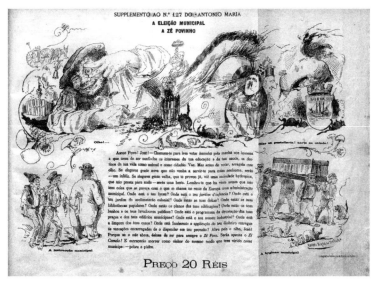

Zé Povinho (top left)

Pinheiro to stand for all those intriguing contradictions and idiosyncrasies in the national character—what the historian Oliveira Martins called Portugal's "intrinsic madness."

Providing a conduit for his creator's humorous social comment on injustice and corruption and the Portuguese response to it, Zé Povinho started out as a drawing and is now often represented in a glazed clay statuette on display in bars and cafés, posing in a rude gesture that lets customers know what the chances are of drinking on credit. He is a caricature, painted in broad brush strokes. He is swarthy, with thick forearms, a ruddy face, and a five o'clock shadow, and wears a traditional round black hat and waistcoat. He embodies the Portuguese impulses that sometimes are hard to reconcile—an unstable cocktail of sometimes disabling urges, a kind of Portuguese kryptonite. It is as if any observation of the Portuguese character has to be qualified by its opposite. They are amiable but also irascible, deferential but indomitable, apathetic and humble, tough and dauntless, compassionate but grouchy, submissive and beleaguered, always waiting for fortune to smile on them, good company, conciliatory and tactful as well as effusive and spontaneous, given to blowing their top but eminently reasonable, with a sadness in their soul but joviality in their nature. A century on, Zé Povinho's relevance has not diminished. The historian João Medina believes that Zé Povinho "hasn't aged, because he still represents something which is deep inside us: the apathy, the lack of interest, the lack of collaboration."

While the Portuguese are instinctively tolerant and adaptable, they cannot discount the possibility that they are too tolerant and too adaptable as they go on accepting things that are unacceptable or tolerating the intolerable. After generations of repetition they tend to accept the bizarre as completely normal. There is a thin line between the talent of adaptability and the perils of complacent acceptance. Rather than fighting for a common ideal, the Portuguese, by being compliant and accommodating when in their own interest they should be rigorous and demanding, grant their tacit blessing to outrageous circumstances. They protest about their lot but bear as much responsibility for it as the authorities they readily blame. Indeed, as the columnist Paulo Baldeia asked in 2007: "What's the point in changing governments if we continue to behave in the same way?" Without doubt Portugal has endured long periods of pernicious absolutism, indifferent centralized power, and neglectful governments. But each country has the government it deserves, and the people are the state.

Chapter Ten
Sweet Sorrow
Fado Music and the Soul of Portugal

An old joke about country & western music claims that if you play one of the records backwards, you get your dog back, you get your job back, and you get your wife back. In an equivalent joke about *fado*, Portugal's iconic musical genre, your father would not go off to sea, your long-suffering mother would not break down in tears, and your favorite horse would not get gored by a bull and drop dead. Most countries' traditional music is easy to mock. Limited in range and wed to sometimes outdated mannerisms, it is a soft target for parody.

But *fado* (pronounced far-dough) carries a wealth of cultural baggage, its hard-luck stories affording in many ways a telling glimpse of the Portuguese soul. The country and its centuries-old traditional music are even today bound together so tightly it is hard to appreciate one without comprehending the other. *Fado* narrates life through a Portuguese prism. It is a celebration of "Portugueseness," the distilled essence of a country, as Portuguese as grilled sardines and a jug of sweet sangria at the end of a scorching summer's day.

In the traditional tableau, a lone *fado* singer (*fadista*) stands in front of a pair of seated guitar players, one strumming a classical guitar and the other plucking the Portuguese twelve-string guitar. This distinctive instrument is shaped like a lute, its steel strings strung in pairs producing a shrill and unmistakable resonance. The guitars provide backing for the singer and burst to the fore between the poetic verses in tinkly flourishes. Carlos Paredes, who died in 2004, was a genius on this instrument. The performers usually dress in somber, muted colors.

Fado's lyrics fill in the contours of the country's character. Here is an excerpt from a famous song called "Strange Way of Life":

> It was God's will
> That I should endure this anguish
> …
> What a strange way of life

O FADO

> My heart leads!
> It beats for a wasted life!
> Who shall wave a magic wand?
> What a strange way of life!

That sad tone permeates the music as it does the Portuguese themselves. The lyrical fatalism and victimhood ("God's will") and sense of powerlessness ("a magic wand") are other cultural trademarks. So are the resilience, the lament for the irrecoverable past, and the wistful sentimentality. A cloud of doom and disappointment also hangs over it. *Fado* is an old Portuguese word for fate—something many feel they are up against. When high hopes are dashed and everything goes horribly wrong, they mutter, *Que triste fado* ("What a sad fate"), and groan at cruel destiny.

Mostly it is the sadness that reaches out so emphatically. Indeed, the lyrics possess an intriguing solemnity for a people so evidently life-loving. Performed well, *fado* tugs insistently at the heart-strings. Take this song called "May God Forgive Me":

> If my obscured soul
> Could reveal itself,
> And if my silent suffering
> Could tell all,
> Everyone would see
> How unfortunate I am,
> How I feign happiness,
> How much I weep when I sing...

Another refrain:

> Oh people of my homeland,
> Now I understand—
> This sadness I carry inside me,
> I got it from you.

It is not hard to see why *fado* has been called Portuguese blues.

The sadness has a long history. In the sixteenth century, about a hundred years after the dawn of the exceptional feats of Portuguese explorers in the Age of Discovery, the national epic poet Luís de Camões wrote about his country's "dispirited and vile sadness." Four centuries later, despondency was still in the air. Fernando Pessoa picked up where Camões left off in his famous poem "Nevoeiro" (Mist) from 1934 where he deplores his country's sad and inconsequential life, its "brightness without light," the "land's dull glow." And the modern philosopher José Gil has remarked that visiting foreigners throughout history have reported the Portuguese to be a "taciturn, melancholic, morose" people.

Other Portuguese writers of the last century concurred with this gloomy diagnosis. Domingos Monteiro said his countrymen have a dark soul and consent to "an ambitionless and hopeless destiny." Almeida Faria, in 1980, was scathing in depicting "an exhausted people" who were living in "a deeply sad land." Fernando Dacosta, a late nineteenth-century writer, summed it up: "The destiny—and what a destiny!— that was carved out for us, the Portuguese, was to be sad."

This collective melancholy often was, and is, one of the most striking national characteristics to foreigners. The Spanish philosopher Miguel de Unamuno, on an early twentieth-century trip to Portugal, marveled at "this enormous sadness," going so far as to suggest that the locals might be "a suicidal people." The French writer Antoine de Saint-Exupéry, passing through neutral Portugal during the Second World War, encountered a welcoming and peaceful corner of Europe but decided it was a "sad paradise." A 1959 book entitled *Lisboa, Cidade Triste e Alegre* ("Lisbon, Sad and Happy City") captured this contrast in black-and-white photographs and is regarded as one of the best European photo books of the postwar period.

This does not mean that the Portuguese are incapable of pleasure or *joie de vivre*. When things go well, they briefly erupt in exhilaration and see the error of their ways. Take success on the soccer field, such as at the 2004 European Championship where Portugal reached the final, or the 2006 World Cup where they got to the semi-finals. They lauded their Brazilian coach Luíz Felipe Scolari for his sunny engagement with life and his success in prodding the Portuguese into rallying behind the flag. One television viewer wrote enthusiastically on a broadcaster's blog during the World Cup: "It's not just on the football pitch where we can win! Scolari showed us we can do it in a good mood, with joy, desire and belief. He made us into a cheerful people despite the hardships we face, he showed us that united we can win!" For his part, Scolari, demonstrating that he too had taken the measure of the country's temperament, its disenchantment after four centuries of setbacks that consigned it to the status of one of Europe's poorest countries, observed: "The Portuguese are afraid of feeling happy."

Rather than expressing a dour pessimism, *fado* translates into music the emotional life of a people carrying the sediment of centuries of discouragement that has sapped their spirit, and that downtrodden sentiment sometimes shows.

Sentimental Nature

Fado embraces a theatrical sense of doom and gives it a voice. And it resonates with the Portuguese who regard it as a distillation of their essence. Part of its deep-seated appeal is that *fado* articulates the phenomenon of *saudade*. The Spanish twentieth-century writer Correa Calderon described *saudade* as "the key to an entire people," while the Portuguese writer Teixeira de Pascoães wrote in 1920: "There's one sentiment that sums up the Portuguese. It is *saudade*." (Unfortunately for foreigners trying to grasp the Portuguese character, *saudade* is also The Word that Cannot Be Translated. It springs from ancient Portuguese bloodlines and historical experience and carries such a breadth of meaning, such a rich texture, that no other language can produce an equivalent. In 2004, an international translation company included *saudade* in its list of ten words in the world that were the hardest to render.)

References to this singular, complex sentiment can be found already in Portuguese songs of the thirteenth century. In the fifteenth century it is mentioned (*soidade*) in an account of the taking of Ceuta. King Duarte acknowledged, in the early part of that same century, that *saudade* was untranslatable. Dictionary definitions lamely offer "longing," "homesickness," and "nostalgia" as possible renditions, and the word does draw on the pain of separation from loved ones. But the concept of *saudade* encompasses such a multifaceted range of traits that to get anywhere near deciphering it requires an extensive list—or even a book: Portuguese and foreign writers and thinkers have contributed with volumes, essays, academic papers, and conferences in their effort to get to the bottom of it.

Jorge Dias, writing in 1950 about the national character, reflected that *saudade* stems from a "complex mentality which results from a combination of different factors, some of them opposing"—a reference to the abiding contradictions in the Portuguese character that Zé Povinho exemplifies. Dias identified three roots in Portuguese genealogy that contribute elements of *saudade*: the Celtic lyrical dreamer prone to poetic expression and religious sentiment; Faustian anxiety from the German bloodline; and Arab fatalism. It also contains the features of Atlantic, Mediterranean, and intercontinental influences that are embedded in the national psyche.

At its shallowest, *saudade* conveys a sense of loss. But even then, its expression of pain and sorrow also carries hope for a better tomorrow. It embraces desire as well as memory. *Saudade* casts back to the Age of Discovery, back to the restless tension between those who departed and those left behind. In that fashion, it also evinces the microcosmic, close-knit nature of Portuguese society, the retreat into the interdependent safe havens of kinship and friendship within neighborhood communities known as *bairrismo*. It is a bittersweet emotion. The bonds of home and family do not slacken—witness the tens of thousands of Portuguese emigrants in Europe who each August pour back into the country for their month-long holiday with their families. It is called *matar saudades*, literally "killing off the feeling of *saudade*," by returning to their *terra* ("homeland"—another noun sprinkled generously through *fado* lyrics).

Saudade is often explained with reference to sixteenth-century King Sebastian, slain on the field of battle during his imprudent incursion into North Africa. A popular young monarch, the rumor began in Portugal that he had not in fact died and that he would one day miraculously reappear. King Sebastian's story blends the ingredients of what was and what might be—he, like King Arthur, is the "once and future king" (Barbarossa is another example). Ultimately, *saudade* is a static sentiment, not one that empowers. The writer António José Saraiva said it is like "a state of dissatisfaction."

Still, the Portuguese cherish and nourish it. Almeida Garrett, the nineteenth-century writer, claimed that *saudade* is "perhaps the sweetest, most expressive and most delicate" word in the language. António Nobre, a poet from the same century, wrote that *saudade* is "Such a sad word/And it feels good to hear it." An old popular song goes, "This word *saudade*/Whoever made it up/The first time he said it/He surely must have wept."

The Portuguese are enchanted by the way *fado* endorses their sentimental nature. They are the only people I have seen in tears when they sing their national anthem at major events (though it is a stirring piece and easily one of the best around). Lope de Vega, the playwright and poet of the Spanish Golden Age, was so impressed by this romantic trait during a visit to Portugal that he composed a satirical verse:

A Portuguese who was weeping
Was asked why.
He replied because of his heart
And that he was in love.
To ease his pain,
He was asked with whom he was in love.
He answered: Well, nobody,
I'm crying from pure love.

Jorge Dias commented: "For the Portuguese, the heart is the measure of all things." The star-crossed love affair in the fourteenth century between King Pedro I and Inês de Castro, who are buried in side-by-side tombs at the Alcobaça Monastery, is one of Portugal's favorite romantic tales. Pedro, as prince and heir to the throne, was forced to marry the daughter of a prince of Castile to cement a political alliance, but Inês was his true love. The court frowned upon his romance and Inês was murdered to end it. It is a love story that speaks of devotion, of never giving up.

The melancholy that *fado* captures, though, seems like a fatal attraction and a desire for something unattainable. Just about any Portuguese will tell you that everything is better *lá fora* ("out there")—that is, abroad. The genre presents tales of grief and hard times drawn from a deep well of emotional history and is inspired by privation. There is a visceral expression of emotion, a moment of self-exposure that captures the vulnerability of life. The plaintive tone speaks of torment. One song goes:

> Love, jealousy,
> Ashes and flames,
> Pain and sin.
>
> All this exists,
> All this is sad,
> All this is *fado*.

It is worth noting here that acclaimed Brazilian musicians such as Caetano Veloso have difficulty in delivering an authentic *fado* song. They simply cannot express the mournfulness. (Conversely, the Portuguese cannot really capture the exuberance of Carnival.) The Brazilian writer Angela Dutra de Menezes published a book in 2007 called *The Portuguese who Begat Us* which contemplated an abiding riddle: "I wanted to know who these sad Portuguese were who gave birth to such cheerful people as us," she said.

At its worst, *fado* can sound like a particularly long lament and by the tenth song many outsiders have had enough ennui. It is unfair, however, to convey the impression that all *fado* induces suicidal tendencies. There are, indeed, more than a dozen different forms of *fado*. The *corrido* style, for example, is much more cheerful, and can even be danced to, while the version popular in Coimbra is performed only by men. The style called *desgarrada* involves two singers who engage in a playful duet.

The best-known type, however, is *fado menor*—the more melancholic brand of the genre. Though some can find it mawkish, the songs can be tremendously moving, at their best packing an emotional charge that gives the audience goose bumps. Even foreigners who do not understand a word of Portuguese have been known to leap to their feet and shout "Bravo!"

Although certainly mournful and lachrymose, *fado* is not about resignation. There is an assenting rapture in it. It is about fortitude, about a celebration of life despite the hardships, about faith. The passion of life lurks in its belly. It is a joyous lament. That is what makes the skin tingle even if you cannot understand the words. *Fado* singers may wail about their plight but they do not give up, and never would. Raging at misfortune, it is intimate suffering recounted, *forte*, in public, and the defiantly lone singer is still standing at end of it in a metaphorical display of Portuguese resilience. A *fado* performance offers a gripping soliloquy—the performer against the elements.

Tunes from the Docks

The best place to witness authentic *fado* is in the old taverns of Lisbon, though those once smoky dens are becoming scarce and you usually have to know someone to get in. At the more serious places, where they take tourists, traditionalists huddle in sombre reverence. There are ancient rules to be followed, strict conventions to be obeyed. Anyone who dares to make a noise during a performance is quickly shushed with the famous phrase *Silêncio, que se canta o fado!* ("Be quiet, *fado* is being sung!").

The home of *fado* is in the capital's small, earthy venues where the heavy wine is served out of barrels lined up along the wall behind the bar and the barman does not say please or thank you. At these places the locals get up one after another and let rip with their favorite song. The Portuguese are a private people but a good lament breaks down inhibitions. A friend took us to a place where one of the impromptu amateur performers was a judge (minus his black robe). Another time at another place, a local man stood up and started singing a song that began with a line about weeping for his mother. But he kept getting a frog in his throat and starting again. By the third time he sang the line someone shouted out, "What a cry baby!" and everyone broke down in laughter.

These places feel much more authentic than the sometimes contrived tourist locations, as well as comfortingly irreverent. *Fado* started out, apparently, in just these kinds of venues. It is said to have grown out of Lisbon's rough dockside neighborhoods in the early nineteenth century. The tunes are from the docks, and it is said that some prostitutes were also admired *fadistas*. The roots go deeper, though, perhaps stretching back centuries. Sailing ships anchored in the River Tagus brought home Portuguese seafarers, many of whom plied colonial Atlantic routes between Africa and Brazil. Their sung stories and laments crystallized into a style that borrowed from the music they heard on their voyages. *Fado* also distilled the musical features brought by foreign sailors who passed through Lisbon and could hold an entertaining tune on the tavern floor. All those influences, brewed together, made *fado* unique. There are strains of African slave songs, Brazilian rhythms, popular Portuguese tunes, as well as other European and even Arab elements.

Inevitably the national music, occupying a central place in the national culture, is knitted tightly into the national history, especially during the last century. Portugal's prolonged twentieth-century dictatorship used *fado* as a tool to stir nationalistic passion, a symbol and a guard against the encroachment of toxic foreign influences such as rock 'n' roll. The art form was co-opted. On the one hand, performers had to request licenses and the lyrics of their songs had to pass the censor. On the other, popular performers were encouraged to perform abroad, especially in the colonies, and state television held an annual *fado* festival as part of an effort to cement national cultural values. It was one of António Salazar's "Three Fs," even though the dictator reportedly confided to a friend that he found *fado* depressing.

After the 1974 coup the country's new leaders—eager to wipe away vestiges of the hated ruler—looked upon *fado* with distaste and cold-shouldered it. It was unofficially labeled out-of-date and inappropriate for the New Times. Even Amália Rodrigues, the most famous *fadista*, known simply as Amália, was a victim of that new mood. She was accused of having been an informant for the dictatorship's secret police. Astonished by the allegations, she vigorously denied them but by association was still for a time marginalized by the hostility of Portugal's new leaders towards the previous regime. Yet her international success—

Amália Rodrigues, commemorated in street art

she made the cover of *Variety* magazine in 1959—and the people's abiding fondness for her helped to keep *fado* out of the ghetto. She was a black-shawl *fadista*, one of the old school and legendary queen of the genre. After Amália's death in 1999 a new generation of mostly women *fado* singers blossomed. Mariza, a slender blonde-haired mulatta from Lisbon, has made the strongest popular impact. She has sold widely abroad under the world music category and her world tours have included sell-out concerts at the Royal Albert Hall in London, Carnegie Hall in New York, and the Sydney Opera House. To her credit, Mariza has taken *fado* beyond the predictable phrasing and weary rhythms of previous eras and, in doing so, has returned it to the playlist of popular radio stations. In her, and other, hands *fado* has become something sweeter, more cheerful and upbeat. She teases out the music's roots, handing Brazilian and African percussion a prominent role alongside the traditional guitars.

The repetitive rhythms of drum-led African music make for an infectious beat, like reggae, and Lisbon's African nightclubs have long proved a strong draw, to some extent rivalling the appeal of *fado* dens. Some of the old, established African clubs were until recent times in wooden-floored ballrooms and had an old-fashioned dance-hall feel, with mirror balls dangling from the ceiling, as if tethered to the city's past. The most talked-about of these clubs was called B.Leza and occupied a battered seventeenth-century Lisbon manor house where Europeans and Africans could perform dances such as the *kizomba* (a slow, sensual smooch), the *funaná* (a hopping, swinging movement) and the more sedate and genteel *coladeira*. Shut since 2007, Lisbon still mourns its passing. Today many clubs are restaurants by day, with the tables pushed aside at night to make room for dancing. The capital's modern Angolan discotheques are tougher, edgier places.

As tastes changed after the end of the dictatorship and with Portugal's move into the modernizing European mainstream, Brazilian culture became another competitor for the popular attention once heaped on *fado*. Brazilian performers such as Caetano Veloso, Ivete Sangalo, and Maria Bethânia have topped the charts, part of an influx of Brazilian culture witnessed especially from the 1980s when imported

Brazilian *telenovelas* began to command prime-time viewing and Brazilian accents—the hard consonants and broad vowels being unmistakable, like an American drawl to a British ear—poured forth from television sets. Those Brazilian soaps also brought the first naked breasts to Portuguese screens, in the wildly successful *Gabriela* in 1977, underscoring the post-Revolution cultural sea change and recalling the startled response of early seafarers to the half-naked natives they encountered in Terra de Vera Cruz.

Other *fado* singers who, like Mariza, have helped check Portuguese youth's defection to British and American pop and rock include Camané, Kátia Guerreiro, and Dulce Pontes. Some of them have experimented with mingling other musical forms, including Portuguese rap and hip-hop artists: Mariza cut a single with Boss AC, and Jorge Fernando hooked up with Sam the Kid. *Fado* traditionalists shuddered; neither genre's fans queued up to buy. A bigger shot-in-the-arm for *fado* came at the end of 2009 with the launch of an FM radio station called, not surprisingly, Amália.

For all the attempts at modernization, the baleful chronicles of a downtrodden people still resonate through the nostalgic lyrics of the old *fado* songs. The Portuguese at times seem to revel in their cherished sadness. It is worth noting, though, that *fadistas* often smile when they recount their bleak narratives. It is as if they are happy to be sad. I was once chatting from the back seat with a Lisbon taxi driver about some enormous construction going on in the city center. The work was never-ending and exasperating for anyone who had to drive in the area. As we drove by, the taxi driver pondered the traffic jam and shook his head in resignation. It was unfair, but there was nothing he could do about it—the Portuguese malaise of passive complaint. "Portugal is so sad," he said. Then he looked at me in the rear-view mirror and added with a broad smile: "That's why I love it."

Chapter Eleven
Slow-Food Nation
The Importance of Eating Well

On a state visit to Lisbon in the summer of 2008, Venezuelan President Hugo Chávez took his motorcade to Lisbon's main avenue for a wreath-laying ceremony at a statue of South America's nineteenth-century independence hero Simón Bolívar. As he stepped out of his armored limousine (late, as ever—we were already deep into lunchtime) and proceeded beneath the shade of the broad plane trees, some two dozen grey-haired leftist veterans of Portugal's 1974 Revolution broke into cheers of "Viva! Viva!" Evidently regarding Venezuela as the New Jerusalem of the Left, they punched the air with their fists as they chanted the 34-year-old Portuguese revolutionary slogan: *O povo, unido, jamais será vencido.* After a while one of these chanting men who was standing in front of me turned away and, still pumping his fist, muttered, "but when it's time to eat..." Brimming with purpose, he strode off to the nearest restaurant. Even great revolutionary ideals, it seemed, have to compete for attention with a good meal.

The Portuguese are serious about their food. It is a national feature that any visitor will quickly spot and one which splendidly captures their *joie de vivre*. William Beckford, on his journey through Portugal in the eighteenth century, exclaimed: "The Portuguese need to have the stomachs of ostriches to digest the loads of savoury viands with which they cram themselves." Visiting the Alcobaça Monastery, which catered to some 400 monks, Beckford is said to have marveled at the plump fish swimming in the watercourse that ran through the kitchen, the heaps of game, the brimming saucepans of fresh vegetables, and the lay brothers who, perhaps in salivary anticipation, sang while they rolled out pastry.

Fondness for good food cuts across class differences and is a great common denominator. Think of the tea and marmalade Catherine of Bragança took to England in the seventeenth century and the record-breaking bean stew (eight tons) for 15,000 Lisbon locals at the inaugu-

Dried, salted cod in a grocery store

ration of the new bridge over the Tagus in 1998. Even the humblest gathering merits some culinary effort. A German businessman who has an office in Lisbon and other European capitals told me that once his Portuguese staff asked him if they could bring in some food for a colleague's birthday lunch. Envisioning a cake and some snacks he readily agreed. Coming in the next day, he encountered a mountain of food piled on a desk. It was the Portuguese full buffet: olives, cheeses, smoked ham, sausages, roast chicken, roast suckling pig, fishcakes, meat rolls, salad, cake, bread, wine. "I couldn't believe it," he said, laughing. As a northern European he had expected some paper plates with modest bits of cheese and pineapple or tinned sausages on sticks.

Weekday lunch breaks may no longer last from 1 until 3 p.m. (though they may), but a full-blown three-course meal is not unusual by any means. Restaurants in Lisbon at lunchtime are full of office workers and laborers having a proper sit-down meal. During the police investigation into the 2007 disappearance of Madeleine McCann in the Algarve, the British media expressed shock and horror at Portuguese detectives who took a two-hour Friday lunch break complete with wine and whisky.

The poorly-educated Portuguese emigrants who have been forced to go and live abroad to make a decent living may in some aspects be deracinated, but food is one of the things that helps keep the cultural bonds tight. When they return to France or wherever they work after their August holiday at home, their car trunks and roof-racks are loaded with "*saudade*-killing" hometown delicacies.

You overhear, in the street, on the bus, in queues, people telling each other about some mouthwatering dish they had at a restaurant or had cooked or heard about. (Curiously, cooking programs are not common on Portuguese television.) They go into great detail and squint and rub their fingers at the recollection of flavors. A 1990 census showed that the Portuguese spent almost 30 percent of their household income on food, compared with the EU average of just over 12 percent. The prominent essayist Eduardo Lourenço wrote in 1978, when Portugal was in the grip of the post-revolution economic crisis, that "entire families, those we say are of modest means, calmly spend on lunch a tenth of what one of them earns in a month." A study in 2008 revealed that

Portuguese families spend 9.5 percent of their family income on eating and drinking out—more than double the EU average. That statistic helps to explain why Portugal has three times more restaurants per capita than in the rest of the EU (one for every 131 people; the EU average is one per 374).

Eating out in Portugal can be laughably cheap, especially if you opt for the robust home cooking offered at *tascas*—modest, often family-run restaurants that elsewhere might be termed cheap-and-cheerful or "greasy spoons." The unpretentiousness is often charming; you could be forgiven for thinking that their heavy frying pans are impregnated with garlic after so much use, and the house wine can seem so heavy you could chew it. For many years the bill would be scribbled on the paper tablecloth in a rough totting-up, though that habit is disappearing in an overdue crackdown on chronic tax evasion. They are still the cheapest places to dine, however. On a 2006 visit to Santa Comba Dão in central Portugal, where António Salazar's grave lies, a colleague and I ordered (by mistake) three dishes of the day, a bottle of wine and one of water, and coffee. When I asked for the bill, the waitress looked at our table, mumbled some sums to herself and said, "Give me €5 each."

This happened in the countryside, of course, where living standards are a far cry from those in the capital, although in 2009 you could still get a square meal in Lisbon for under €10. A colleague and I popped into a run-of-the-mill city-center restaurant, for example, and ordered the broad-bean stew with sausages and the cod fishcakes with bean rice. Each cost €5.50 and each portion was big enough for two people (which would have made it less than €3 each dish). Together with wine, water, and coffee the bill came to about €16. That is why tourists often exclaim about Portugal, "It's so cheap!"

The size of portions, especially in rural areas, can even be alarming. At the deservedly famous Fialho restaurant in Évora, in the Alentejo region, the appetizers alone could fell a bull. There is a restaurant in an out-of-the-way part of the Algarve that has no menu but puts eight consecutive courses (each better than the last) in front of the diner. In Porto, there is a restaurant specializing in grilled meat where I can never get more than halfway through the half-portion—conduct which the waiters regard as unmanly. Porto also specializes in a dish called a *francesinha*, a hot sandwich on a plate that is gargantuan: stack alternate slices of sausage, ham, and beef and/or pork between two slices of bread, coat it with melted cheese and pour over a tomato and chili sauce. Add a fried egg or chips if you dare. I once introduced an Irish friend to this tasty morsel and after polishing it off he sat there in stunned silence, staring at the table.

The relish for good food is instilled at an early age. My eldest daughter enthused about her secondary school cafeteria. The meals—always featuring soup, fish or meat, salad, and fruit—are carefully prepared and appetizing and, apparently, devoured. That is not to say, however, that young people are not seduced by fast-food chains as in any other European country.

Land of Plenty

The Portuguese will often make a detour on a long car ride to sample a prized local dish. On the Lisbon-Porto route, for instance, you might time your journey so you hit Mealhada, roughly the midway point, around lunchtime. There, you can tuck into the local speciality of succulent suckling pig (*leitão*) roasted whole on spits that are slid into huge, head-high ovens. It comes with handmade crisps, a spicy sauce on the crackling, and a sparkling white wine from the local vineyards.

With such an amenable climate, eating outside is possible for much of the year. The outdoor life is a facet of the culture that helps make the Portuguese such a convivial, sociable people. There is nothing like sitting in the sunshine at a busy restaurant by the sea and feasting on a platter of fresh fish amid the chatter and laughter. The other option is a picnic, though this being Portugal it does not involve a sandwich and paper cups on a car rug but more typically an elaborate barbecue-and-buffet event with all the trimmings as well as cutlery, glasses, and a folding table. Oddly for such a picturesque country, the Portuguese happily pitch their table at the side of a road when a grassy, wooded area is close by.

Some of Portugal's most delectable specialities afford a glimpse of how seriously food is taken—and why. Among the many cheeses, for example, Azeitão and Serra da Estrela (both taking their names from the places they are made) are exceptional. Both are made with curdled raw sheep's milk and cured. You cut out a hole in the top of the rind and lift the lid on a creamy paste that is scooped out with a spoon, preferably onto some fresh, crunchy bread (and Portugal has excellent bread). In 2008 the American magazine *Vanity Fair* singled out a cheese from northeastern Portugal called Queijo Amarelo da Beira Baixa—a soft, cured blend of sheep and goat's milk—for special praise; and the same month *Wine Spectator* magazine placed Nisa among the top cheeses in the world. Nisa, taking its name from the Alentejo town where it is made, is given an infusion of cardoon and is tangy and hard.

Cornbread is exceptional in Portugal, as are the Alentejo-style loaves baked in a wood-fired oven. Homemade versions may come with crunchy bits of charcoal in them, like a bizarre version of chocolate chips. Sausage bread, where slices of sausage are rolled into the dough before baking and leak a fatty flavor, is also a favorite. It should be noted, though, that Portuguese bread is very salty. Experts say that because refrigeration became widespread in Portugal only in the 1970s, salt was widely used to preserve food and that the taste for salt has remained. Others say it is because unscrupulous bakers want to make more money: salt retains the water and makes the bread, which is sold by weight, heavier.

Nobody eats canned soup in Portugal, as superior homemade versions are common, either in the shape of broths, consommés, or loaded with meat and/or vegetables to make meals in themselves. Take *sopa da pedra* (stone soup)—misleadingly named as far as its ingredients are concerned, but sincere in its suggestion about how you will feel after eating it. In the two hard decades after the Second World War vegetable soups were a staple and required some imagination. Especially for poor people in the country, where meat and fish were hard to come by, soup was the main dish of the day. People of that generation tend to be short, unlike their well-fed children and grandchildren—the EU generation—who have had a broader diet. These youngsters are as tall as other Europeans and dwarf their grandparents.

Depleted stocks have made fresh fish and shellfish more expensive but still they are a central part of the national diet. In fact, the Portuguese are the biggest fish eaters in the EU, consuming 123 pounds a year per person, more than double the EU average of 48 pounds. Dried salted cod (*bacalhau*) has been a staple since the Age of Exploration, when it was valued by sailors because it kept for so long, and is the traditional Christmas Eve dish. It used to be eaten mostly on Mondays when there was no fresh fish because fishermen do not go out to sea on Sundays. Nicknamed the Faithful Friend, it may not look much in a shop (its appearance has been likened to a piece of cardboard) but after immersing it in water for a couple of days (skin side up) and mixing in some milk the flaky white flesh is fit for a king. Some say there are 1,000 ways of cooking it; others that there is a different cod recipe for each day of the year. Either way, its place in Portuguese lore is undoubted. The downside is the powerful cod smell. A walk down a street called Rua do Arsenal in Lisbon, where boxes of dried cod are stacked outside a row of fishmongers, is a sensory experience. Even the breeze off the River Tagus cannot shift this aroma.

Tinned sardines have for many decades been a national export, but the Portuguese keep the best for themselves. The whiff of grilling sardines is common in months with no letter "r" in their name (that is, May–August), when the fish are fattest, and is especially frequent during the Lisbon summer *festas* when crowds squeeze into the narrow alleyways of the old Alfama quarter for jugs of sangria, bowls of steaming cabbage soup and sardines served on a slice of bread so that, standing in the busy night-time street, you can use your fingers to peel off the flesh.

Jaquinzinhos (deep-fried whitebait) are also eaten with your fingers, biting off the crunchy head and body to leave the crispy tail between index finger and thumb. Seafood such as clams, mussels, or limpets may come as appetizers, cooked briefly in olive oil, white wine, and garlic, or as a main dish in rice with tomato. A common sight along the coast is amateur scuba divers hunting for octopus. They haul them out from beneath rocks with a grapple-like device and pull them inside out, like a glove, to kill them. Oddly, octopus is softer if it is frozen before it is boiled. Crab, too, is another favorite. Children and adults alike have great fun at seafood restaurants where they are armed with a little wooden mallet. As you hit the crab to open is shell, its legs and bits of white crab meat fly like shrapnel across the tables, prompting broad smiles from adults and giggles from their children.

Such fare can, of course, be disconcerting for anyone accustomed to more sanitized versions of seafood. My wife and I once witnessed a German tourist break down in tears when the waiter unceremoniously placed a boiled fish head in front of her. It is actually a popular dish: the tastiest bits of flesh are in the cheeks and in the top of the head.

Jewish Sausage and Convent Desserts

Portugal's most popular dishes were invented in its peasant past. *Açorda*, for example, is bread mashed up with garlic and olive oil and cooked in a saucepan. In the old days it was a way of using up stale bread but now it has a place in mainstream gastronomy. The same applies to *migas*, an Alentejo specialty that is essentially the same recipe but with the addition of lard and, possibly, asparagus or tomato.

The broad variety of traditional smoked sausages, too, has survived through the centuries, and these are now being adapted into more modern, nouvelle cuisine-type dishes. They are not the pallid, factory-produced sausages (called *salsichas* in Portuguese) readily recognizable elsewhere, but rather full-flavored, nourishing additions to stews and soups. Most are mass-produced these days, but some are still handmade.

It has been said that nobody likes watching sausages being made. The *matança do porco* (slaying of the pig) gives that expression a whole new meaning. This bloody, informal tradition still goes on, and is publicly advertised, though it is a medieval ritual that is not for the faint-hearted or the animal-lover. In rural areas when a pig is ready for slaughter, families and friends gather outdoors and light a bonfire in a festive atmosphere. The men grapple with the panicked pig, lay it on a bench and tie it down. After the women have moved in closer with their buckets and bowls, one of the men jabs a long, dagger-like knife into the pig's jugular. The air becomes fraught with the animal's harrowing squeals as the blood drains from its body. The women catch the gushing blood in bowls to make sausages known as *morcela*. After singeing off the dead pig's hair (traditionally with burning straw but today sometimes with a blow torch) the animal is hung upside down and its belly slit open, being careful not to nick the intestines, which are used to make the sausages. Different parts of the animal are carved out for use in different sausages—*farinheiras, linguiças, chouriços*—or as cuts of meat. Such broad-daylight drama is permitted by law within certain parameters; a vet is supposed to inspect the animal and the meat cannot be sold, for example. Still, it is hard to square the practice with hallowed EU hygiene rules. For Portuguese countryfolk, meanwhile, it is run-of-the-mill stuff. Invited once for lunch to the farm of a family at whose Lisbon market stall we did our weekly shopping, my wife, children, and I sat on planks along a makeshift table in their garage and tucked into a memorable meal with them while right next to us an eviscerated pig slaughtered shortly after dawn dangled from the ceiling by a rope, cooling. We ate heartily as the pale pig twisted gently in the draught. A popular cookbook from the 1980s called *Traditional Portuguese Cooking*, which is also available in English translation, offers color pictures of a strung-up pig being disemboweled in a rural street and women washing the bloody tripe in a river. "If possible, prepare the tripe next to a watercourse or, if you can't, find a place with plenty of running water and drainage," the recipe cautions.

A more heartwarming story than rural pig-slaying is provided by the tale of the sausage that helped spare Jews from the Inquisition. When 500 years ago King Manuel I offered Jews in Portugal a choice between expulsion or conversion to Catholicism, some took the second option. However, they secretly kept their faith. With the Church police prowling and always keen to resort to torture and bonfires, the Jews attempted to conceal their true religious belief by pretending to make the same pork sausages their Catholic neighbors made. In fact, what they produced and hung out for smoking was a lookalike sausage, the *alheira*, which contained other meat such as rabbit, veal, or chicken. A residual community of these Jews in the town of Belmonte, in northcentral Portugal, today oversees the production of kosher wine and olive oil.

Several types of sausage are included in a dish called *cozido à portuguesa*, which is the perfect Sunday lunchtime meal to be followed by a long walk or a nap, though it is also an occasional dish-of-the-day at city restaurants—goodness knows how people work afterwards. The dish is composed of a mountain of various boiled meats, including pig's ear and snout, boiled sausages, boiled vegetables and rice. It offers several unique taste sensations—*chouriço de sangue* (blood sausage) with the rice, and the paprika-colored *farinheira* with the boiled potatoes. At a place in the Azores called Lagoa das Furnas locals have a unique way of making *cozido*: a big, lidded saucepan full of meaty ingredients is lowered on a string into a pit, which is heated by a volcano and after five hours the steaming mass is pulled out.

Sausages also go into the bean stew called *feijoada* (Brazilians do a particularly good version of this dish) and can be added to other traditional fare such as tripe and trotters. Pig's blood is the main ingredient in *papa de serrabulho*, while chicken blood is used to cook the rice in *arroz de cabidela*. Tripe dishes are a speciality of Porto, whose citizens are known as *tripeiros* (roughly, tripe-eaters). Tradition has it that they earned this nickname because on two occasions—the Portuguese army's march on Castile in the late fourteenth century and the sailing from Porto of a fleet to capture Ceuta in North Africa in 1415—townspeople gave up their meat for the soldiers and lived on what was left. The people of Lisbon, meanwhile, are known as *alfacinhos*, presumably taken from the word for lettuce, *alface*, which is said to have grown abundantly in and around the capital in the times it was occupied by North African Muslims. Unfortunately, salads are one area where the Portuguese today definitely do not excel, rarely straying beyond what is called a "mixed salad"—tomato, lettuce, with maybe a bit of onion and some grated carrot thrown on top. The exception to this rule is the grilled pepper salad that is served with sardines.

Goat is a commonplace dish. One of the best ways to eat it is in a version called *chanfana*, a kind of casserole where the meat is placed in earthenware pots, immersed in red wine and herbs and cooked for hours in the oven. This recipe allegedly dates from the nineteenth-century invasions of Portugal by Napoleon's armies. The hated French troops plundered the land, stealing food at gunpoint. The Portuguese retaliated by poisoning the local wells and stuck with wine—which they hid—for cooking.

The traditional dishes have two things in common: they are tasty and they are heavy. And as if all this carbohydrate-rich fare was not enough, the Portuguese also have a sweet tooth. Perhaps the best-

known pastry, certainly among tourists, is a kind of little custard pie called a *pastel de Belém*, made in the Lisbon riverside quarter of the same name. Bakeries in the low back rooms of cafés there make thousands of them each day, and on Sundays locals line up in the street. The tarts come with little sachets of sugar and ground cinnamon to dust the pie's top.

Most typical are the *doces conventuais*, orange-colored desserts once made in Catholic convents where, it is said, egg yolks were left over after using the whites to make wafers for Mass. The only other ingredient apart from the yolks is sugar—a plentiful commodity from the cane crops the Portuguese encountered during the Age of Discovery. Today made commercially, the different types of convent desserts—drier or more succulent, molded into different shapes and textures—have kept their curious old names, such as nun's belly, nun's kisses, abbot's ears, and blessed mothers.

Another egg-based delight is the *pastel de Tentúgal*, a delicate affair said to date from the sixteenth century and a speciality of the town of the same name near Coimbra. The secret lies in the wafer-thin, crispy pastry. It starts out as a huge ball of dough, which is rolled out over a wooden floor the size of an average living room and gradually, and exhaustingly, stretched and thinned out.

Other staples are just as sugary. Any summer fair or sport event worth the name in Portugal features someone selling *farturas*—fistfuls of flour and egg that are deep-fried and then coated in sugar. And on the beach at end of a summer afternoon, when the shadows are lengthening, men and women dressed in white and carrying cloth-covered trays trudge across the sand selling sugar-dusted doughnuts called *bolas*. Locals and visitors sit on their towels, chewing and wiping sugar-freckled lips with the back of their hand.

Wine and Firewater

It used to be said that wine provides work for a million Portuguese, but that was before the advent of the EU's wine lake and the uprooting of vines. For a long time the quality of Portuguese wine, outside the famed ports, was distinctly patchy. Consequently, Portuguese wine had trouble making its presence felt abroad. Only Mateus Rosé built up a following. (Significantly, few in Portugal drink it.)

Much has changed in recent years. From the 1990s producers began to embrace previously foreign practices such as sophisticated production techniques and professional marketing. Today there is a breadth of choice never previously seen in Portugal. Even so, the country's relatively low production, compared to France or Spain for example, means that it falls short of the economies of scale achievable in competing nations. That, in turn, means that it cannot aspire to the same shelf space at foreign supermarket chains, which deal in high-volume, low-price business strategies. Though there are some gems in the Portuguese wine sector, it is not worth the producers' while spending millions on international marketing campaigns for an output of, say, 100,000 bottles.

Experts such as Jancis Robinson and Richard Mayson have written extensively, and admiringly, about the changing landscape of the Portuguese wine sector and the pearls that can be found, especially given the rare grape varieties. Jancis Robinson wrote on her website in

2007 that "since the country has kept so many of its exciting arsenal of indigenous grape varieties in the ground, sensibly resisting the temptation to replace them all with Cabernet Sauvignon and Chardonnay, Portugal can offer the wine drinker really distinctive flavours and styles that cannot be found anywhere else—until the Touriga Nacional cuttings imported from Portugal by growers in places such as Australia and Spain mature, of course."

Port wine remains unique to the enchanting Douro Valley. This is where the world's first demarcated wine region was established by royal charter in 1756, though the first written references to wine from this region date from the mid-seventeenth century. The local export business boomed in the eighteenth century as England procured alternatives to French wine whose supply was uncertain because of trade disputes and war. While some of the most famous brands consequently have a British heritage, today multinationals are often behind the old names. By 1799 wine from the Douro made up more than half of Portugal's total exports. The thinly populated region is still important, its 106,000 acres of vineyards producing about 70 percent of wine exports, worth more than $500 million annually.

There are many grape varieties here that cannot be found in any other country, among them *tinta barroca, tinta roriz, touriga nacional, tinto cão, rufete* and *bastardo*. They grow amid often majestic scenery. Terraced vineyards, where every autumn grape-pickers slowly zigzag uphill, follow the contours of the land, rippling back from the river in corrugated lines. The Douro region carries neither the glamour nor the prominence of Bordeaux, Tuscany, or Spain's Rioja but it boasts some great wines. Port vintages, denoting that the wine is made from a grape harvest of exceptionally high quality, fetch handsome prices, and the older vintages can sell for hundreds of euros.

Madeira's fortified wine is also singular. It was first put in barrels in the fifteenth century and won a following among passing sailors who were fond of a wine which, notably, keeps well once opened. Madeira wine's fame spread with them. The signatories of the American Declaration of Independence in 1776, among them Thomas Jefferson and Benjamin Franklin, raised a glass of Madeira in a toast after laying down their quill pens. The British, too, developed a taste for Madeira which, like sherry, comes in sweet and dry varieties. They also saw that there was money in its sale and have been engaged in the local export trade since the nineteenth century. The history of Madeira includes the names of merchants such as Charles Blandy and Thomas Leacock, who helped the business overcome a nineteenth-century blight. The vineyards cling to slopes of volcanic soil, and the wine—because centuries ago it was found to improve on sweltering voyages to the tropics—is placed for several months in hot houses, which subject it to an accelerated, pseudo-tropical aging process.

To round off a meal, Portugal has the best coffee in Europe, alongside Italy, and, if you dare, an aid to digestion is the home-brewed firewater (*aguardente, bagaço,* or *medronho*), which the restaurant owner brings from his home town and keeps aside for regular customers and friends. It is an innocently clear liquid. And it burns all the way down.

Chapter Twelve
That Sinking Feeling
Old Problems, New Crisis

The annual Lisbon Book Fair almost did not happen in 2008. The country's publishers locked horns in a passionate row that looked likely to culminate in the cancelation of the traditional summer event in one of the capital's parks. The cause: a publishing group had created controversy by planning to set up a sophisticated modern stand at the fair instead of occupying one of the about 200 identical, draughty wooden shacks that everyone had been using for the previous 78 years. The publishing group—a commercially aggressive outfit that had gobbled up more than a dozen rivals—drew up a stylish layout for its new stand that resembled what might be found at book fairs in Frankfurt and other European cities. The other publishers flew into a rage. The break with tradition was regarded as an affront to sacred egalitarianism. Nobel laureate José Saramago joined the fray, complaining that the fair was supposed to be a "democratic celebration" and that by breaking ranks the publisher would highlight "class differences." The majority of publishers threatened to boycott the event in protest. Eventually, this being Portugal, the antagonists stepped back from the brink, reached a compromise and the fair opened. Saramago, visiting the brash publisher's new installations, decided they were actually quite acceptable. And in 2009 the fair received a comprehensive makeover with the introduction of smart new stands for all.

Newspapers recorded each salvo fired by the country's cultural heavy artillery with voyeuristic glee, but most missed the bigger point—that the quarrel showcased a broader national malaise that was arresting Portugal's progress. The reluctance to change, the suspicion of ambition and drive and vision, had conspired to shackle the country. Old orthodoxies travelled across the millennial threshold into the new century and choked natural talents. Consequently, Portugal became an analog country in a digital age. And after the spend-happy years of post-EU membership, there was a reckoning. It engendered one of the country's grimmest economic periods in living memory, bringing more

Boom and bust: Portuguese economic indicators

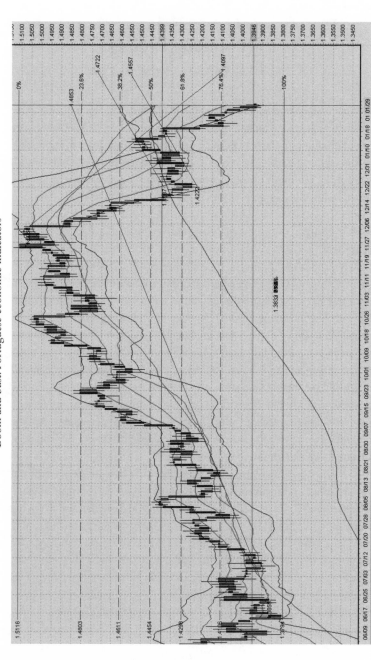

torment for the long-suffering Portuguese.

In the late twentieth century Portugal's national wealth peaked at over 78 percent of the EU average. After that, bit by bit, it slipped back until by 2008 it stood at 76 percent. Portugal, stuck in reverse gear, was overtaken by the Czech Republic and Malta. Between 2001 and 2008 Portugal's economy grew on average less than 1 percent a year while wages continued to rise by about 3 percent a year, pushing up production costs. The 2009 Global Competitiveness Index placed Portugal 17th in the EU, behind burgeoning Cyprus, Estonia, and Slovenia. Foreign analysts branded it "chronically uncompetitive" as it remained the poorest nation among countries using the euro currency. Lisbon was the only Portuguese region that came anywhere near matching wealth levels in richer EU countries (the old saying about the rest of Portugal being countryside still holds true). In the unforgiving mirror of comparative EU statistics, Portugal's reflection was unflattering. Figures on education, welfare, productivity, and other benchmarks were disheartening and read like an accusation—somebody could almost have written a *fado* song about them.

Bingo halls offer an illustration of the kind of difficulties the Portuguese face in being competitive. The announcer offers no "Clickety-click 66," no "Legs Eleven," no "Dancing Queen 17." He just stands there pulling out the little balls and calling out the numbers in a colorless drone: 6-6, 66, 1-1, 11, 1-7, 17... It is a lack of imagination about how things could be, an acceptance of—and resignation to—how things are. The poet Fernando Pessoa wrote in a 1915 article that the Portuguese "are always waiting for someone else to do everything."

Modernity, in some key respects, felt bolted-on rather than a natural growth or progression, and the decline was bewildering. It was as if Portugal had dashed ahead and left the Portuguese behind. Manuel João Ramos, a Lisbon University anthropologist, observed: "We have changed a lot, but too quickly and without having the cultural background or education to be able to digest it or keep up with it. That has distorted Portugal." Michael Porter, a Harvard Business School professor hired by the government in 1994 to map out a future for the fragile Portuguese economy, returned in 2002 to judge how the project had worked out. His assessment was gloomy: "Portugal has wasted the past eight years." Competition from new, and poorer, EU members in Central and Eastern Europe and from globalized trade exposed abiding Portuguese weaknesses.

The fall was all the harder because in the preceding years the Portuguese had glimpsed what might have been. In a sober and stunning appraisal, the European Commission in 2006 exhibited Portugal as a cautionary tale for the EU's new eastern members. It had gone from being tagged as a "good pupil" to being held up as a bad example. A damning six-page report spoke grimly of "inadequate reforms"—a failure, that is, to move with the times—which left Portugal out of kilter. It was an old problem, discernible already in the later period of the Age of Discovery when Portuguese shipbuilding failed to keep pace with other countries' improvements. It was also the case in the early 1900s when the intellectual António Sérgio remarked, "The big mistake the Portuguese made was not breaking with tradition, but rather only having broken with tradition superficially."

The Portuguese economy recorded periods of recession in 2003, 2004, 2008, and 2009—four in six years. It was the worst economic performance since the Second World War. In late 2008 President Aníbal Cavaco Silva advised: "For us to be able to compete in the global marketplace, we have to change our productive structure as fast as we can." The slowness to switch from a low-wage economy to innovative manufacturing made Portugal vulnerable. Acutely aware of their country's diminishing stature, the Portuguese felt fragile and despondent. It would be a dire decade.

Portugal for too long persevered with a misguided economic policy based on cheap labor. The Economy and Innovation Minister, on an official visit to China to woo investors in 2007, tried to impress businessmen there with the meagerness of Portuguese salaries compared with the rest of the EU. In 2009 some 342,000 people—twice as many as in 2006—took home the minimum salary of just €475 a month. The average salary stood at just under €900, about a third of the level in the UK. At the same time, Portugal kept in place post-revolutionary labor laws that protected jobs and made it hard to fire or lay off workers, even if their productivity levels were found wanting—another shortcoming censured by international institutions.

The hoped-for influx of foreign investment in high-grade industry did not materialize in any substantial way. The AutoEuropa plant stood as testimony to what might have been. Traditional industries such as footwear and fabrics, meanwhile, shrank, especially the textile sector, which reeled under the impact of cheap Chinese imports and shed thousands of jobs as companies went bankrupt. In 1990 the textile sector accounted for 33 percent of Portugal's exports; fifteen years later it was 12 percent, and the industry's workforce of about 300,000 workers had shrunk to about half that. The government launched technological education courses for more than 5,000 textile workers in an effort to stem the tide, but with the global financial crisis and a bruising recession in 2009 the sector continued to shed jobs. The erosion of manufacturing led to services contributing about two thirds of GDP. The search for viable industries that might lift Portugal's economy continued.

The Portuguese, those gentle anarchists, also had had difficulty in adjusting to the disciplined financial life imposed on them by Northern European countries through inclusion in the euro. Within ten years of the currency's 1999 debut, Portugal had three times broken the membership rules, fluctuating between obedient compliance and reckless laxity as it was repeatedly tempted to spend more than it earned. Under the euro membership conditions the state budget deficit could not exceed 3 percent of the country's GDP, as countries were supposed to live prudently within their means. But as the columnist Henrique Raposo wrote in 2008: "The typical Portuguese is a walking contradiction: he works like a Moroccan but expects the luxury of a Scandinavian"—the kind of biting remark that could have been made by the sixteenth-century Flemish traveller Nicolas Cleynaert.

The global economic downturn worsened the Portuguese debt burden in 2009, as low growth and extra spending undermined its fiscal planning, though this time Portugal was not alone as a handful of other countries, including Greece, Spain, and Ireland, joined it on the economic casualty list. Portugal, though, was perceived internationally as being the euro system's "weakest link" after Greece, even if the Portuguese do not vent their anger as violently as the Greeks.

International bodies and analysts warned that Portugal risked "a slow death" amid mounting debts and feeble growth. There was talk of it possibly defaulting on its foreign debt, while comparisons were drawn between its growing difficulties and Argentina's 2001 default crisis.

Portugal did not become a victim of the international crisis because of toxic debts nor due to a boom-and-bust property market. It fell because some aspects of the country's configuration were fundamentally flawed and it was vulnerable to contagious jitters. "This crisis has at least one virtue," Ricardo Reis, a Portuguese economics professor at Columbia University in New York, commented wryly. "It has brought to the attention of the Portuguese that the way they have been living for the past ten years is unsustainable."

Amid the theoretical debate about the economic way forward, the plight of some Portuguese became acute. The Portuguese Food Bank, a volunteer organization that is the largest of its kind on the continent, was in 2008 handing out food to almost 250,000 needy people who could not make ends meet. In early 2010 Portuguese bishops urged action to combat what they dramatically called "scandalous levels of misery."

Bad Habits

Despite all the progress it had recorded in the 1990s, Portugal could not rid itself of the perception abroad that it was inclined to political disorder. It did not help that after 1999 it had a series of four governments in six years. In 2008, as the global financial crisis gathered pace, finance minister Fernando Teixeira dos Santos told Parliament that the country had to keep a careful eye on its international credit rating used for loans on foreign money markets. "Unfortunately not all countries are equal. They have different reputations, and Portugal's isn't the best," he conceded.

Globalization, which the Portuguese initiated in the fifteenth century, rewards flexibility and innovation. But Portugal can be an inhospitable place for business. The former finance minister Miguel Cadilhe, when he was head of the Portuguese Investment Agency, an official body that sought to lure foreign companies, grumbled in 2005 that some aspects of life were like those of a Third World country. Cadilhe enumerated his list of complaints: entrepreneurs were up against a self-defeating bureaucracy, plodding political decisionmakers who held up billions of euros of investment for years, and a discouraging legal system that made potential investors think twice about risking their money. For all the pleasantness of the unrushed pace of life in Portugal, conducive to business it is not. "The ideal," the economist Sérgio Rebelo commented, "would be to live in Portugal and work in the United States."

Portugal, with its handicaps, was easily snared in the world economic crisis but the roots of its malaise stemmed more from the inside than the outside. Passivity and acquiescence run deep. The fear of speaking out, of demanding one's rights, is part of what the philosopher José Gil, in his incisive book *Portugal Today: the Fear of Existing*, called the "non-enrolment" in civic life and part of António Salazar's legacy. The non-participation, or disengagement, he said, has been inherited by a country that recently, in historical terms, spent four decades under a dictatorship and still bears its scars. The terror of reprisals for stepping out of line fostered cunning, not confrontation. Gil believes that little, truly, has changed, "from the fear, which has survived in different forms, to the 'irresponsibility' which still marks out Portuguese behaviour." A 1997 survey found that only 3 percent of Portuguese had ever written a letter to a newspaper about something they disagreed with. Under Salazar, and before him, the people were kept away from power—power that allows action, affirmation, decision-making, autonomy—and have stayed away from it. Gil unflinchingly and angrily calls his countrymen "childish adults." The Portuguese resist change and cling to centuries-old survival strategies. The EU brought a new era, "but if Europe entered us, we haven't yet entered Europe," Gil concludes.

The historian João Medina also detected a temperament that can be traced back through the family tree. "We still have flaws which come from way back, a lack of initiative, a lack of participation in collective life," he wrote. The essayist Eduardo Lourenço also identified a "long tradition of civic passivity." It would, he argued, be absurd to think the

Portuguese, in their late twentieth-century switch to democracy, could quickly offload their cultural baggage.

The absence of a collective, strategic vision means that the Portuguese coagulate into defensive squares of self-interest—that closed circuit of factional allegiances known as *bairrismo*, which is replicated in family ties, trade unions, and elites. The social elite, once referred to by a friend of mine as "the one-kiss brigade" because they give only one kiss in greeting instead of the usual two, recall those characters in Eça de Queirós's novels who look abroad for inspiration. For all the post-revolutionary rhetoric of egalitarianism, Portugal remains the EU country where the distance between the richest and the poorest is greatest, according to the OECD. Villaverde Cabral, the social scientist, concluded after a 1997 survey that the advent of democracy with the Carnation Revolution had not closed the gap between the rulers and the ruled. Measuring what sociologists call the "power distance index," he drew the following conclusion: "For about two-thirds of Portuguese people, power is exercised in exactly the opposite way they think it should be—that is, in an autocratic way instead of participatory."

A 2008 report by the Association for Social and Economic Development, an august independent institution, pulled no punches. "On a political level, there has been a sharpening of the decline in public trust in politicians which just about crosses the entire political spectrum," it noted. It regretted the lack of high-caliber individuals in political parties and the fact that party officials had become increasingly focused on managing their own interests rather than improving the quality of people's lives. It drew attention to opinion polls that found politicians were the members of society people trusted the least, reflecting a sense of disenfranchisement, and suggested that the state was part of the problem, not the solution. It concluded that "the State has a suffocating effect on the whole of society, to such an extent that it is no exaggeration to say that the space truly left free for private initiative is increasingly narrow."

The state seems undeniably inattentive. Politicians appear to live in their own *bairro*. At general elections party favorites are parachuted into constituencies where they have never been seen before and rarely return once elected (there are no weekly MP surgeries here). Members of

The informal economy: a shoeshine in the street

parliament can "suspend" their mandate to go and do something else, including private-sector jobs, being replaced by other party appa-ratchiks. In the four-year parliamentary term up to 2009, 133 of the 230 elected MPs left their posts, at least for a spell. It conveys the idea to the people that their democracy is a sham.

Meanwhile the state feeds, inefficiently, on the country's resources. It takes half the wealth produced and then disburses it with largesse, creating a dependence on state subsidies. The wages and pensions of civil servants devour about 15 percent of GDP, double the EU average. The Lisbon Council, it turned out in 2007, was being run by twice as many staff, in proportional terms, as Madrid.

The Portuguese, though, have an unhealthy love–hate relationship with the state. Companies in financial trouble dash to seek its help, and landing a job in the civil service is prized because it is for life, with plenty of perks, such as broad entitlements to days off. The writer Vasco Pulido Valente says the lack of enterprise in Portuguese society, as sep-arate from the state, is "the specific tragedy of the Portuguese destiny." That is despite the state's manifest unfairness. The National Federation of Construction Companies protested in 2007 that councils owed building companies more than €900 million and took more than seven months to pay their bills. As far back as the sixteenth century the authorities were setting the same bad example, prompting that old complaint about the state paying either late, only in part, or never.

Evidence of the state's shortcomings is all around. An annual survey in 2008 on the efficiency of European welfare systems placed Portugal near the bottom of the table, ahead only of Romania, Bulgaria, and Latvia. For the Portuguese that means that when they make an appointment with their family GP they often have to spend hours in the waiting room for the doctor, who on arrival offers no apology, or the doctor may not turn up at all, without warning. Grievance is piled upon grievance, and many people feel forsaken.

The medical profession also has its own *bairro*. So does the legal profession. The wheels of Portuguese justice turn at a glacial pace. According to figures compiled by the sociologist António Barreto, in the 1990s the expiry of the statute of limitations denied plaintiffs a verdict in up to 10,000 cases a year. It is not uncommon to wait five or more years for a trial verdict, as with the Casa Pia pedophile case. The Portuguese Bar Association once invited people angered by ineptness in the legal system to send in their stories for what it called a "Gallery of Horrors" on its website. It was soon filled with excruciating examples of minor litigation that took up to two decades to resolve. Cue that frequent Portuguese gripe: *Isto é uma desgraça* ("It's a disgrace").

Statistics from 2006 showed that cases stacked up at courts amounted, in money terms, to €13 billion—almost 10 percent of GDP. In 2008 a judge at the Supreme Administrative Court confided that there was a backlog of 37,000 cases. Such a debilitated system is wide open to abuse. It is also a shortcoming that eats away at the fabric of a society. As George Washington once observed, the administration of justice is "the firmest pillar of government." The Portuguese legal system too often encourages doubt instead of clearing it up. Its feebleness has the result of weakening authority, weakening public trust, and contributing to general ill-feeling.

Justice delayed is justice denied, fueling resentment. A 2008 report by a government watchdog body found that almost 80 percent of Portuguese did not expect justice to be done through the courts.

Barreto wrote: "The lack of justice is a passport to everything that's wrong with us: impunity, backwardness, the lack of responsibility, the disregard for citizens' rights and a belief that liberty merely amounts to being able to say whatever you want."

There are times when the neglect is unpardonable. In 2001 a tour bus and cars were crossing a bridge over the River Douro at Entre-os-Rios. The bus, carrying families from a day trip to see almond trees in bloom, was returning home in the dark when the bridge gave way, tipping the vehicles into the swollen river far below. Fifty-nine people perished. For days afterwards bodies washed up on the riverbank, prolonging the agony for bereaving families. The bridge had become weak over time, allegedly due to the authorities' poor oversight. It was a scandal, regarded as a deadly example of what was wrong with Portugal: Lisbon authorities' condescension towards the countryside; official inertia and incompetence; uneven development and abandoned people in what had become a two-speed country. But there were no convictions. Nobody was held responsible. In 2008, on the seventh anniversary of the tragedy, the association of families of the victims gave up on their legal bid to get compensation from the state. It would be too long and complicated, they said. They shrugged and got on with their lives—a peaceful collective, as the poet Miguel Torga said of the Portuguese, of outraged people.

Rui Ramos, a historian, reckons that because of negative cultural traits such as post-revolution entitlements and the country's hallmark conservatism, politicians have in large part been unable to engineer the economic and social transformations that took place in Nordic countries, Britain, or Ireland at the end of the twentieth century. The lingering fear of insurrection that haunts post-revolutionary political leaders also makes them surrender perhaps too quickly to noisy opposition. "It's hard to get consensus in Portugal...The ghosts of the past jump back to life," Ramos says. "Foreigners don't understand this. They say, why can't Portugal be like Ireland?"

Low education levels are one of the main contributors to Portugal's predicament. In 2008 only about 27 percent of Portuguese between 25 and 64 had completed secondary school—by far the worst rate in the EU. (The next worst was Spain, with 51 percent, and the best was the

Czech Republic, with 91 percent.) Portugal's figures compared very unfavorably with those in the Eastern European countries that became EU members. Highly qualified immigrants from those countries came to look for work in Portugal in the late 1990s, often finding employment on building sites, and for many of them the tragic state of the local education system was one of the country's striking details. In an excellent 2006 documentary called *Lisboetas*, about immigrants who were now residents of the capital, a weighty Russian woman sits on her towel on the beach at Caparica watching her children playing at the water's edge as she talks on a cell phone to friends in Russia who are coming over. "I'm on a beach!" she says. "It's sunny and there's the beach and the sea. It's really nice here," she continues. "But schooling is very difficult. Portuguese education is really bad."

A Negative Miracle

Low education levels do not just stunt productivity, they also bring everyday torments. A psychologist at one of Lisbon's biggest hospitals lodged a formal complaint against ancillary staff who twice a week strode into the crowded hospital waiting room and shouted, "Alcoholics Anonymous, first floor!" The handful of suddenly not-so-anonymous patients shuffled off under the gaze of curious onlookers. "It's largely because of a lack of schooling, not knowing how things are supposed to be done," the psychologist said of the staff.

While immigrants from even poorer nations came to Portugal, the Portuguese were heading to wealthier countries. Portugal has long been a country of emigrants, going abroad in search of a better life that does not seem possible at home. There are some five million Portuguese living abroad, roughly equivalent to half Portugal's population. A study in 2007 found that in the EU Portugal had the highest number of workers in jobs outside the country. An OECD migration report the same year found that there were 1.3 million Portuguese in the United States, 800,000 in France, and 700,000 in Brazil.

The Portuguese have become adept at getting by—a talent for adaptability, called *desenrascanço*, honed over centuries of difficulties.

Odd jobs on the side help to keep the wolf from the door. Outside the cities people usually have a bit of land where they plant vegetables, and even in cities you might come across a vegetable patch on a verge amid heavy traffic. Society appears to obey informal rules. Help comes from family or neighbors bonded in an informal network that makes up for the system's shortcomings. It is not the modern EU model, but more a drawing on the past. Getting something you need entails a few calls to friends of friends—useful connections known as *cunhas*—because the state, people think, will never gladly give you anything. These relations replace the yardsticks of merit and justice because, the Portuguese say, "it's not about know-how, it's about know-who." And, hoping for a miracle such as the return of King Sebastião, the Portuguese are the Europeans who spend the most, in relative terms, on the Euromillions continental lottery. Like those who brush aside concern about a repeat of the 1755 earthquake, these gamblers place their faith in providence and set little store by the possibility of triumphing on their own initiative.

Yet it is unlikely that any Portuguese government will be able to enact the reforms Portugal needs. As the writer Vasco Pulido Valente remarked, Portugal has been talking about the need for reforms for the past 800 years. The necessary changes, when they come, will be bottom-up, not top-down.

Just as importantly, Portugal is still finding its feet as a European country. As the philosopher José Gil noted, Portugal entered Europe, metaphorically, less than thirty years ago, and its "Europeanization" is still in its infancy. Portugal was for many centuries an Atlantic country that always looked outwards for its well-being. It is still trying to figure out how to get along with continental ways of doing things.

The Portuguese are not, on the whole, an especially ambitious people. They are attractively peaceable, humble, and content with their good things in life—eating out at one of the many restaurants in good weather with family and friends, for example. The absence of any discernible burning ambition goes hand-in-hand with modest expectations of life. Polish pianist Piotr Anderszewski, who lived for a period in Lisbon, wrote in *Gramophone* magazine in June 2007 about the city: "It's like nothing has changed and nothing will change that's in human power; it's the most extreme city in that respect... in Lisbon, you look at what you have—you are not blind, you have two arms, you have two legs, you have a brain—there is not much more ambition to have more, or to be better or more beautiful."

Such languor is not a modern phenomenon. The Duke of Wellington, in a perceptive dispatch from Portugal 200 years ago during the invasions by Napoleon's armies, wrote:

> There exists in the people of Portugal an unconquerable love of their ease, which is superior even to their fear and detestation of the enemy. Neither will they, or their magistrates, or the Government, see that the temporary indulgence of this passion for tranquility must occasion the greatest misfortunes to the state and hardships to the individuals themselves; and no person in the country likes to have his tranquility and habits disturbed for any purpose, however important, or to be the instrument for the disturbing those of others. Thus every arrangement is defeated...

The German author Hans Magnus Enzensberger, in an article about Portugal in the Spanish daily *El País* in 1987 entitled "The Pleasure of Being Sad," marveled at how the Portuguese way of life had endured in modern Europe. "They cling to their indolent generosity, to virtues which may be utopian and which carry a heavy penalty because, in a world of progress, they are considered mortal sins," he wrote. "What do these people live on? Nobody shouts, nobody starts shooting, nobody dies of hunger. This is the true Portuguese miracle, a negative miracle."

Chapter Thirteen
New Horizons
Confronting the Twenty-First Century

A few weeks before Christmas in 2004 an employee of the Confecções Afonso (Afonso Garments) company in northern Portugal was driving past the company's low, prefab factory about an hour after she and the rest of the staff had left for the day. Through the wintry murk she spotted representatives of the company's Switzerland-based owners reversing an empty articulated truck through the shirt factory's back gate. Her suspicions aroused, she called some coworkers on her cell phone. They rushed over and a confrontation ensued. In the tense standoff the workers learned that the truck was taking the factory's machinery to Slovakia. In what the workers described as a midnight flit, the company was shutting down its Portuguese operation and shifting production thousands of miles to the east.

About to become the latest casualties of an international economic trend—the relocation of manufacturing to lower-wage economies— the workers decided to fight for their livelihoods and threw up an impromptu blockade with their cars. If the owners did not want the factory, they decided, they would take it over themselves. In the region of white-water rivers and dark pine forests, where livelihoods in the male-dominated culture come mainly from small-time farming, few of the factory's ninety women workers had a chance of finding another job. "All the workers wanted to stay. They had nowhere else to go," said Conceição Pinhao, a middle-aged mother who was the factory manager. She took charge of production after the staff had paid a sym- bolic €1 for the Portuguese branch of the company—and its heavy debts.

The Swiss owners of Afonso Garments argued that Portugal's appeal as a place to do business had lapsed and they were losing money. They said they were pulling out because over the previous ten years Portugal's competitive edge had become blunt as wages rose. They complained that outdated employment laws aimed at job protection had handicapped the Portuguese in crucial business benchmarks. A company, for example, could not alter employment terms such as working hours without negotiating with the worker, who can refuse. Layoffs can entail demonstrating to labor authorities that there is "just cause"—possibly a lengthy and costly bureaucratic procedure—and negotiating severance packages which entitle employees to the equivalent of at least six weeks' pay for each year worked. Another arrow in the company's side was the EU's 2005 decision to scrap its textile quotas, inviting a surge in cheap Chinese imports that engulfed the continent.

The workers at Afonso Garments, however, kept faith. They began by taking a risk on new machinery and then producing top-range goods for discerning clients in the United States, Britain, Spain, and Germany. They worked whatever hours they needed to. While local flat-earthers—companies that stuck with low production costs as a business strategy—were doomed, two years after the staff took over Afonso's production was up by a third and business was flourishing. "I always believed it was possible and now I believe it more than ever," Conceição Pinhao said.

Afonso Garments was a case study in how to avoid the twenty-first-century pitfalls of company relocation and global trade liberalization. And it demonstrated how Portugal Inc. is a viable enterprise whenever the Portuguese draw on their often neglected reservoirs of talent. Their adaptability, resilience, and resourcefulness are traits that have shown themselves throughout Portuguese history. Luís Ferreira Lopes, a financial journalist, suggested that the Portuguese, confronted by their contemporary difficulties, needed to conjure back up the qualities that inspired the astounding maritime feats of the fifteenth and sixteenth centuries. He wrote in a 2007 book called *sucesso.pt*, which listed internationally successful Portuguese companies: "We are living through a time I call 'the point of no return': if we step backwards, we will die as a country; if we look ahead, with daring and more confidence in our abilities, with a spirit of enterprise... we will find the path towards sustained growth of the most dynamic sectors of our economy and our society."

The EU Generation

The familiar slings and arrows of national misfortune waylaid the Portuguese once more during the 2008-9 financial crisis. But some good may have come out of the hardship, as it compelled Portugal to accept the change which so long it had resisted. And through the gloom, promising new horizons were discernible. Portugal's modernization, though belated, showed signs of gaining impetus. A new, younger generation—what might be termed the EU Generation—matured and started taking its place in society. Unscarred by dictatorship and uncompromised by revolution, these people's points of reference and their expectations were sharply different from those of their parents. Young university graduates, smart, ambitious, and tutored in how things are done elsewhere, were each weekday morning filing into Lisbon's sleek new office blocks. Many of them worked for multinational companies. Outside work they went to fashionable bars, fancy shops, and sophisticated restaurants, which sprang up as the Portuguese capital took on a vibrantly modern feel. The intake of new executives called each other by their first names, eschewing the archaic forms of address such as *Senhor Doutor*—the cap-doffing epithet long applied to anyone who has been to university. Like the Afonso Garments staff, they were not handicapped by the long-standing malaise that former president and prime minister Mário Soares identified when he observed that the Portuguese "suffer from a terrible illness: they don't believe in themselves."

The blue-collar Afonso Garments staff and the white-collar city executives were among those fighting to remedy that shortcoming, and such self-belief paid dividends. Witness the Grupo Jerónimo Martins, one of Portugal's leading food distribution companies, which in 1997 bought a minor supermarket chain in Poland called, in Polish, Ladybird. Setting up a business on the other side of the continent was a bold and risky move. It seemed quixotic at the time for a Portuguese company to be going head-to-head with much bigger German and French rivals who were also expanding there. Yet it was the kind of audacity and intrepidness that once led the Portuguese into the Atlantic. Operation Ladybird was a triumph, thanks to the company's ambition and drive.

By 2010 the chain had expanded to almost 1,500 shops, becoming one of Poland's biggest companies. The average age of the Portuguese executives who had triumphed in Poland, Grupo Jerónimo Martins president Alexandre Soares dos Santos proudly pointed out, was 35 or 36. "This shows the depth of talent that Portugal possesses," he said. He also recalled what a Unilever executive once said to him, referring to Portugal's untapped potential: "You Portuguese always underestimate yourselves."

An international social network called Star Tracking aimed to restore national self-confidence and self-esteem (its slogan: "Saying bad things about Portugal is prohibited"). It linked, via the internet, more than 15,000 Portuguese expatriates around the world, most of them educated and successful young people. Their common denominator was a determination to nurture Portuguese strengths, to look on the bright side, to strive for betterment and to spurn the jaundiced mentality of the past. Instead of waiting for change they were bringing it about. Others, too, sought to deliver Portugal from apathy and inaction. Patriotic civic movements sprouted, such as *Compromisso Portugal* (Portugal Commitment) and *Acredita Portugal* (Believe Portugal). The marketing expert Carlos Coelho, in his book *Portugal Genial*, pointed to 82 areas where Portugal—which "always felt, on the inside, universal and, outside, insignificant and marginalized"—could claim uniqueness, such as the admired Lusitanian thoroughbred horse, *fado,* and the famous custard tarts. The book *sucesso.pt*, meanwhile, listed Portuguese companies that were world-beaters, including one that provided special paint for ships and catered to the entire US Navy fleet, and another that sold felt for hats, including Stetsons for former US president George W. Bush.

Several Portuguese companies have pioneered international innovation. Highway builder and operator Brisa in the 1990s introduced Europe's first nationwide electronic toll payment system, called Via Verde. It tracks where vehicles get on the motorway and where they get off and deducts—with prior consent—the amount due from each motorist's bank account. The Multibanco ATM network grew to deliver some sixty functions, making it one of the most sophisticated electronic banking systems in the world. Critical Software in Coimbra was picked to provide essential systems for NASA and the London

Underground. Lisbon-based Vision-Box installed the biometric security systems at British airports. Portuguese mobile phone company TMN invented pre-paid phone cards. EdP Renováveis, the green energy division of national energy company Energias de Portugal, became a world leader in wind energy and committed $4 billion to building wind farms in the United States by 2012.

Portugal has also produced plenty of individuals with world-class credentials. To select just a few: the Porto-based architect Álvaro Siza Vieira collected the prestigious Pritzker prize in 1992 and in 2009 became the first Portuguese to scoop Britain's Royal Gold Medal for Architecture, even though he had built nothing there; the sociologist António Barreto received the esteemed Montaigne prize in 2004; José Gil, the philosopher, was in 2005 named among the top 25 thinkers in the world by *Le Nouvel Observateur*; Cristiano Ronaldo, like Luís Figo before him, became world player of the year and a recognizable name around the globe; José Manuel Barroso was appointed to the EU's top job; José Saramago captured the Nobel literature prize while works by artists Paula Rego and Joana Vasconcelos drew six-figure price tags, and art-house favorite Manoel de Oliveira was the world's oldest working filmmaker in 2010 at the age of 101; António Damásio was an acclaimed neuroscientist at the University of Southern California who in 1994 published the landmark work *Descartes' Error*; in a 2010 survey by US business magazine *Institutional Investor*, which consulted more than 1,700 analysts about European companies, the CEOs of Energias de Portugal and Portugal Telecom were rated the best in their sectors on the continent; Carlos Tavares was a highly-regarded executive vice-president of Nissan in Tokyo; a team led by Elvira Fortunato, a researcher at Lisbon's New University, won international awards for important breakthroughs in the fast-growing field of transparent electronics; Miguel Soares of the Gulbenkian Science Institute in Lisbon recorded important advances in the study of malaria, which blights Africa; cosmologist João Magueijo was a theoretical physicist at Imperial College London who famously questioned Einstein's theory of relativity. The Portuguese are, QED, no less estimable than others. Unfortunately, as Magueijo remarked, many of these world-beaters had been forced to go abroad to encounter the kind of dynamic, free-thinking atmosphere that encouraged new ways of looking at things. They, like the Star Trackers, were part of a brain drain that Portugal needed to reverse.

There are many blue-collar achievers, too. Those emigrants who stepped aboard the Sud Express in Portugal and alighted at Paris' Gare d'Austerlitz needed guts and hard work to establish themselves in France. These workers proudly recount how French employers quip that they like to have a Portuguese on hand for when things get tough ("Break glass in case of emergency," they say with reference to the Portuguese). That said, these Portuguese emigrants are still widely regarded as the Africans of Europe. Even white-collar staff grumble that they often have to work twice as hard as, say, the British, Germans, or French to prove themselves.

Breaking the Mold

Work also began on revamping the Portuguese economy. The socialist government that came to power in 2005 under Prime Minister José Sócrates—a 48-year-old divorcee whose daily jogging and taste for designer suits seemed to fit the idea of new times—launched a grand Technological Plan. Its goal was to accelerate the development of Portugal's high-tech capabilities. Previously paltry spending on research and development surged to 1.2 percent of GDP, above Spain, Ireland and Italy by 2007, with the private sector's R&D overtaking the public sector's for the first time. By the next year Portugal featured fifth in a list of EU countries that had made the most progress in innovation and was placed top in the growth of private-sector research and development. The authorities recruited the Massachusetts Institute of Technology, Harvard University, and Carnegie Mellon to help guide the overhaul. More than one million free or discounted laptops were distributed to primary and secondary schools; English was made an obligatory subject at elementary schools. An initiative called New Opportunities drew about a million adults back into the classroom to complete their secondary education and help lift Portugal from the foot of the European league table on education statistics. The government also took scissors to the red tape. It reduced the time taken to set up a company from more than two months to a day with an on-the-spot procedure, impressing the World Bank. Government online services quickly expanded and by 2007 more tax returns were being filed online than in hard copies—further evidence of Portuguese adaptability.

Portugal also recorded notable successes in the introduction of clean energy technology, setting itself apart as one of the continent's more forward-looking nations. It deployed the world's first wave energy farm hooked up to a national grid, though it had some teething problems, and at one point boasted the world's largest solar power plant and Europe's biggest wind energy farm. It also set up factories producing innovative green technology and started building a national grid to recharge electric cars. The Azores archipelago joined MIT's Green Islands Project, becoming an open-air laboratory as scientists devised ways of providing sustainable energy. The prime minister announced that in 2007 Portugal had, for the first time in its history, sold more technology than it imported, largely due to its renewable energy projects. On a landmark day in January 2010, Portugal produced enough green energy to power the entire country. By that year almost 40 percent of national electricity consumption came from renewable sources—about double the EU average.

Renewable energy: solar panels in the countryside

A Portuguese-German Chamber of Commerce survey in 2008 found that German companies were happier with their investments in Portugal than with those they had made in Spain, France, and Italy. The survey described its members' appraisal of their investments in Portugal as "very positive." The head of a British company that based its European operations in Portugal the same year remarked that the country should sell itself better abroad to shed its undeservedly negative image. Among other things, the Portuguese could tempt foreign investors with some quality workers and good infrastructures—all those new, and rather empty, highways. Portugal, he said, is "a great country with incredible talent and it just has to show companies what it's good at."

The ethnologist Jorge Dias, writing in 1950, provided an explanation for the psychological asymmetry—often self-defeating behavior at home and excellence abroad—that recalls that fictional archetype Zé Povinho: "Once the Portuguese are called upon to play some important role, they throw into it all their qualities of action, abnegation, sacrifice and courage and carry it out better than most. But if you ask them to take a mediocre role, which doesn't satisfy their imagination, they wilt and do only whatever it takes to get by."

An opportunity for the Portuguese to show that they have such "qualities of action" came with the 2004 European soccer championship. Portugal had to build seven modern stadiums from scratch and renovate three others in time for the continental soccer competition. The passion for soccer welded the Portuguese together in one of those rare displays of unity when they become a mighty force. They passed the litmus test. The stadiums were ready on time, whereas London's effort to build a new Wembley stadium, by way of interesting comparison, ran over deadline by two years.

The quest for modernization spread beyond the economy into society. The quality of public services improved noticeably, perhaps swayed by new expectations. Staff on the Lisbon underground, called the Metropolitano, and with the national rail company CP, once infamous for their lack of customer services, received training in how to deal with the public and developed a kinder, gentler demeanor. Civil servants at public offices were more often reported to be friendly and efficient.

People started pulling together, like the bull-wrestling *forcados*. As the economic crisis deepened and an increasing number of people felt its impact, the Portuguese Food Bank announced that public donations for its efforts had grown. On a weekend in 2010 some 100,000 people turned out with garbage bags to clean up dirty public spaces around the country. Schoolchildren badgered their parents to recycle waste, and parents nationwide joined a voluntary internet-linked organization to press for a better deal for the handicapped. The evidence of a new collective attitude signaled a turning tide among a people once reluctant to sign petitions or participate in referendums.

In business, too, there was a harnessing of pooled strengths. ViniPortugal grouped associations and federations involved in wine production as part of a joint national effort to raise Portugal's profile on the shelves of foreign shops. Producers of Portuguese olive oil, which is undoubtedly among the best in Europe, adopted more sophisticated branding and marketing techniques in a new drive for attention.

Lisbon experienced exciting new cultural developments as the modernization process gathered pace: the Orient Museum, featuring exhibits from Asia, and the Design Museum, for example. It also acquired, after what seemed to be an obligatory period of political squabbling, the Berardo Collection. Housed at the Belém Cultural Centre (that extremely understated building next to the Jerónimos Monastery), this assembly of modern art placed Portugal, in one fell swoop, on the international circuit. It features works by Picasso, Dalí, Mondrian, Modigliani, Andy Warhol, Francis Bacon, Jackson Pollock, Henry Moore, Willem de Kooning, Jean-Michel Basquiat, David Hockney, Jeff Koons, Roy Lichtenstein, Man Ray, and many more. The collection of more than 4,000 works was put together by Joe Berardo who, with trademark Portuguese pluck, emigrated from his native Madeira at the age of nineteen to seek his fortune. He started out selling fruit in South Africa, went on to make a fortune in mining there, and today has stakes in vineyards, hotels and banks and the media. Wealth has allowed him to speak his mind, and he has a reputation as a philanthropic rough diamond, but his vocal bullying of political procrastinators as he fought for a Lisbon home (with free admission) for his art collection achieved results and earned him applause.

The Berardo Collection in many ways put Lisbon's other great museum, at the Gulbenkian Foundation, in the shade. The Gulbenkian, as the extensive cultural center is known in shorthand, was long Portugal's only museum of international renown. It was founded on a bequest by Calouste Gulbenkian, an early twentieth-century Armenian oil financier known as Mr. Five Percent. He was one of the world's wealthiest men and built up a fabulous private art collection. He shrank from publicity, preferring obscurity, and the out-of-the-way Portuguese capital suited him fine. He arrived in Lisbon in 1942 *en route* to the United States and decided he would stay in the peaceful, hospitable city with low taxes and no media harassment. Up to his death in 1955, at 86, he spent thirteen years in a modest suite at the Hotel Aviz and rode around Lisbon in a rented car. He bequeathed part of his fortune to a Lisbon-based international arts foundation in a gesture of thanks to the Portuguese.

New Departures

New opportunities have presented themselves to the Portuguese. After a long stagnation in relations Portugal remembered its long career in Africa, a continent offering enormous potential for growth. Tens of thousands of Portuguese went back to Angola, for example, in the early years of the twenty-first century, retracing the footsteps of previous generations. In 2004 some 20,000 Portuguese were there; by 2008 they numbered about 100,000 (such levels of emigration helped to keep Portugal's unemployment rate relatively low when compared with, say, Spain). These expatriates not only worked for Portuguese companies: multinationals looking to do business in Africa hired Portuguese because of the common language and because after centuries of shared history they were familiar with how those African countries work.

In the three years from 2007 Portugal invested about US$1 billion in Angola, making it the second biggest foreign investor after China. Portuguese exports to Angola jumped by 35 percent in 2008. In a cultural context, the return to Africa makes sense. The former colonies long held promise for the Portuguese. In a period of particular crisis in the late 1800s, when Portugal was being squeezed out of Africa by bigger European powers, Eça de Queirós in his novel *The Illustrious House of Ramires* portrayed a loser called Gonçalo who sails—on a ship called *Portugal*—to Mozambique. He comes back four years later, a wealthy man.

Predicted population growth in the Community of Portuguese Language Countries opened another door for Portugal. The group's total population was forecast to reach 350 million by 2030, establishing a huge market from which the Portuguese were well placed to profit.

Looking back to the country's halcyon days, a return to the sea was mooted as one of the central priorities of economic strategy. A 400-page study in 2009 by former finance minister Ernâni Lopes decided that fishing and other maritime activity had become a neglected sector since Portugal turned its attention inwards, to mainland Europe, beginning in the 1980s (the Grupo Jerónimo Martins' move into Poland was an instance of this trend). The country had turned its back on the ocean as it once had, a long time ago, on Europe. Maritime activities still accounted for 5 or 6 percent of GDP and 75,000 jobs, but, the study projected, the sea could account for 12 percent of GDP by 2025 if there was a concerted effort to develop leisure activities for tourists, transport logistics, fishing, and aquaculture along the country's ample coastline, which once had yielded so much.

Tourism, meanwhile, diversified away from the sun-and-sand package holidays associated with the Algarve and, though vulnerable to the international economic climate, the sector showed great promise. A staple Portuguese industry for decades, tourism already represented around ten per cent of GDP, in a country where services made up more than sixty per cent of the economy. The country held several advantages over its competitors, though not all of them had been planned. For a start, its lopsided development had left virtually pristine landscapes within easy striking distance—along the new highways—of the cities, and its countryside offered deeply varied geographical features within a relatively small space, from the Alentejo plains to the Douro Valley and the mountains of Trás-os-Montes. It has simple, wholesome food and wine at very reasonable prices when compared with similarly handsome regions such as Tuscany. Much of this produce is on sale at old-

The beach at Albufeira

fashioned open-air markets where family farmers offer fresh produce from the soil and the sea.

Portugal's exceptional appeal to vacationers gradually began to earn wider attention. Lisbon's increasingly successful blend of the modern and the ancient earned it the garland of Best European Destination at the 2009 World Travel Awards, and it won the same accolade the following year from European Consumer Choice, a Brussels-based non-profit organization, which based its award on votes from 47 countries. In February 2010, after some one million customers voted, five Lisbon hostels were placed among the best ten options for budget-conscious travellers. These innovative venues mostly catered for sophisticated young travellers who tenderly called Portugal "the Morocco of Europe" in admiration of its low-key, old-fashioned charm. Its metaphorical closeness to Africa had become an advantage.

It is perhaps the Portuguese themselves, though, who should be the main attraction for anyone considering a visit. That "indolent generosity" that German author Hans Magnus Enzensberger spoke of, the "passion for tranquility" that the Duke of Wellington observed, the absence of a rat race that Polish pianist Piotr Anderszewski witnessed, the cherished Portuguese "gentle ways" that seduced Calouste Gulbenkian: these features make the country an ideal refuge from more stressful parts of Europe. It offers that proverbial Portuguese kind-heartedness recounted in the *fado* song *Uma Casa Portuguesa*. A senior Iranian official who came to the Foreign Ministry in 2007 had previously been in Madrid for talks. There, colleagues told me, Spanish officials irritably pushed journalists out into a parking lot where they had to wait hours in the sweltering heat for the much-delayed press conference. In Lisbon, as the wait also stretched into hours, Foreign Ministry officials ordered pizza for everybody and sat around chatting with foreign and local journalists. "The Portuguese are so kind and calm," remarked an impressed foreign colleague who had endured the Madrid episode.

I do not doubt for a moment that the Portuguese will persevere despite the hard times. There is as much chance of Portugal "disappearing," as some have warned, as there is of a snowflake settling on an Algarve beach. The Portuguese remind me of those ancient olive trees you come across around the country—bent out of shape by bigger forces, flawed and suffering, but robustly surviving with an unusual beauty.

This people, as is their wont, can be hard to convince, however. They have scoffed at themselves, predicting that they will soon be fit only for serving grilled sardines to retired people from wealthier EU countries in what is called the Florida Model. But even that cynicism may be misplaced; Florida is by no means a model of failure, and Portugal could do much worse than become a preferred tourist destination in a rapidly aging Europe. Perhaps most importantly, Portugal's enduring appeal to foreigners shows little sign of waning. As the Spanish writer Miguel de Unamuno said after a visit about a hundred years ago: "The more I go there, the more I want to go back."

Further Reading

Bethencourt, Francisco, *Portuguese Oceanic Expansion, 1400-1800*. Cambridge University Press, 2007.

Birmingham, David, *A Concise History of Portugal*. Cambridge University Press, 2003.

—, *Portugal and Africa*. Ohio University Press, 2004.

Brockey, Liam Matthew, Portuguese Colonial Cities in the Early Modern World. Ashgate Publishing, 2008.

Castro e Silva, Miguel de, *The Food and Cooking of Portugal*. Aquamarine, 2007.

Disney, A. R., *A History of Portugal and the Portuguese Empire*. Cambridge University Press, 2009.

Kaplan, Marion, *The Portuguese: the Land and Its People*. Carcanet Press, 2006.

Loude, Jean-Yves, *Lisbonne, dans la ville noire*. Actes Sud, 2003.

Mayson, Richard, *Port and the Douro*. Mitchell Beazley, 2004.

—, *The Wines and Vineyards of Portugal*. Mitchell Beazley, 2003.

Metcalfe, Charles and McWhirter, Kathryn, *The Wine and Food Lover's Guide to Portugal*. Inn House Publishing, 2007.

Ribeiro de Meneses, Filipe, *Salazar: A Political Biography*. Enigma Books, 2010.

Robertson, Carol, *Portuguese Cooking*. North Atlantic Books, 2008.

Russell, Peter, *Prince Henry "The Navigator": A Life*. Yale University Press, 2001.

Russel-Wood, A. J. R., *The Portuguese Empire 1415–1808*. Johns Hopkins University Press, 1998.

Saraiva, José Hermano, *Portugal: A Companion History*. Carcanet Press, 1997.

Vieira, Edite, *The Taste of Portugal*. Grub Street, 2000.

Zimmler, Richard, *The Last Kabbalist of Lisbon*. Arcadia Books, 2000.

Literature in Translation

Lobo Antunes, António, *The Inquisitor's Manual*. Grove Press, 2004.

Lobo Antunes, António, *The Natural Order of Things*. Grove Press, 2001.

Lobo Antunes, António, *The Return of the Caravels*. Grove Press, 2003.

Pessoa, Fernando, *The Book of Disquiet*. Serpent's Tail, 2010.

Pessoa, Fernando, *Message*. Shearsman Books, 2007.

Pessoa, Fernando, *Selected Poems*. Dedalus Press, 2009.

Queiróz, Eça de, *The City and the Mountains*. Dedalus, 2008.

Queiróz, Eça de, *The Maias*. Dedalus, 2007.

Saramago, José, *Baltasar and Blimunda*. The Harvill Press, 2001.

Saramago, José, *The Gospel According to Jesus Christ*. The Harvill Press, 1999.

Saramago, José, *Journey to Portugal*. The Harvill Press, 2002.

Saramago, José, *The Stone Raft*. The Harvill Press, 2000.

Saramago, José, *The Year of the Death of Ricardo Reis*. The Harvill Press, 1998.

Sousa Tavares, Miguel, *Equator*. Bloomsbury, 2009.

Films

In the White City, Alain Tanner, 1983
Lisbon Story, Wim Wenders, 1994
Slightly Smaller than Indiana, Daniel Blaufuks, 2006

Websites

Tourism:
    www.visitportugal.com
Monuments:
    www.igespar.pt
Government:
    www.portugal.gov.pt
Finance and Investment:
    www.portugalglobal.pt
English-language Newspapers:
    www.algarveresident.com
    www.theportugalnews.com

Index